Security

Sociology and Social Worlds

Edited by Simon Carter, Tim Jordan and Sophie Watson

Manchester University Press
Manchester and New York
distributed exclusively in the USA by Palgrave
in association with

This book is part of a series published by Manchester University Press in association with The Open University. The three books in the Making Social Worlds series are:

Security: Sociology and Social Worlds (edited by Simon Carter, Tim Jordan and Sophie Watson)

Attachment: Sociology and Social Worlds (edited by Peter Redman)

Conduct: Sociology and Social Worlds (edited by Liz McFall, Paul du Gay and Simon Carter)

This publication forms part of the Open University course *Making social worlds* (DD308). Details of this and other Open University courses can be obtained from the Student Registration and Enquiry Service, The Open University, PO Box 197, Milton Keynes, MK7 6BJ, United Kingdom; tel. +44 (0)845 300 6090; email general-enquiries@open.ac.uk.

Alternatively, you may visit The Open University website at http://www.open.ac.uk where you can learn more about the wide range of courses and packs offered at all levels by The Open University.

To purchase a selection of Open University course materials visit http://www.ouw.co.uk, or contact Open University Worldwide Ltd, Walton Hall, Milton Keynes MK7 6AA, United Kingdom for a brochure, tel. +44 (0)1908 858785; fax +44 (0)1908 858787; email ouw-customer-services@open.ac.uk

Security

Sociology and Social Worlds

Manchester University Press
Oxford Road
Manchester M13 9NR, UK
and Room 400, 175 Fifth Avenue, New York, NY 10010, USA

www.manchesteruniversitypress.co.uk

First published 2008

A catalogue record of this book is available from the British Library

ISBN 978 0 7190 7811 8 *paperback*

Library of Congress Cataloguing-in-Publication Data

CIP data applied for

Edited and designed by The Open University.

Typeset in India by Alden Prepress Services, Chennai.

Printed and bound in the United Kingdom by Alden Group, Oxfordshire.

1.1

Contents

Notes on contributors vi

Series preface vii

Liz McFall

Introduction 1

Simon Carter, Tim Jordan and Sophie Watson

Chapter 1 Security in the social: gardens and Harry Potter 17

Tim Jordan

Chapter 2 Global security after 11 September 2001 47

Matt McDonald

Chapter 3 Security, the self and the home 81

Elizabeth B. Silva

Chapter 4 Security in the city 111

Sophie Watson

Chapter 5 Health and security 145

Simon Carter and George Davey Smith

Afterword 179

Simon Carter, Tim Jordan and Sophie Watson

Acknowledgements 188

Index 190

Notes on contributors

Simon Carter is Lecturer in Sociology at The Open University. He has a particular interest in Science and Technology Studies, especially as applied to issues of health and medicine. He is the author of *Rise and Shine: Sunlight, Technology and Health* (Berg, 2007) and many articles in sociological and medical journals.

George Davey Smith is Professor of Clinical Epidemiology at the University of Bristol Department of Social Medicine and Scientific Director of the Avon Longitudinal Study of Parents and their Children. His research interests include socio-economic inequalities in health, genetic epidemiology and the historical origins of social medicine.

Tim Jordan is Reader in Sociology at The Open University. He is the author of *Activism!: Direct Action, Hacktivism and the Future of Society* (Reaktion, 2002), *Hacktivism and Cyberwars: Rebels with a Cause?* (with Paul Taylor) (Routledge, 2004) and the forthcoming book *Hacking* (Polity, 2008). He is a founder and former editor of *Social Movement Studies: Journal of Social, Cultural and Political Protest.*

Matt McDonald is Assistant Professor in International Security at The University of Warwick. He has a particular interest in critical theoretical approaches to security, and has researched and published on the relationship between security and environmental change, immigration and Australian foreign policy. He is currently writing a book on the construction of security regarding the environment, and is co-editor (with Anthony Burke) of *Critical Security in the Asia-Pacific* (Manchester University Press, 2007).

Liz McFall is Lecturer in Sociology at The Open University. Her work is situated within the historical sociology of economic life with particular emphasis on the role of promotional practices in the 'making' of markets and consumers. She is the author of *Advertising: A Cultural Economy* (Sage, 2004) and a number of articles exploring nineteenth-century promotional culture, consumption and life assurance.

Elizabeth B. Silva is Senior Lecturer in Sociology at The Open University. Recent publications include 'Homologies of social space and elective affinities: researching cultural capital' (*Sociology*, 2007, vol. 41, no. 1), 'Gender, home and family in cultural capital theory' (*British Journal of Sociology*, 2005, vol. 56, no. 1), and the co-edited book, *Contemporary Culture and Everyday Life* (Sociology Press, 2004).

Sophie Watson is Professor of Sociology, The Open University, and has held Chairs at Bristol University, The University of Sydney and the University of East London. She has written a number of books, including *City Publics: The (Dis) Enchantments of Urban Encounters* (Routledge, 2006), *The Blackwell City Reader* (Blackwell, 2002) and *A Companion to the City* (Blackwell, 2000) (both edited with Gary Bridge), and *Markets as Sites for Social Interaction: Spaces of Diversity* (co-authored with David Studdert; Policy Press, 2006).

Series preface

Sociology and Social Worlds is a series of three stand-alone books designed to explore the characteristics and benefits of sociological approaches to the social worlds in which we live. The books form the main study materials for the Open University course *Making social worlds* (DD308), which aims to demonstrate the insights that sociology offers into everyday life, individual behaviour, the relationships between people and between people and things. The series considers how social worlds meet – and sometimes fail to meet – individual needs for security, attachment and order. Supported by examples ranging from Harry Potter to concentration camps, the books demonstrate that sociological approaches can help explain how individuals operate in the world, how social experience is shaped by nature and the material world, and how individual, social lives are made meaningful through culture and the media. The series takes account of the way in which sociology has been shaped by other disciplines and intellectual approaches, including cultural studies, media studies, history, psychology, anthropology and women's studies.

The first book in the series, *Security*, examines what security means in a variety of social and individual contexts. Authors consider issues ranging from geopolitical concerns such as global warming, terrorism and asylum seekers through to the intimate world of home and psychological development to help explain how security intersects with the making of social worlds. Through critical, sociological analyses of the character of material, natural, political and psychological 'threats' the authors show how security is constructed at different times and places.

The second book, *Attachment*, addresses attachment as a fundamental – and frequently overlooked – dimension of social life. Attachments between people, and between people and objects, make up the social worlds we inhabit. This book brings together a range of approaches (such as social constructionism, psychoanalysis and the anthropology of material culture) to investigate how the processes of attachment and detachment occur. Exploring a number of areas – including the nature of attachment to characters and plotlines in reality television shows, intimacy in parent–child relationships, and sport and the masculine body – the book offers a clear and accessible introduction to attachment as an issue of sociological concern.

Conduct, the final book in the series, offers an innovative perspective on how individual behaviour is ordered in social worlds. It aims to show that matters of conduct – habits, attributes, capacities, manners, skills and behaviours – and the norms, techniques, laws and rules which regulate them offer a crucial means through which sociologists can understand how social worlds are put together, change and break apart. Topics including self-service shopping, personal finance, violence and drunkenness are used as part of a sustained analysis of the close links between individual conduct and particular social worlds.

Open University courses are produced by course teams. These teams involve authors from The Open University as well as other institutions, course and project managers, tutors, external assessors, editors, designers, audio and video producers, administrators and secretaries. Academics on the *Making social worlds* course team were based mainly in the Sociology department within The Open University's Faculty of Social Sciences, but the course team also drew upon the expertise of colleagues in the Economic and Social Research Council (ESRC) Centre for Research on Socio-cultural Change (CRESC) and from other universities and institutions in order to construct a course with interdisciplinary foundations and appeal. While book editors have primary responsibility for the content of each book, the assignment of editors' names to books does not adequately convey the collective nature of production at The Open University. I'd like to thank all my colleagues on the course team for their intellectual energy, hard work and unfailing good humour. Particular thanks are due to Lucy Morris, who has, among many other things, been a resourceful, professional and efficient Course Manager.

Liz McFall, Course Chair

On behalf of the *Making social worlds* course team

Introduction

Simon Carter, Tim Jordan and Sophie Watson

Contents

1 Security and social worlds **2**

2 Sociological concerns: mediation, matter, the individual **6**

2.1 Mediation 7

2.2 Matter 8

2.3 The individual 9

3 Security and the airport **10**

4 Structure of the book **14**

References **16**

1 Security and social worlds

Security is part of all our lives. At the beginning of the twenty-first century, following terrorist attacks and a second war in Iraq, security seems to be growing in importance by the day. Security now frames a range of newspaper, radio and television news items. An editorial in a daily newspaper recently argued convincingly that we need a better government response in dealing with domestic and foreign security threats. Another newspaper argued that the security services (such as MI5 and MI6, the intelligence-gathering arms of the UK government) must be restructured to deal with the consequences of climate change, which may prove to be an unprecedented threat to Britain's security. Elsewhere, the House of Lords Science and Technology Committee was reported to be increasingly concerned about personal internet security and the threat that this may pose to the international banking system, with an alleged 8000 per cent increase in online fraud over an eighteen-month period. Beyond the UK, we learned that the Russian government had forced the oil company Shell to surrender its majority stake in the Shtokman gas field to a Russian monopoly, and further reports explored how this takeover may 'hurt' European energy security.

These reports, which all appeared over the space of a few days, made it seem that we may be under threat. But is an increase in security really a way to address these threats? These papers also reported concerns about increased security measures. Some reports covered legislative changes that may be seen as eroding civil liberties. But other reports described the more mundane and everyday annoyances that security procedures can cause, and how these are increasingly making the negotiation of everyday life unmanageable, possibly creating a desire for less security. For example, it was reported that the drive to increase internet security was affecting our sanity with many people commonly having to remember up to twenty different passwords and even needing passwords to protect passwords, an experience that many of us already share. In other reports we discovered that expanded security measures at the world's airports were having an adverse effect on the tourist industry, with many travellers discouraged from visiting the United States of America because of the reported surliness of US immigration officials and long queues at airports. The pettiness of often poorly paid security staff dealing with harassed and annoyed travellers was also frequently mentioned. The aim of this book is to establish the complexity of security's operation across different social settings, ranging from the psychic to the geopolitical.

We can begin to appreciate the multilayered complexity of security issues through the example of travel. On the one hand, travellers are increasingly delayed and restricted by additional security measures which can address everything from the threat of terrorism through to disease prevention. On the other hand, there has been a dramatic increase in the number of air travellers over the last two decades – an increase that is projected to carry on into the future. As more and more travellers need to be processed through ever tighter security controls, the greater are the opportunities for breaching security. According to some commentators, the increase in global travel is simultaneously damaging both local and global environments, and this undermines security in unexpected ways. Anthropological studies undertaken since the growth of mass tourism began in the 1970s have warned about the deleterious effects that an influx of large numbers of temporary visitors can have on local communities and their sense of security (Boissevain, 1978; Stott, 1978). More recently the increasing capacity of the air transportation industry has been implicated in the production of emissions which may increase global warming. While this damage threatens our environmental security, any change in economic practices which restricts air travel may bring about economic insecurity, as tourism and travel are currently the world's leading export earner, ahead of automotive products, chemicals, petroleum and food. International tourism receipts, combined with passenger transport, is currently worth more than US$680 billion (€547 billion) every year (World Tourism Organisation, 2007).

How can we understand the complexity of security? The beginning of an answer lies in thinking about what we mean by security. A standard dictionary definition defines security, or being secure, as a state of 'being free' or 'untroubled' by danger, in short as being safe. Using this as a starting point, we might think of security as safety. We feel secure when we feel safe. Yet there seems to be more to security than this. If we describe a personal computer as safe in this sense it could mean that someone will not be electrocuted while using it, or that it will not catch fire if left unattended (as happened in 2006 when a number of laptop batteries burst unexpectedly into flames). But is this sense of security really the same as describing a computer as secure?

If someone says their computer is secure, this seems to mean something more than the fact that it will not cause physical injury. It also includes other kinds of claims, such as the computer being free from outside interference. This could mean that any records or files kept on the computer could only be accessed by those with the appropriate authority, or that any sensitive transactions such as online banking could not be intercepted by others. Thinking more broadly, we should all be aware that our computers need to be kept safe from various malicious entities, from software such as viruses or key loggers to plain and simple theft. A computer can be secured by a variety of social and material means. Material protection may include software programs (such as a virus checker, a firewall and spyware checkers), together with more simple devices such as locking the room in which the computer is kept. Social measures to ensure security may involve training users to set appropriate passwords or to avoid running dangerous software on their computer. This expanded understanding of security in no way denies the importance of computers not endangering physical security. Having a laptop that suddenly bursts into flames would cause anyone a very real sense of insecurity. The point is that in this case the physical is only one aspect of what is meant by security. Indeed it could be argued that what is meant by the idea of security has a relevant purchase on nearly any social interaction, and that what is meant by security will inevitably be complex. Consequently, in the first decade of the twenty-first century – the time of terrorist attacks such as those of 11 September 2001 in New York or July 2005 in London, and wars in Iraq and Afghanistan – security will always be a key factor in our lives, even if global society subsequently moves into what are felt to be calmer times.

In summary, security may refer to a wide range of matters that are broadly related to safety: physical, financial, social and psychological. But security may also refer to a range of concepts other than safety; we would expect concepts such as risk, danger and isolation to be relevant at various times to the understanding of security. Security is therefore complex both in what it means in any particular situation and in the types of social interaction it may refer to. Within the social sciences, security has often traditionally been examined by political scientists. However, this book will demonstrate that a critical sociological inquiry into security, as broadly conceived, is crucial in understanding the range of relevant social and cultural phenomena.

To open up these discussions we will employ the concept of 'social worlds'. In particular, we are interested in how we 'make' our social worlds. The concept of the 'social world' emerged from what is now commonly called the Chicago School of Sociology. The University of Chicago founded one of the first ever sociology departments in 1892. One important and influential perspective to come out of this was the idea that people's conduct towards both things and other people is based on the meaning that these various entities have for them. These meanings are gained from social interaction. This is part of a perspective often called 'symbolic interactionism' (Blumer, 1969; Goffman, 1958). The use of social worlds as a conceptual tool came out of this tradition in which a 'social world' can broadly be understood as a unit or set of social interactions that is not confined by geography or formal membership of organisations or institutions, but rather is an assemblage or association with shared commitments or practices. For example, everyday life may be made up of a mosaic of social worlds, with all of us having multiple memberships. Someone who travels to work on a train and happens to meet work colleagues on the train may be seen as simultaneously living as a member of the social world of train travellers (who all have common understandings of tickets and how they are inspected, of how frequent delays are, and so on) and of the social world of the workplace (given that work colleagues are highly likely to discuss work). Membership of any social world may be both a highly complex and a highly contingent process.

Let us think for a moment about the social world of art and ask, who does art? The answer may seem simple, if alarmingly circular; artists do art! But a much wider range of people is involved in the world of art than just the artist (Becker, 1982). The curator of a gallery or museum decides which art to display, academic or popular critics define various art forms into categories and qualities, buyers define the value of specific artworks, and caretakers and porters hang works of art in particular positions in a gallery and tell us not to touch them as we wander around galleries. Are not all these people, in a sense, also doing art? Certainly the social world of art may well not exist, or would at least be significantly changed, if one of these groups did not exist. If we examine art from the perspective of social worlds, then 'art' rapidly segments into multiple sub-worlds of artists, curators, critics, wealthy patrons and caretakers whose intricate interactions create the overall social world of art. Of interest to sociologists is what happens when we look at how these worlds operate by identifying and analysing all the interactions that create a social world. One particular interest is how these different groups legitimate or de-legitimate one another. For example, when a well-known collector suddenly pays high prices for the work of an artist, that artist is often 'legitimated', leading to closer critical and commercial attention as their status rises. This example of the social world of art suggests that the essential analytic moment is not to begin enquiry with an established and ready-made category of art (or security) but with the messy multitude of practices, individuals and material artefacts that mediate and construct the category of art (or security) in the first place. It is this spirit of social worlds analysis that we pursue in relation to security by exploring how security makes our social worlds (Gieryn, 1995; Latour, 1987; Star and Griesemer, 1989).

We are not suggesting that this is an exhaustive explanation of the contemporary social world's literature (see Clarke, 1997; Fujimura, 1987), rather it is an introduction and opens out a way in which each author approaches the intricacies of security. The question that faces us is to explore security in society without over-simplifying, but also without the complexities of security overwhelming the discussion. Social worlds can be thought of as a 'framing device'. Such devices are ideas that structure investigations; they allow disparate analyses to launch themselves from similar questions. In a sense you will find that all the authors in this book have looked through a very similar conceptual window. Thus we will constantly return to the question: 'what role does security play in the making of our social worlds?' This means that the following chapters will employ varying notions of 'social worlds'. But this is deliberate and is one of the key points we are making: social worlds and the various commitments and practices around the notion of security do not exist independently of one another; rather each helps to make the other in specific and particular ways. In this sense, the idea of social worlds allows us to ask questions rather than to reach constraining conclusions.

We have already warned about the difficulties of fully recognising and grasping the complexity of security and it would be all too easy to either propose an over-simplified notion of security or lose the specificities of security as we follow up a multitude of possible relevant threads. The strategy of this book is to explore the nature of security through a wide range of case studies, allowing us to demonstrate and analyse the richness of security. The chapters that follow deal with case studies on geopolitical issues and international relations in the post-Cold War era, on how security is made and unmade in urban social worlds, on how a sense of the secure self is achieved within the space of the home, on health and disease in the body and the psyche and on many more factors. Security is complex both in 'where' we find it (the home, the nation, the microbe, the unconscious) and in what it means when we have identified a 'security' issue (physical danger, illness, psychic threat, risk or safety). The framing device of social worlds is one way of channelling this wide-ranging discussion.

2 Sociological concerns: mediation, matter, the individual

All the contributions to this book show how a variety of local practices and material artefacts mediate different experiences and understandings of the (in)security of individuals as they go about making their social worlds. Three sociological concerns – mediation, matter and the individual – will also frame the discussion of security. Like the concept of social worlds, not all the following chapters will use exactly the same understandings of these concerns, nor will they deal with these concerns evenly within each chapter. Contributors will use them as tools to crack open sociological analysis of security in a number of different social worlds.

In a sense, our use of these three terms is arbitrary but they also have a very real resonance with wider discussions going on in sociology and the social sciences.

2.1 Mediation

Mediation is used in a variety of ways within sociology and the related field of media studies. We can think of mediation both as media and as translation. Mediation as media offers the potential to address the role of the media in the making of social worlds. Different forms of media are involved in the production, circulation and reproduction of social imaginations and meanings through such media objects as films, television, books or radio. For example, the US satellite channel 'Fox News' was widely seen as having a conservative or right-wing political agenda and typically framed debates on security in particular ways: a comparative study of US and Arab news coverage of the 2003 Iraq War 'revealed a strong bias in support of the American-led war effort at Fox News Channel and important differences in how the various networks covered the war' (Aday et al., 2005).

A related sense of mediation is that it refers to the ways meaning is created, particularly through the translation of one thing into another thing. Meaning is never outside of the social worlds that make it; even the very languages we use to convey meaning to each other are socially and culturally specific. As has often been pointed out, different languages dissect the world into different objects. For example, in French, *aimer* cannot be simply translated into English, as it refers both to 'to like' and 'to love'. In Russian, we find that what the English language calls light blue and dark blue are treated as two distinct primary colours and not as shades of one colour (Culler, 1976). This demonstrates the ways in which communication is never free from social, cultural and material influences. It could even be argued that every social experience is in some sense mediated.

If all experience is indeed mediated, what kinds of mediation occur and what is the role of translation? Here we begin to move away from the common-sense use of the term (the transparent meaning exchange of one language for another) to where translation can refer to both statements and material objects. It describes those processes that allow statements or artefacts to pass from one social world into another, stabilising their existence in different social worlds (Star, 1991). For example, one problem in managing security has always been how to document or translate identity. By the twenty-first century, the most common solution was to create a document that included various forms of identification, crucially a photograph of the individual. The passport has proven a remarkably durable tactic for translating a person into a document or physical object. Despite the weaknesses of photographs (people's appearances change, not everyone resembles their photograph) they have allowed someone's identity to be translated into a document, which can then be further translated by security procedures to identify a safe or unsafe person. A chain of translations now exists: person – photograph – document – security procedures – safety/unsafety.

Mediation as media and mediation as translation are closely related because the media carries translations. For example, if we consider a news source to be biased, we could be seen to accuse that source of translating news in ways that benefit one politics over another politics. As we shall see, there are many ways in which mediation can affect security in social worlds.

2.2 Matter

Matter is also used to analyse society and social worlds in a number of ways. It helps us to explore the practices through which people make their social worlds in relation to various objects and artefacts, which we can call material practices. Matter also refers us to things in the world that we might think of as being 'real' and 'objective', that is objects that are used within societies but which are not themselves believed to be social, like rocks or wind. Matter allows sociologists to explore things that seem to exist outside social influence and to examine how they may or may not be made in particular social worlds. In practice it is never easy to draw a line between the social and the material. It may seem obvious that a rock is simply a rock. But the hard green lump that I call a 'paperweight' (a definition based on use and practice) may be something entirely different to a geologist who may subject the object to a series of tests and classificatory systems and declare it to be a 'mantle-peridotite-xenolith'. We attribute entirely different properties and practices to this material object: for me it simply holds papers down when the window is open, but it tells the geologist a story about the formation of the earth while also confirming a disciplinary classification system.

Passports are not only mediators of identity and security, but they also make this translation happen through material practices. The passport itself will be made from particular sorts of materials, stamped with various government insignia and including words that anyone can understand (name, age, etc.), together with machine-readable type (like a barcode). A security official can swipe the passport through a non-human reader to check records held in databases in order to confirm a traveller's identity. This example of a material practice may be repeated thousands of times a day. Throughout this book we will return to matter and how it is created and used in material practices.

For sociologists, matter also opens up issues of 'reality'. Such issues are particularly acute around notions of science and technology, which are often seen as producing an objective account of social worlds. For example, case studies in this book will look at how the safety or danger of soil for growing vegetables is established and at the causes of coronary heart disease. We will confront the detail of certain scientific techniques for telling us the 'truth' about something. But we also are able to open up the scientific production of truth, by exploring the social and material context around specific scientific practices. Sociologists and social scientists are increasingly investigating the material in order to examine how different social and material practices contribute to the making of social worlds.

2.3 The individual

The individual is a common object of analysis for sociologists. Sometimes sociologists employ the individual as a basis for social analysis and at other times they may dispute the existence of the 'individual' outside of the various social and cultural norms that allow the nature of individuality to be defined in any particular social world. A famous assertion exists, supported by followers of some economics schools of thought, that there is no such thing as society, only individual people making (or failing to make) rational decisions to better themselves. The individual is sometimes used as an assertion against sociological analysis. However, most social scientists would wish to argue for some connection between the individual and the various social worlds that produce and maintain them.

Considering the passport again allows us to illustrate how individuals are always embedded within the social world in which they move. The passport helps to illustrate how a person, at a point when they are clearly constituted as an individual, is simultaneously surrounded by social factors such as the material practices that constitute the passport. The moment when someone produces their passport to an official on entry to a nation can be seen as one of individualisation; even a group such as a family must produce a passport for each individual (even for a baby who is only several weeks old). Yet we can also see that it is surrounded and made by a range of material practices. When we find individuals in social worlds we also tend to find various social and cultural norms which surround their individuality. This features in the analyses of security in this book.

We can also see that forms or types of individuality differ across social worlds. What it means to be an 'individual' often shifts according to the various relations that create particular social worlds. Security is caught up in such constitutions, perhaps most obviously in relation to the creation, or not, of psychic security. For example, the moment of individualisation when looking at a passport means that an individual is produced as secure or insecure, and only certain types of practices are allowed by individuals; people are expected to wait patiently in line, not to take photographs, to enter the correct queue, to move forward only when a customs officer is free, not to move in groups unless they are in some way related (both blood and friendship), and so on. Not all customs entry points will have exactly these (and only these) practices, but each entry point will have a set of practices that defines the individuality that is allowed to travellers as they seek entry to a nation.

Figure 1
People queueing at passport control

The three concerns we have chosen to help examine security will recur across the various chapters presented in this book. They will allow us to prise open in a range of ways what may seem to be the natural or assumed features of our lives but which are in need of, or are susceptible to, sociological analysis. Combined with the ideas of what a 'social world' is, we now have a number of interesting tools that we can use to begin to make sense of security. As tools, they will be used and understood differently, depending on their utility in any particular form of analysis. A hammer can bang nails, pull out nails and be used as a weight; in the same sense, mediation, matter and the individual will be recurrently used in our work but not always in the same way.

3 Security and the airport

International airports like Schiphol or Heathrow can illustrate some of our earlier points. Like cities, they have a remarkably high number of temporary residents, and comprise complex social worlds that subdivide into ever-smaller worlds: travellers, such as business travellers, tourists, migrants, those visiting families; airlines and their workers, such as check-in workers, airline pilots, baggage handlers; government agencies with police, security services, customs officials, immigration officials, public health officials, safety inspectors, and fire officers; and all the various commercial industries to service and profit from the food and shopping needs of travellers and airport workers. Many of these social worlds will have their own practices and cultures. One particular such world would be that inhabited by airline pilots. How does someone become a pilot? Or, put another way, how does someone enter the social world of pilots?

Gaining membership of the social world of airline pilots is a complex and contingent process, governed not only by a pilot's licence but also by employment and social practices. An individual may gradually become a member even though at the start they may have no more than a vague interest in flying. If such an individual enters a range of mediating practices, such as studying certain topics like how to read navigation or how to land a plane, s/he may gain admission to certain relevant qualifications. Having qualified, a pilot would engage in the existing communities of practice of pilots. For example, they might read magazines devoted to flying or take time to find and look at relevant websites. Finally, someone's status as a member of this social world could be formally recognised through employment as a pilot. Or one may participate in this world simply as a leisure activity. Other routes into this social world may be taken: for example, it is not uncommon for pilots trained in national air forces to enter commercial employment once they are released from the armed services. Yet in all cases, an individual becomes a pilot not just by being able to fly a plane but by passing into the social world of pilots, which is mediated by a range of material practices. The social world of pilots also exists in a number of places – the key one is, of course, the airport. In the airport, we see how many different social worlds exist in the same place.

The social world of the airport has become increasingly familiar to many people. In the past fifty years there has been a dramatic increase in mobility and flow of people and things through airports. In 1960 around three million trips abroad were made by British residents. By 1992 this figure had grown to twenty-two million. By 2005 this had risen to more than sixty-six million (Office for National Statistics, 2006). The majority of these trips were made using aeroplanes and the airport has long been iconic of global mobility and movement. However, the rise in travel presents a problem for those who manage and regulate airports as the movement of people and things can be both desirable (for example, business travellers, tourists, goods and foods) and undesirable (for example, criminals and organised crime, 'unregulated' migrants, guns, drugs, diseases and food). Security and surveillance become central to such flows of people and things through airports, together with checking the access of various entities to each nation-state or regional body (like the European Union). Airports have become the modern frontier towns of the nation-state. Yet these new frontiers are not on the geographical periphery but are often located very close to the economic centres of a nation-state. It is often in the economic interest of a nation-state to facilitate quick access by tourists or business-people to the areas of most interest to these travellers. The airport becomes both the security border of a nation and a place that aims to create quick and easy access to specific and often sensitive regions of the nation-state.

Such a contradiction exists on top of the fact that airports must constantly organise for the possibility of catastrophe, whether that be a plane crash, severe weather or a terrorist attack. Various emergency teams perpetually practise handling fire, accident, epidemics, hazardous materials and other civil and military disaster contingencies. Yet in the same place the normal activities of shopping and eating are heavily promoted to a captive audience. Trying to combine such seemingly contradictory functions means the airport has been described as being in a ceaseless state of emergency (Fuller and Harley, 2004).

The airport is also one of the most surveilled spaces in modern everyday life. This surveillance is highly mediated by a number of material artefacts, for example: CCTV cameras, metal detectors, baggage scanners and passport readers. For the individual travelling through an airport, documentation of identity becomes central to the control of security and mobility. Various material artefacts such as the passport and the boarding card are needed to align an individual's identity with the name on the airline records and with various state agencies. The passport controls access at key gateways and 'choke points' (for example, in the transition from landside to airside, on arrival, on boarding the plane) and it identifies the traveller to both the airline and state agencies. Identification via the use of passports or quasi-passports has become the primary means of translating individuals as secure or insecure, as threats or non-threats.

Identification of individuals via a passport was previously a simple matter of matching an individual body to one specific document via a photograph. The advent of increasingly complex biometric systems of surveillance and identification – iris scans, facial recognition systems, fingerprint scanners – introduces new forms of mediation. Visual representations of the body such as the striations of the iris are rendered into numeric or digital form. Once 'virtualised' in this form, a body can become attached to a global information exchange. An increasingly complex and mediated virtual identity now follows the individual passenger through the airport. In identification procedures we see all three concerns – mediation, matter and the individual – interacting in ways that produce security in the social world of the airport.

The passport is just one of the material objects found in an airport. Other artefacts mediate the flows and movements of people around the airport. Airports are places where large numbers of people come from diverse cultural backgrounds and have differing understandings of verbal and non-verbal communication. The behaviour of individuals, and in particular their smooth flow through the airport, is created in part by signs that have gradually been made internationally comprehensible. We need only think of the common ways that pictures denote male and female toilets. These signs direct passengers, vehicles and aircraft alike. For example, all users of the airport (whether pilots taxiing aircraft, car drivers or foot passengers) are assumed to be unfamiliar with the particular geography and language of the specific airport and in need of frequent reminders of where they are and how to get where they want to go. The signs used in airports mediate and separate the various flows of people and things by creating a series of decision points that constantly split routes for passengers, cars and aircraft in order to direct all these entities to their temporary destinations. Such signs are all part of airport design, which stabilises both the system of the airport and the temporary users of the airport.

Airports exist within the geophysical borders of nation-states but are also detached from these locations. Many people may pass through the airports at Los Angeles (LAX), Amsterdam (AMS), Frankfurt (FRA) or Chicago (ORD) without ever really being in these cities because they are 'flight hubs' used by many to connect from one flight to another. Yet the generic airport as a 'place', with its shopping malls, bars, cafés, and waiting areas is entirely familiar to most travellers – in a sense one never visits a strange airport. This familiarity with the social world of the airport is achieved by the multiple material entities that mediate the individual's passage through this social world.

The mediated familiarity and ordinariness of the airport is an enormous achievement, given that visible technologies of fear (guns, barriers, one-way mirrors, uniforms) sit next to familiar spaces of pleasure and consumption (coffee bars and shops). In the space of a few short steps travellers can be asked to remove their shoes and/or belt then be subjected to body search by a total stranger, before being sprayed with complimentary perfume or given a free sample of a liqueur: 'Airports mix multiple forms of life, matter and information into a series of new and constantly changing relations between bodies and the sky, between local landscapes and global capital' (Fuller and Harley, 2004, p. 104). Airports achieve this by creating spaces in which disparate systems can meet each other and coexist: high-speed jet routes meet slow urban motorways; shopping malls meet high security systems; high-speed mass transit systems are integrated with slow-speed individualised means of transport, such as walking (Fuller and Harley, 2004).

Airports demonstrate how security can be found and explored if we look at how it plays a role in the creation of social worlds. We are particularly helped in such analyses by the concern we have to look at issues of matter, mediation and the individual in relation to security.

4 Structure of the book

We will now give a brief outline of the remainder of the book.

In Chapter 1, Tim Jordan explores security by using the three concerns of matter, mediation and the individual. First, a case study of soil poisoning on an allotment explores food security and the matter of soil. Second, a case study of psycho-social analysis of the Harry Potter series will be used to explore mediation and to demonstrate sociological analysis of the psyche. Finally, security and the individual will be examined in relation to both the matter of poisoned soil and the mediations of the Potter books.

In Chapter 2, Matt McDonald takes as his starting point the global security dynamics and processes of a world dominated by the aftermath of 11 September 2001. This chapter briefly sketches changes in dominant understandings of security in international relations from the cold war to the present, suggesting that the traditional association of 'security' with the preservation of state sovereignty remains the most powerful discourse of security in international politics. This association, however, is problematic on both analytical and ethical grounds. Analytically, as the example of asylum seekers shows, it fails to account for the ways in which security is constructed, for example, through designations of some things as a threat and other things as safe. And ethically, as the example of climate change shows, such an understanding of security reinforces a context in which states and their interests are taken as boundaries of ethical responsibility, denying obligations to vulnerable outsiders and future generations. This chapter concludes by suggesting that to recognise the constructed nature of security in global politics means taking seriously several core but often overlooked questions, such as 'whose security are we talking about?', 'from what do they need protecting?' and 'by whom?'

In Chapter 3, Elizabeth Silva addresses how security has become a major part of the domestic social world. She explores senses of self and security in the context of the home. Relations within homes, she argues, provide a specific context for broadening the discussion of sociological understandings of social practices of security. She focuses on the relevance of a sense of personal, internal and assumed security in the face of actual and symbolic risks and threats entailed by rapid social change. Silva discusses the importance of routines and normality for social life, together with concerns about the rapid changes in information and communication technologies on home life. This chapter also explores how a sense of 'ontological security' is developed and maintained, this being the sense of personal physical and psychic safety our everyday routines are partly designed to foster.

In Chapter 4, Sophie Watson outlines a number of pro-urban and anti-urban discourses that have articulated the city variously as a site of intermingling, difference and heterogeneity, or of heightened sensibility and excitement. She explores how security is made and unmade in urban social worlds. The city is examined as a potential site of social interaction and democratic civic life on the one hand, but also as a site of contamination, unruly forces, dangerous others and chaos on the other. These tensions between negative and positive imaginaries of the city have been played out in the way cities have been planned and made. Strategies for security are a crucial aspect of these imaginaries of the city. In particular Watson illustrates how the fear of different others in the city underpins social–spatial segregation and division. Three case studies – gated communities, sports utility vehicles and surveillance cameras – illustrate the contribution of psycho-social and sociological accounts to understanding the fear of others in the city.

In Chapter 5, Simon Carter and George Davey Smith use a number of historical and contemporary case studies on the subjects of health and disease to examine various aspects of security. These include cholera in the nineteenth century, the emergence of the 'risk factor' while studying coronary heart disease in the mid-twentieth century and the contemporary use of the metered dose inhaler to control asthma. This chapter uses these case studies to introduce and develop a number of relevant contemporary sociological issues. These can be broadly characterised as those approaches and methods associated with Science and Technology Studies (S&TS), the study and investigation of the part played by science and technology in society.

The Afterword summarises the concerns of each chapter and draws them together into a debate about the sociological concerns of matter, mediation and the individual. These summaries are connected to understandings of social worlds. This is used as a basis to reflect on the engagement of sociological thought with security.

References

Aday, S., Livingston, S. and Hebert, M. (2005) 'Embedding the truth: a cross-cultural analysis of objectivity and television coverage of the Iraq war', *Harvard International Journal of Press-Politics*, vol. 10, pp. 3–21.

Becker, H. (1982) *Art Worlds*, Berkeley, CA, University of California Press.

Blumer, H. (1969) *Symbolic Interactionism: Perspective and Method*, Englewood Cliffs, NJ, Prentice-Hall.

Boissevain, J. (1978) 'Tourism and the European periphery: the case of the Mediterranean' in Seers, D.E.A. (ed.) *Underdeveloped Europe: Studies in Core Periphery Relations*, London, Harvester Press.

Clarke, A. (1997) 'A social worlds research adventure: the case of reproductive science' in Strauss, A. and Corbin, J. (eds) *Grounded Theory in Practice*, London, Sage.

Culler, J. (1976) *Saussaure*, Glasgow, Fontana.

Fujimura, J. (1987) 'Constructing "do-able" problems in cancer research: articulating alignment', *Social Studies of Science*, vol. 17, pp. 257–93.

Fuller, G. and Harley, R. (2004) *Aviopolis: A Book About Airports*, London, Black Dog Publishing.

Gieryn, T. (1995) 'Boundaries of science' in Jasanoff, S., Markle, G., Petersen, J. and Pinch, T. (eds) *Handbook of Science and Technology Studies*, London, Sage.

Goffman, E. (1958) *The Presentation of Self in Everyday Life*, Edinburgh, University of Edinburgh, Social Sciences Research Centre.

Latour, B. (1987) *Science in Action: How to Follow Scientists and Engineers Through Society*, Milton Keynes, Open University Press.

Office for National Statistics (2006) 'Travel trends: a report on the 2005 international passenger survey', London, National Statistics Office.

Star, S. (1991) 'Power, technology and the phenomenology of conventions: on being allergic to onions' in Law, J. (ed.) *A Sociology of Monsters: Essays on Power, Technlogy and Domination*, London, Routledge.

Star, S. and Griesemer, J. (1989) 'Institutional ecology, "translations" and boundary objects: amateurs and professionals in Berkeley's museum of vertebrate zoology', *Social Studies of Science*, vol. 19, pp. 387–420.

Stott, M. (1978) 'Tourism in Mykonos: some social and cultural responses', *Mediterranean Studies*, vol. 1, pp. 122–33.

World Tourism Organisation (2007) *World Tourism Highlights: 2006 Edition*, Madrid, World Tourism Organisation.

Chapter 1
Security in the social: gardens and Harry Potter

Tim Jordan

Contents

1 **Introduction** **18**

1.1 Allotting security 18

1.2 Teaching aims 19

2 **Matter and security** **19**

3 **Harry Potter and the security of the psycho-social** **27**

4 **The individual: digging and reading** **39**

5 **Conclusion** **44**

References **44**

1 Introduction

1.1 Allotting security

Our gardening allotment was one of twenty-nine, set out one by one, side by side, in a long snaking line in inner-city London. Each allotment was around ten metres by ten metres and was mainly devoted to growing vegetables. We had successfully grown carrots, borlotti beans, several kinds of lettuce, green beans and potatoes. In addition to feeding ourselves, the allotment provided exercise and leisure; I particularly found being outdoors and digging in the soil a nice antidote to my usual work practice of sitting at a computer. I had also taken my youngest daughter's school class to the allotment, where twenty-nine five-year-olds had pulled up weeds, dug in the earth, planted seeds, picked vegetables, and then taken them back to the classroom to wash off the dirt and eat them (although one child insisted one carrot be saved for his rabbit).

Figure 1.1
A typical allotment

It came as a disturbing surprise when, in late 2004, a letter from the London Borough of Hackney (LBH) arrived, advising us that the soil on our allotment was dangerously contaminated with lead and arsenic, that we should stop eating food grown on the allotment, and stop touching the soil there.

Food that had been a source of security in several ways now became risky and dangerous. We had felt secure with our allotment food, more secure than with other food because our allotment-grown food was organically produced by us. It was not only biologically more secure, it was also emotionally more secure for it was sown, picked and prepared by our hands; watching food grow produced in us a sense of safety that was unconscious and felt, rather than articulated and rational. These different appreciations of our food produced in us a complex sense of security which had now been radically and utterly inverted into a sense of insecurity. Had we poisoned ourselves? Had we poisoned our children? What terrible environment had we been unknowingly working in, where touching the soil was considered a danger to health? Security turned to insecurity, safety to danger, comfort to risk, pleasure to pain; all this from one letter.

This chapter will explore how security is made and unmade in our lives through two case studies. In addition, it will explore three concerns that sociologists often address: matter, mediation and the individual. Matter will be examined in relation to the first case study – our allotment. Mediation will be explored in relation to the second case study – the Harry Potter series and brand. Finally, it will examine the individual, drawing on both these case studies.

1.2 Teaching aims

The aims of this chapter are to explain:

- how security is part of our social world
- sociological interpretations of security and matter through a case study of allotment gardening
- psycho-social interpretations of security and mediation through a case study of the Harry Potter novels and brand
- sociological interpretations of the individual by drawing on both case studies.

2 Matter and security

The central factor in the allotment story is matter – the soil itself; one day it was secure, allowing vegetables to be grown, and the next day it was unsafe. As you might expect, there was initially a strong reaction to the LBH letter. A loud and argumentative public meeting occurred, as well as a number of meetings involving the Hackney Allotment Society, local government representatives, various national government agencies, some news reporters, and myriad discussions by gardeners over the vegetables. One question asked was *why* the tests had been done. LBH had originally decided to carry out borough-wide tests to meet new environmental protection rules that came into force in 2000, through the Environment Protection Act 1990, although the tests were not conducted until 2004.

LBH appointed an external consultant, who took soil samples from all the Hackney allotments, and also from a local park to act as a cross-check. The samples were tested for poisons in a laboratory by dissolving the soil in test tubes. The allotment had been transformed from a series of gardens, first to a series of soil samples, and then to a series of test tubes, each containing the soil's dispersed chemical fragments. From these test tubes, the consultant was able to derive figures for the levels of various poisons in the soil. All these stages involve various social conventions particular to the experts who work on them. For example, there is extensive debate among soil contamination experts about how many soil samples and where to take them.

Our matter had now been acted on by a range of social actors of wildly different sizes – from the British Parliament to the trowel that dug. At this point, an inversion took place – the soil began to act back and take on a role of its own. Sociologists Michel Callon and Bruno Latour have described this process of social acting and the construction of social sizes:

> What then is a sociologist? Someone who studies associations and dissociations, that is all, as the word 'social' itself implies. Associations between men [*sic*]? Not solely, since for a long time now associations between men have been expanded and extended through other allies: words, rituals, iron, wood, seeds and rain. The sociologist studies all associations, but in particular the transformation of weak interactions into strong ones and vice versa. This is of special interest because here the relative dimensions of the actors are altered.
>
> ...
>
> For the sociologist then the question of method boils down to knowing where to place oneself. ... [H]e or she sits just at the point where the contract is made, just where forces are translated, and the difference between the technical and the social is fought out, just where the irreversible becomes reversible[.]
>
> (Callon and Latour, 1981, pp. 300–1)

We can read Latour and Callon's term **association** to mean connection. The production of numbers from our soil is just such a moment of the transformation – through connections of social into technical and of reversibility into irreversibility – that Callon and Latour describe. For example, the numbers that resulted from the tests of our soil were then connected by LBH staff to the Soil Guidance Values (SGV), which set out acceptable and unacceptable levels of certain chemicals in soil. This connection showed that our soil contained dangerous levels of lead and arsenic. These numbers prompted LBH to act and send out health warnings, which in turn acted on us to reassess what the matter meant to us.

Little then changed over the next nine months. The medical advice was softened because it was believed the soil would be decontaminated, and eating vegetables and touching soil in our allotment for a year or so was not considered hazardous. People worked, or not, on their allotments and the Allotment Society consulted with the local government workers who, in turn, sought further advice and explored funding opportunities. Here was a set of social connections that were stable but, everyone knew, could not last. Matter, the soil, would have to be settled one way or another – the most likely option being the expensive removal of the soil and replacing it with clean matter. The irreversible (that the soil was poisoned) was now driving the security of our soil. But, just as Callon and Latour suggest, a social moment may emerge out of which the irreversible is reversed. Sociologists are well equipped to notice and record such moments. Out of the interactions of different actors, a focus emerged on a different soil test: physiologically based extraction tests (PBET).

PBET springs from a simple idea. It measures the take-up of poisons in the soil, based on the assumption that only a certain percentage of the poison in the soil would enter a human. For example, the US authorities assume that 100 per cent of arsenic contained in soil will be absorbed into a body (Ruby et al., 1996, p. 422). PBET challenges this assumption by arguing that a great deal of poison is bound to other elements in the soil and much less might be taken into the human system than the level of poison in the soil suggests. The term for this is bioaccessibility, that is, the amount of poison in any bit of matter that is accessible to human biology. Changing our soil's nature from poisonous to non-poisonous might then be achieved by arguing that all the poison in a soil might not transfer to humans.

PBET has emerged as the leading contender in its field. It was first proposed in 1996 and consists of mimicking the digestive system of a two- to three-year-old child who has eaten contaminated soil. This particular digestive system was chosen because it was claimed to be the most at risk. The test reduces this digestive system to its three major stages (stomach, large intestine, small intestine) and tracks the passage of the soil through the digestive process. Each of the major stages is represented by a flask into which chemicals are added that mimic the human body. The soil progresses through the flasks and the remaining amount of poison can be measured (Ruby et al., 1996).

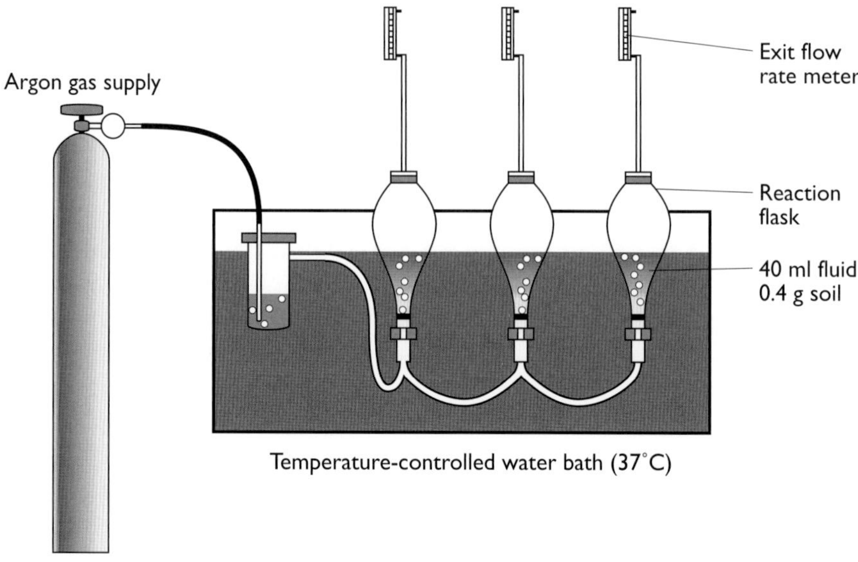

Figure 1.2
Schematic of the PBET experiment

However, proponents of such a test cannot simply expect it to be taken up. They have to create connections beyond the technical alliances made between flasks in their simulated digestive system. Most importantly, the reliability of the test must be assessed. The ultimate test of the test is for a human to eat some poisoned soil and compare the results with the simulated system's results from the same soil. Of course this would be unethical. A stand-in for the human must be created; a second simulation of a human digestive system is needed to test the reliability of the first. The standard procedure here is animal testing, a controversial practice due to the deleterious effect on the animals in question, but it is a widely used procedure, particularly in medical testing (Ruby et al., 1996, p. 429). We can now see that a test-tube (or *in vitro*) simulation of a human digestive system can be validated by being compared to an animal (or *in vivo*) simulation of a human digestive system.

Science and technology here provide a series of connections between humans and objects, which construct a particular social understanding of danger through the PBET test, which claims to measure more accurately than other tests the danger a soil might pose to humans. The magic of science is often to conceal these social interactions in the objectivity of test results. For example, it might now be claimed that PBET tests the harm that soil might do to humans, but this is an objectification of a series of choices that have been made over ideas and objects in a quest to simulate parts of the human digestive system.

PBET, when used on soil from our allotment, showed it to have less poison than the previous test – our soil was declared safe again.

LBH issued new advice clearly stating that the soil did not pose a risk to human health (London Borough of Hackrey, 2005). A little later, sacks of compost were delivered, to be dug into the soil to further dilute any poison that might be lurking in the no-longer-infected matter. Security was restored, and everyone could treat the sequence as a strange interlude in their gardening.

This result was announced at a meeting of the Allotment Society, prompting many representatives immediately and spontaneously to express their relief that they could get back to normal. One or two even began to complain mutinously that they had been put through months of worry and uncertainty for no reason. It seemed to me that the relief that LBH felt (after all, expensive, complicated and time-consuming works had now been avoided) was matched by the relief that the representatives of allotment holders felt. This was a pivotal moment, in which the PBET test created a focus for relations between LBH and allotment holders who accepted the tests as valid and allowed a return to normality. Security emerged from the laboratories, and our soil magically turned from poisonous to healthy. All the agencies – from the national to the local, which had coalesced into the moment when LBH tested the safety of our allotment – were now dispersed. As sociologists we can see not only the moment when the irreversible (soil is poisonous) is reversed (soil is healthy) but also, by looking more closely, the fragility of this moment.

In February 2005 the Environment Agency (EA, a UK government department) issued a report on bioaccessibility, concluding that 'on the basis of the information currently available, the Agency cannot recommend the use of bioaccessibility testing in a risk assessment at this time' (Environment Agency, 2005). In short, the EA refused to endorse PBET, pointing out that standard laboratory procedures had not yet been defined and accepted, meaning that different laboratories might produce different results. However, the EA's report is ambivalent in parts and records good results for PBET on a number of studies. The EA concluded that PBET was unproven just seven months before LBH adopted PBET to 'unpoison' our soil.

A further worry is the emphasis some companies that sell PBET as a service may put on their product. One company advertised with a leaflet using a case study that claimed to demonstrate that use of a PBET allowed a developer to show that the land they were developing for housing was less polluted than standard tests showed, meaning that 'Our client was able to complete the development without incurring substantial additional costs' (Ground Investigation Limited, undated). Such a claim in no way undermines the scientific legitimacy of PBET, but its fairly consistent ability to show lower levels of poison compared to the standard tests make it attractive to many for a range of reasons.

The pivotal moment in the unpoisoning of our soil occurred when PBET managed to connect LBH (whose interests were the health of allotment holders, its legal obligations, to control costs of fixing soil and to eliminate the problem of poisoned soil) and the allotment holders, particularly the society that represented them (whose interests were their health and a return to gardening on healthy soil). This was the key moment in the making of this social world as secure or insecure, the moment when the social was made and unmade.

I have already quoted Callon and Latour on how sociologists are capable of seeing the moments when the social is made and unmade; these are moments when we can see how our world is social and how that social world is made in the particular way it is. The following reading from their work continues this theme by introducing the notion of the **black box**. A black box means something that has been made through social interaction that has been hidden – put inside a black box which no one can see into – and what has been made can thus appear asocial.

Read the following extract by Michel Callon and Bruno Latour, paying particular attention to the way they describe the construction of different 'social actors'. Reflect on what is meant by a 'black box' and try to identify moments in the story of the allotment when a black box is opened or closed. Callon and Latour's work is often called 'actor-network theory' and will be discussed further in Chapter 5.

Reading 1.1 Michel Callon and Bruno Latour, 'Unscrewing the big Leviathan'

A difference in relative size is obtained when a micro-actor can, in addition to enlisting bodies, also enlist the greatest number of durable materials. He or she thus creates greatness and longevity making the others small and provisional in comparison. ... Instead of dividing the subject with the social/technical, or with the human/animal, or with the micro/macro dichotomies, we will only retain for the analysis *gradients of resistivity* and consider only the *variations in relative solidity and durability of different sorts of materials.*

By associating materials of different durability, a set of practices is placed in a hierarchy in such a way that some become stable and need no longer be considered. Only thus can one 'grow'. ... An actor grows with the number of relations he or she can put, as we say, in black boxes. A black box contains that which no longer needs to be reconsidered, those things whose contents have become a matter of indifference. The more elements one can place in black boxes – modes of thoughts, habits, forces and objects – the broader the construction one can raise. Of course, black boxes never remain fully closed or properly fastened ... but macro-actors can do *as if* they were closed and dark. Although, as ethnomethodologists have shown, we are all constantly struggling for closing leaky black boxes, macro-actors, to say the least, do not have to negotiate with *equal intensity* everything. They can go on and count on a force while negotiating for another. If they were not successful at that, they could not simplify the social world. In mechanical terms, they could not make a machine, that is hide the continued exercise of a will to give the impression of forces that move by themselves. In logical terms, they could not make chains of arguments, that is stabilize discussion of certain premises to allow deductions or establish order between different elements.

...

The paradox with which we ended the introduction has now been resolved. We end up with actors of different size even though they are all isomorphic, because some have been able to put into black boxes more elements durably to alter their relative size. The question of method is also resolved. How can we examine macro-actors and micro-actors, we were wondering, without confirming differences in size? Reply: by directing our attention not to the social but towards the processes by which an actor creates lasting asymmetries. That among these processes some lead to associations which are sometimes called 'social' (associations of bodies), and that some of the others are sometimes called 'technical' (associations of materials), need *not* concern us further. Only the differences between what can be put in black boxes and what remains open for future negotiations are now relevant for us.

To summarize, macro-actors are micro-actors seated on top of many (leaky) black boxes. They are neither larger, nor more complex than micro-actors; on the contrary, they are of the same size and, as we shall see, they are in fact simpler than micro-actors.

...

The rules of sociological method

... Sociological analysis is nevertheless involved, since it follows the associations and dissociations, but it follows them wherever they are produced by the actors. The actors can bond together in a block comprising millions of individuals, they can enter alliances with iron, with grains of sand, neurons, words, opinions and affects. All this is of little importance, providing they can be followed with the same freedom as they themselves practise. We cannot analyse the [social] if we give precedence to a certain type of association, for example associations of men with men, iron with iron, neurons with neurons, or a specific size of factors. Sociology is only lively and productive when it examines *all associations with at least the same daring as the actors who make them.*

...

How to slip between two mistakes

A macro-actor, as we have seen, is a micro-actor seated on black boxes, a force capable of associating so many other forces that it acts like a 'single man'. The result is that a macro-actor is by definition no more difficult to examine than a micro-actor. Growth is only possible if one can associate long lasting forces with oneself and thereby simplify existence. Hence a macro-actor is at least as simple as a micro-actor *since otherwise it could not have become bigger.* We do not draw closer to social reality by descending to micro-negotiations or by rising towards the macro-actors. We must leave behind the preconceptions which lead us to believe that macro-actors are more complicated than micro-actors. ... A macro-actor can only grow if it simplifies itself. As it simplifies its existence, it simplifies the work of the sociologist. It is no more difficult to send tanks into Kabul than to dial 999. It is no more difficult to describe Renault than the secretary who takes telephone calls at the Houston police station. If it were much more difficult the tanks would not move and Renault would not exist. There would be no macro-actors. By claiming that macro-actors are more complex than micro-actors sociologists discourage analysis, and hamstring investigators. And they prevent the secret of the macro-actors' growth from being revealed: making operations childishly simple. The king is not only naked, he is a child playing with (leaky) black boxes.

Reading source

Callon and Latour, 1981, pp. 284–99

A social world, according to Callon and Latour, is made of a series of black boxes. The various 'actors' in a social world are able to act according to the black boxes they can command. In our example of the soil, the most important black boxes were the soil tests. Interpreted more generally, Callon and Latour argue that our social worlds operate when we partially forget the social nature of many things that we use. We operate by taking the sociality of many things – soil tests, for example – for granted. For Callon and Latour, the power of sociology is to remind us of this.

You may be curious to know how the allotment story turned out for us. We abandoned our allotment and handed the keys back. You can probably guess our reasons; we were not convinced that we should bet our and our children's long-term health on the superiority of PBET (even though we knew PBET might well be a reliable test). We had also had some very serious illnesses in our family in the same period and were undoubtedly feeling insecure about health generally. We also noticed the closing of ranks around the PBET results by the Allotment Society and LBH and, although we could see nothing specifically wrong about this, it felt uncomfortable. There was something intangible about the sudden transition from insecurity back to security that we could not trust.

Our own assessment of the security of our allotment was, as you can see, based on conscious and unconscious reasons. I cannot fully explain it, chiefly because I can see that the PBET test is most likely something to be trusted (Wynne, 1996). Yet our decision was clear and not in question: the only question that remained was whether we assessed the threat to our security rationally, or were being driven by less conscious motives.

3 Harry Potter and the security of the psycho-social

Sociological thought has, particularly in recent years, developed an increasingly influential strand of work under the name '**psycho-social** thought'. This strand draws together psychoanalytical insights with sociological interpretations. To further our understanding of how security is an integral part of our ongoing creation of social worlds, it will help to turn to this body of work. To do this I will use a second case study, this one concerning Harry Potter, teenage wizard and hero of novels, films and countless marketing goods. Potter is a useful example because, as psychoanalyst Margaret Rustin and sociologist Michael Rustin put it: 'The fluidity of the boundary between the imaginary and the real in the lives of children, and the uncertainties and openness surrounding both, make children especially capable of being moved by stories which give form to the experience of their inner worlds' (Rustin and Rustin, 2001, p. 15).

A case study involving children's psychic development and fiction makes it easier for psychic and social dimensions in security to be examined simultaneously. It also introduces the second sociological concern of this chapter, mediation. Understandings of mediation will be developed throughout this book, but initially you can take it to mean social moments when one thing turns into another, just like the moments that Callon and Latour identify when the irreversible is reversed. For example, in the allotment story our soil was turned from secure to insecure and back again. This mediation, the transformation of one thing into another, was performed (or mediated) through the soil tests. A key form of mediation that contributes substantially to security is the media. This book is a form of media that allows ideas about security explored by the authors to be mediated to you, the reader. Media such as television, films or video games all mediate various social and cultural messages between different bodies. If one advantage of using a psycho-social analysis of Harry Potter to explore security is the ease with which such an analysis allows us access to issues of security, social worlds and the psyche, then a further advantage is that the young wizard is, above all, a creature of the media and mediation. After all, Harry exists only in media – in print, film, computer games, websites, playing cards, and so on.

Rustin and Rustin explore children's literature, particularly that aimed at children aged from ten to the mid-teens. They argue that this period poses a number of key inner emotional developmental tasks in relation to emerging independence. First, independence from the family must be gradually gained and this involves knowing 'How to deal with the loss of the near-exclusive attention of mother, initiated in the process of weaning but extending beyond this in terms of emotional intimacy' (Rustin and Rustin, 2001, p. 9). Second, in this period children normally become increasingly involved with other children, producing sets of anxieties about how to relate to peers. Third, this period includes enormous changes in sex and sexuality. In all these areas children need to develop unconscious and inner emotions, as well as articulated and outer emotions, to cope with the creation and maintenance of their own sense of self – of being someone – and their relationships with others. Such developments intimately involve a sense of security or insecurity in one's self, dealing as they do with the necessary loss of loved ones – in growth away from parents – which is part of the development of a secure personality. For these reasons, the Rustins argue that the key elements of children's fantasy fiction revolve around love and loss with, in particular, the near-universal of children's fiction being children who no longer have, or who lose, or who must regain their parents while simultaneously learning to develop ethical and fulfilling relationships beyond their family.

Such elements lie at the core of the Potter series. Harry is an orphan who begins the story living with his uncle and aunt; coming to know his parents and dealing with his feelings for them is a central theme throughout the stories (Rowling, 1997). Another of the most prominent themes is Harry's relationship with his closest friends, Ron Weasley and Hermione Granger. As with his feelings for his parents, Harry and his friends struggle to develop their relationships and to understand how to act with each other. For example, at the time when sexuality is beginning to make its presence felt, Ron and Harry must ask a girl to go to a ball at their school, Hogwarts, but Harry finds it extremely difficult and embarrassing:

> [I]t was amazing how many girls Hogwarts suddenly seemed to hold; he had never quite noticed that before. Girls giggling and whispering in the corridors, girls shrieking with laughter as boys passed them, girls excitedly comparing notes on what they were going to wear on Christmas night ...
>
> 'Why do they have to move in packs?' Harry asked Ron, as a dozen or so girls walked past them, sniggering and staring at Harry. 'How're you supposed to get one on their own to ask them?'
>
> (Rowling, 2000, pp. 338–9)

A match exists here between the emotional issues facing children generally and the issues facing the fictional Harry and Ron. But how does one affect the other? How are the author J.K. Rowling's words mediated into real emotional developments in psychic security and insecurity? What mediation occurs to allow fiction to aid fact?

Rustin and Rustin argue that:

> One way in which [children's] writers explore children's inner experience ... is by describing the meaning for the child of feeling contained and understood in symbolic terms. The capacity to think, to maintain an internal resilience to temporarily bad experiences through the memory of the good, is crucial to development, and depends in part on powers of language, play, and imagination.
>
> (Rustin and Rustin, 2001, p. 11)

The themes in fiction of loss of parental figures and fears about developing peer-relations become central to symbolically representing the emotional difficulties faced by children. The argument is that stories provide what might be called 'symbolic containers' for the confused and developing feelings of children and thus provide ways of exploring, understanding and developing these feelings. Harry's fictional orphaning can be mediated by readers into a vehicle through which they can project their own worries about becoming independent. As Rustin and Rustin argue, the central component of much children's literature addresses 'the pains evoked in children by loss of loved people and places and the loss of present security which all growth and change entails' (Rustin and Rustin, 2001, p. 249), because such themes offer imaginative resources for children to explore their changing feelings.

I have so far offered a small-scale example from Harry Potter of how symbols of emotional development are present and available to readers.

Further evidence of the potential emotional impact of Harry Potter lies in the overarching story (some of which I must give away to those who do not know the Potter story). Rowling says that she has been working to a pre-set plotline covering seven volumes, each volume covering a year in Harry's school life from eleven until he leaves school. The potential in such a plan for covering the years in which independence develops is obvious. The first volume begins with readers understanding that Harry is a magical and special child, as he is placed on the doorstep of his aunt and uncle's house as an orphan, because an evil wizard failed in an attempt to kill him. Harry is unaware of his powers, and is deliberately misled by his aunt and uncle who wish to banish magic from their world. This relies on Rowling's fantasy world-building device that there is a magical wizarding world hidden from the non-magical or 'muggle' world. When Harry turns eleven he begins receiving invitations to the Hogwarts' school of magic, but these are hidden from him. He is finally tracked down by the first of several father (and mother) figures that Harry encounters – Hagrid, the half-giant school gamekeeper. Only at this stage does Harry find out that his parents were killed while trying to defend him from the evil wizard Voldemort and, after their death, the spell to kill Harry backfired somehow and Voldemort disappeared.

We can note the complexity of this situation. Harry is offered the guilt of having lived while his parents died and the loss of not knowing them. His path to independence is opened up by going to secondary school and finding out he is a wizard, and he is immediately plunged into the complexities of good and evil. The Potter story unfolds over seven volumes with each volume posing physical and psychic threats to Harry's security, offering a rich symbolism for his readers. Each book begins with Harry trapped at his magic-hating aunt and uncle's, then follows Harry through an adventure and ends with him discussing the events with Hogwarts' headmaster and father-figure, Albus Dumbledore.

Take for example one of the climactic moments in the third book, *Harry Potter and the Prisoner of Azkaban* (Rowling, 1999). In this plot, Harry initially finds out that escaped mass murderer Sirius Black was a friend of his parents, who then betrayed their whereabouts to Voldemort, leading ultimately to their deaths. In a confrontation with Harry, it is revealed that Black is innocent, and it was another friend who betrayed his parents. As they take the guilty party towards justice, Black tells Harry that he is his godfather and asks whether, once declared innocent, Harry would like to come and live with him. But the guilty party escapes in the confusion. Black is assaulted by Dementors, who suck out a person's soul. Harry tries to defend Black but is himself assaulted and both find themselves near to death. At this crucial moment, someone that Harry can barely see performs a powerful and difficult piece of magic called a

Patronus which saves them. Unfortunately this delivers Black into the authorities' hands, who still believe him guilty of murder and refuse to believe the claims of thirteen-year-old Harry and his friends that Black is innocent. Hermione has a device that allows her to time-travel, so she and Harry go back to three hours earlier to try and save Black. Hermione asks Harry who saved him and Black from the Dementors:

> Harry didn't say anything. He was thinking back to the person he'd seen on the other bank of the lake. He knew who he thought it had been ... but how *could* it have been?
>
> 'Didn't you see what they looked like?' said Hermione eagerly. 'Was it one of the teachers?'
>
> 'No,' said Harry. 'He wasn't a teacher.'
>
> 'But it must have been a really powerful wizard, to drive all those Dementors away ... If the Patronus was shining so brightly, didn't it light him up? Couldn't you see –?'
>
> 'Yeah, I saw him,' said Harry slowly. 'But ... maybe I imagined it ... I wasn't thinking straight ... I passed out right afterwards ...'
>
> '*Who did you think it was?*'
>
> 'I think –' Harry swallowed, knowing how strange this was going to sound. 'I think it was my dad.'
>
> Harry glanced up at Hermione and saw that her mouth was fully open now. She was gazing at him with a mixture of alarm and pity.
>
> 'Harry, your dad's – well – *dead*,' she said quietly.
>
> 'I know that,' said Harry quickly.
>
> (Rowling, 1999, p. 297)

Having gone back in time and being understandably tempted, Harry sneaks down to see the Patronus being performed and get a glimpse, he hopes, of his dad. But no one appears and he watches himself and Sirius close to disaster, when he suddenly realises that he had seen himself. Harry then performs the Patronus that saves the day. Harry had recently found out that his father had been able to shapeshift into the shape of a stag, which earned him the nickname Prongs. Harry's Patronus appears in the form of a stag. Later in the novel Harry discusses this with Dumbledore and is dejected because, although they saved Sirius' life, he is still considered a criminal and has to hide. Having been offered the chance of a family, Harry is again, symbolically, orphaned. Harry tells Dumbledore he had expected to see his father again:

> 'It was stupid, thinking it was him,' he muttered. 'I mean, I knew he was dead.'

> 'You think the dead we have loved ever truly leave us? You think that we don't recall them more clearly than ever in times of great trouble? Your father is alive in you, Harry, and shows himself most plainly when you have need of him. How else could you produce that *particular* Patronus? Prongs rode again last night. ... So you did see your father last night, Harry ... you found him inside yourself.'
>
> And Dumbledore left the office, leaving Harry to his very confused thoughts.
>
> (Rowling, 1999, p. 312)

Harry thus has to find and lose one father-figure (his godfather), only to find in himself the strength and skill to save himself and his godfather by drawing on the memory of his father's love. The potential for children to take these symbols and explore issues of independence, evil, self-reliance and security seems clear and perhaps goes some way to explaining the power that the Harry Potter series has to engage readers.

At the time of writing, the seventh and last, according to Rowling, Potter book is being written, so we do not yet know how the Potter saga ends. However, by the end of the sixth book (*Half-Blood Prince*) Harry has reached a state of some independence, including achieving his first emotionally satisfying relationship of love (with Ron's sister Ginny) and having to endure the loss of further parental figures with Sirius's death in volume five (*Order of the Phoenix*) and Dumbledore's death in volume six. Harry's developing independence is overlaid with a drama that is absent from most children's journeys; his protectors have been murdered and the murderer is the most powerful man in his world, who also wishes Harry dead. The emotions of readers are mediated through the symbolic containers available in the Potter story, the books and movies that make up the media of Potter, and provide ways of helping to generate secure emotions or deal with the insecurities that growing up inevitably produces.

Exploration of the Harry Potter saga demonstrates how intimately security is involved in psychic development. To make this a more clearly psycho-social rather than psychoanalytic analysis, it can be broadened out to include more social factors, of which I wish to touch on just one – Potter as a **brand**.

We are surrounded now by brands and every agency, from Nike to The Open University, feels compelled to 'brand' itself. If we remember that branding refers to the marking of a symbol onto flesh with a red-hot iron in order to identify that flesh as owned, we might wonder why so many agencies feel compelled to symbolically scar themselves. The vice president of marketing at the coffee chain Starbucks, who then became head of marketing at sportsgoods seller Nike, claimed that because consumers did not believe there was a great difference between many products it was important for companies to:

> [E]stablish emotional ties ... Nike, for example, is leveraging the deep emotional connection that people have with sports and fitness. With Starbucks, we see how coffee has woven itself into the fabric of people's lives, and that's our opportunity for emotional leverage ... A great brand raises the bar – it adds a greater sense of purpose to the experience, whether it's the challenge to do your best in sport and fitness or the affirmation that the cup of coffee you're drinking really matters.
>
> (Scott Bedbury, cited in Klein, 2000, pp. 20–1)

The 'experience' that Bedbury talks about adding purpose to is the purchase of commodities branded by Nike (sport) or Starbucks (coffee and cake). Brands provide a symbolic means of connecting a wide range of commodities to an emotional content, which creates the desire within consumers to purchase those products. Brands manage difference (all the different types of commodities) through emotion (for Nike the emotions associated with sport) and symbols into a reliable and loyal customer base who create profits for the Nike corporation.

If Potter is now thought of as a brand, it is easy to understand the emotional leverage that Harry Potter potentially offers; it is the exploration of psychic developments that are necessary and pressing. As a brand Potter can be turned into a vast array of purchasing opportunities. Brand analyst Stephen Brown points out that while the three main Potter commodities are the books themselves (often issued in varying editions, including ones aimed at adults), movies (including DVDs) and video games, there are at least six further types of Potter commodities: apparel, from T-shirts to halloween costumes; education supplies, from pens and pencils to a troll-shaped glue dispenser in which the glue is dispensed as snot; household goods – Harry and his friends can appear on your mug, towel and glow-in-the-dark band aids; sweets and food, some of which mimics items from the books; toys and games, from Lego sets to scale models; and sundries – purses, keyrings, kites, and more (Brown, 2005, pp. 97–101; Blake, 2002).

The emergence of Potter as a brand dates from the moment Rowling agreed a film deal with Warner and signed over some merchandising rights. Undoubtedly this was successful. Just prior to the release of the sixth of the Harry Potter books, there had already been 250 million books sold, the first three films had earned close to £1 billion, there were £430 million DVD and video sales and more than 400 items of Harry Potter merchandise were available, with a valuation of £2.2 billion (Simmons, 2005). All these commodities are grouped together under various symbols of Harry Potter; in particular the lightning mark that is

Figure 1.3
The Nike 'swoosh' symbol, in use on various commodities

the shape of Harry's scar on his forehead. Potter as a brand participates in an early twenty-first century economic phenomenon, whereby vast ranges of very different products are brought together and emotionally connected to the buyer through a set of symbols. The brand is an economic phenomenon fully in tune with economies of the twenty-first century and Potter is merely one example among many (Lury, 2004).

Figure 1.4
Harry Potter's logo on a variety of merchandise

It's now possible to see how a psycho-social analysis of Potter might work, although this is by no means a comprehensive analysis. On the one hand, the Potter stories may gain an emotional hold on children through the resources that Potter provides for children to imagine themselves in various emotional positions. On the other hand, a brand that needs to generate an emotional connection to its customers can use symbols to encourage people to buy particular goods. Such goods may not only empty parents' wallets, but also become a part of children's development by creating further opportunities for imagination. Psyche and commerce are mediated by the brand in the interests of profit, but such profits, no matter how large, do not necessarily undermine the emotional power of Potter.

Understanding this connection of profit and psyche might make a parent feel insecure about the effect of Potter as a brand. After all, one result of this psycho-social analysis is that not only does Potter have some power to intervene in children's emotional development, but this power can also be turned into a desire to buy. Finding out that children's emotional development is being mined for profit by large corporations is a thought to make many people queasy. However, the power of this psycho-social analysis is that while this is true, the brand does rely on the ways that Potter may help children to feel more emotionally secure. If Potter fails to assist emotional development, the brand also loses its emotional hold over the child.

This section has pursued the boy wizard to explore notions of psychic security; the ways in which we might 'feel' more or less secure. We have also seen how security and insecurity can be analysed in relation to mediation in our social worlds, even if security is lodged at least partially in our unconscious. Mediations were initially identified in the media which create the fictional world of Potter and extended into seeing inner psychic security through symbolic encounters with Potter. We were also able to see how this emotional mediation could itself be taken up and mediated into a brand which sought to extract financial profit.

Read the following extract by Margaret Rustin and Michael Rustin. Do you think they are successful in providing both a social and a psychoanalytic account of Harry Potter? You might like to reflect on any other children's stories you know and think about whether issues of love and loss appear in them.

Reading 1.2 Margaret Rustin and Michael Rustin, 'The inner world of Harry Potter'

We believe that the source of the richness and emotional power of Rowling's stories lies in her empathy with and understanding of children's unconscious emotional life, and that it is this that makes these books more than merely entertaining adventures. It is this depth of feeling, and their evocation of the fundamental anxieties of childhood, which places these books in this particular tradition of significant writing for children. Our title, *Narratives of Love and Loss*, points to the experience of separation from, and actual or imagined loss of, parents as a central issue in the stories we discuss, and the *Harry Potter* books in this respect follow the pattern of the earlier books we wrote about. It is the relationship in Harry's mind with his lost parents which is crucial to his sense of identity, and which is put to the test at the crises of the narratives of each of these books. This reaches particularly intense moments in *Harry Potter and the Prisoner of Azkaban* (vol. 3) and again in *Harry Potter and the Goblet of Fire* (vol. 4), but ... this theme is also at the centre of the first book in the series.

Some of the themes to be revisited in the text that follows are introduced in the first few pages. Harry is a very special child – the child who survived Voldemort's murderous attack on his family, as we learn a little later – and we are straight away in the territory of what Freud (1909) called 'Family romances'. Here is Harry in the stiflingly ordinary world of the Dursleys, whose major concern is to be 'normal'. It is immediately clear that Harry does not belong in this family. In fact, Harry is described as having dreamt and dreamt when he was younger that some unknown relations would come and take him away. Freud wrote about this common children's fantasy of really belonging to another family, a superior family in which the hateful aspects of one's everyday parents and one's own limitations would be replaced by the discovery that one's real parents are of royal blood or its equivalent. In Harry's case, there is the wonder of discovering his magical powers. Some of the feelings evoked in children who have been brought up in substitute families bring this idea strongly to the fore – even an actually neglectful or abusive birth-family can be idealized by a foster-child having to bear the painful disappointments of life. The gross splitting between the representation of the Dursleys who seem to have no redeeming qualities and the alternative and substitute families (the Weasleys and the Hogwarts school community) who welcome Harry and are full of life and generosity are reminders that we are in a world of absolutes. This is the world of a child who is not yet able to think in more complex and subtle ways about himself or others. There is only good and bad, and both are extreme – only victim, persecutor, heroic rescuer. Harry's discoveries about moral possibilities record his emotional growth and the gradual realization that living involves confronting internal as well as external wrongs, and that wizard's magic has to be allied to more than self-assertion and the desire for survival if it is to have a good outcome.

...

Arriving at school, Harry's own experience of panic surfaces alongside hope and excitement ... As the children cross the lake, we think perhaps of souls crossing the Styx – into the Underworld. The idea that this is what Harry must confront has already been suggested by Harry's incarceration in the dark cupboard under the stairs with the spiders, at number four, Privet Drive. This is the world beneath the surface, the unconscious, the difficult-to-integrate elements in human nature and experience. Harry now has the sense of a direct link to his famous parents. This is their old place, and for the first time the weight of parental hopes bears down on him. These are not the pressures of social expectation and of parental injunction in the present, but are related to Harry's feelings of indebtedness to others – parents who gave him life, the Wizard world that has kept alive an interest in his future, teachers who now offer him opportunities. These feelings give rise to anxieties about being worthy of all these efforts on his behalf. Harry's conscience is tender, as we see repeatedly in the story whenever fundamentals are at issue. This is not the conscience of a goody-goody. In fact, much of Harry's charm (for child readers) lies in his ordinary naughtiness, but when serious evil threatens, Harry is unable to turn a blind eye. His is the conscience of a young child whose anxieties about his goodness have been intensified by his life experiences, a child who is easily persecuted by a sense of guilt and who feels that there is something wrong that must be put right.

For the first time as he confronts the possibility of making friends, he has a background sense of being cared for. This functions at many levels, including that of physical care – Hogwarts is secure, the children are warm and well-fed (and food is very important in the story), and the teachers seem to be everywhere. Parental couples concerned with Harry's welfare abound: it is soon obvious that Professors McGonagall and Dumbledore are one such, and Hagrid the gamekeeper and Harry's owl Hedwig (a Celtic pair) are a second.

Reference

Freud, S. (1909) 'Family romances' in Standard Edition, *vol. 9, London, Croom Helm, pp. 237–41.*

Reading source

Rustin and Rustin, 2001, pp. 273–7

A number of elements come together in this psycho-social tale of Harry Potter, which the reading from Rustin and Rustin further explores. First, security involves inner emotional states, but such states are not immune from outer cultural, economic and social states; indeed, we might say that inner states are necessarily connected to outer states. Second, mediation plays an important role in constructing our social worlds and is closely implicated in the construction of security. You first came across inner dimensions of security when exploring the nature of matter in our social world and you can now add mediation to that world. Yet there remain questions. Who is it that digs? Who is it that reads? Where are the individuals who dig, eat, read and imagine?

4 The individual: digging and reading

We already have a great deal of sociological material in front of us and, instead of introducing another substantive topic comparable to the allotment story or the Potter saga, I will draw on these two case studies to outline the role of the individual. This will also have the benefit of allowing us to see connections between the three sociological concerns of matter, mediation and the individual that you will find discussed throughout this book.

It is tempting to look back over the two case studies and re-read them from the viewpoint of the individuals in those studies. For example, we might think of the Harry Potter series as being made up of individuals including those who produce the series (author, printers, movie directors, producers), those who consume the series (readers, viewers) and those who as fictional characters inhabit the series (Harry, his friends, his enemies). In both cases, we might think that examining all relevant individuals will allow us to create an account by 'adding' them together. Whether digging or reading, a powerful and persistent common-sense view of our social worlds is that they are made up of individuals.

Think of the moment in the allotment story when the second test results came out. The LBH worker who identified and commissioned the tests came to the monthly meeting of the Hackney Allotment Society. This meeting consisted of representatives from each allotment and the usual array of officers – chair, vice chair, secretary, treasurer, and so on. The LBH worker presented the findings of the PBET test, explaining what the test meant. The representatives of the allotment holders questioned and discussed these results. It would seem an obvious interpretation that all the individuals at that meeting contributed to a positive view of the test results, which in turn contributed to the designation of the allotments as safe. The individual agent, who reviews decisions and acts rationally, has a common intuitive understanding of everyday life and, for that reason, the individual is an important concern in sociology, one which we can put alongside matter and mediation.

What sociologists mean by 'the individual' involves a number of elements. Sociologist Barry Barnes suggests three elements are key to everyday or common-sense notions of the individual: rationality, free will and agency. Rationality is simply understood as having a reason for doing something. For example, the publisher of the first Potter book agreed to print it because they expected it to sell and make a profit. Free will is generally understood as the individual having a choice. For example, some people chose to trust the PBET test and continued to grow and eat food from their allotments. Finally, agency means being able to act on the choice that is made, according to some reason. Having decided that we did not trust the tests we gave up our allotment (Barnes, 2000, pp. 3–6).

Yet there is a flaw in this kind of approach because it implies sovereign separate individuals. Rather, sociologists often assert that at no point do individuals act entirely according to the reasons they give for making a particular choice. The account of Harry Potter makes this clear. At one level, the reading of a novel can be engrossing and compelling because it feeds unconscious emotional needs. The reader stands outside that process and can rationalise it, but being inside such a process necessarily means that notions of free will or agency become problematic.

The existence of the unconscious makes the notion of a rational individual problematic, as do social relations. If we think back to the allotment meeting where the results of the PBET test were announced, at no point did someone act as an entirely isolated individual. I talked and listened both in the meeting and later outside to people, and it is certain everyone else did as well. Positing social relations between individuals within which decisions are made seems an accurate understanding of the situation, more accurate than an account which implies that individuals develop their choice with reasons worked out in isolation. We might then be tempted to interpret this sociality as a basis from which individuals make their choices, turning society into a kind of stage before rational choices are made. But rescuing the notion of the rational individual in this way is hard to accept because there are even more basic forms of sociality than discussions, and these forms never leave us. For example, language is a collective endeavour, as are the understandings we all have about how to conduct meetings (such as allowing one person to talk at a time) or the forms of communication we use which rely on other collective endeavours (such as the phone or the internet). A determined individualist might remain unconvinced at this point and continue to argue that in all these collective, social processes, each individual retires to contemplate their rationally enacted free choice, but such a position seems increasingly tenuous.

Those who support the idea of the rational sovereign individual tend to work within a paradigm called 'rational choice theory'. Understandably, rational choice theory has often been argued against by sociologists, who see social worlds as providing a countervailing, if not contradictory, force to individualism. This debate is often structured as one of choosing sides: are you for or against the dominance of the individual over society? Barnes, though a critic of rational choice theory, has suggested that there is a potentially more productive way forward in exploring the intuition or common-sense view that we are all individuals endowed with rationality, choice and agency. The result of his argument is not the disappearance of the individual as a concept into the concept of society or vice versa, but rather an injunction to pay careful attention to how individuality is created and maintained in societies (Barnes, 2000). With this kind of argument, a notion of the individual operates very much like our accounts of matter and mediation, in that these concepts are used to explore the nature of security in social worlds. We can try to give an account of security in the world that is social, but which also focuses on the ways we generate our common perception that we are individuals.

For example, if we take the sociality of the PBET test – that is, the extensive social and cultural choices which lie behind any set of numbers produced out of a PBET test – we can see that individuals who had to discuss the test relied on this sociality. In addition, each person at the Allotment Society meeting would have relied on their knowledge of a common language, knowledge of rules of discussion, knowledge that a particular interpretation of gardening was privileged in allotments (growing food and not decorative flowers), and so on. We could reflect on the new test results, feeling like rational individuals who could make a choice, but feeling that way only because we were reliant on a great range of resources that made up our social world. It is not that our perception of ourselves as individuals was incorrect, but that it forgot social elements. For example, if people had come to that meeting unable to speak English, there would have been great difficulty in constructing oneself as an individual able to make decisions. Similarly, decisions made on the reading or not of Harry Potter novels will have all the hallmarks of individuality, but such moments will be constructed on the basis of a range of psycho-social forces, some of which we can become conscious of and others of which are harder to grasp.

Security seems to be a matter of the individual, yet it is also always bound by the social. Apart from exploring matter and mediation in this book, you will also explore the ways in which security in the construction of our social worlds is affected by individuals whose abilities to be rational, to make choices and to be agents is closely affected by the nature of the social. This argument does not deny the existence of individuals or our clear perception that we and others are individuals, rather it puts it in the context of our social worlds. We can explore this argument further by following Barnes' own articulation of it.

Read the following extract by Barry Barnes. Apply his theory of the individual and the social to the examples given in this chapter. Try to identify points at which an individual clearly appears in those stories and see if you can identify social factors that are closely linked.

Reading 1.3 Barry Barnes, *Understanding Agency*

[I]t is necessary to move on from criticism of asocial individualism, and to reorder the evidence against it into a positive account of the nature of the sociability and interdependence of human beings. As such a positive account is developed, it ought to become clear how individuals' own self-descriptions as responsible agents fit with it, and what the cues are that prompt them to employ voluntaristic notions in those descriptions.

...

How now does accountability relate to responsible agents, capable of rational conduct? It is necessary to ask again what rational conduct entails. What is it, not to be rational or possess rationality, but to rationalise? Perhaps the most important of the senses of this term is that of explaining *ex post facto* how what has been done was rational. To rationalise is to make an action intelligible as reasonable, sensible or judicious. If a responsible agent possesses rationality in this sense, she possesses the ability to give others intelligible, acceptable accounts of her (not necessarily acceptable) actions. If rationality is expected of her in this sense, then it is accountability that is expected. Members who align their relations with each other on the basis of this expectation will engage in communicative interaction and thereby sustain shared language, knowledge and culture. But when individualism cuts the links with others implied by accountability, and hypostasises rationality into an internal power of an independent individual, it forfeits its ability to grasp the nature of communicative interaction and to account for its products. It is then forced to take them as a mysterious 'given' backdrop to the calculative rationality that is its major concern. And this can sometimes lead on to a form of selective perception in which communicative interaction fails to appear altogether.

Members actively align and co-ordinate their accounts, and hence their language, knowledge and cognition, with those of others, in the course of communicative interaction. Of course, this alignment always involves more than 'mere talk'. It emerges from talking and doing, and involves the co-ordination and standardisation of practical actions. Agreement at the level of language requires and implies agreement at the level of practice, a co-ordinated understanding of what is being done as well as what is being said. The disposition to achieve such co-ordination is indeed normal and natural to human beings if work like that of Trevarthen is to be believed. And human beings acknowledge their accountability and expect it of others as a matter of course, as part and parcel of the activity that secures and maintains co-ordination. ... The co-ordination implied by these terms has to arise out of interaction itself: it has to be collectively accomplished as ethnomethodologists tend to say. And as the co-ordination being spoken of is the condition of continuing mutual intelligibility, the interaction that secures it cannot be understood as a rational dialogue wherein mutual intelligibility has already been achieved and is no longer a problem. It is necessary here to understand the relevant interaction causally, and to recognise that members affect each other therein in a causal sense. Agents who are disposed to co-ordinate their understandings with others have to be agents who are affected by others.

Mutual accountability implies co-ordinated understanding, which implies agents who affect each other. It implies, we might say, mutual *susceptibility*. To be capable, as a matter of course, of agreeing in their practice the members of collectives must be understood as mutually accountable and mutually susceptible. But it is important to recognise as well that the co-ordination that is actually achieved in specific collective settings may, and indeed invariably does, extend well beyond what is implied by reference to agreement in practice. Members may agree in how they do things and how they describe what they are doing, yet disagree about what specifically ought to be done. Or they may agree on what ought to be done, yet fail to implement it. Or again they may agree what ought to be done and manage to get it done.

...

How an action could have been otherwise

The hypotheses we have arrived at are these: our sense of the free will of an agent derives from her susceptibility to others, the kind of susceptibility implied in accounts of the deference-emotion system; our characterisation of an action as chosen identifies it as the kind of action that is open to modification through use of the system, that is, through symbolic communications and the evaluations they convey. Clearly, if these are correct hypotheses, then individualistic accounts of free will hypostasise features of social relations and social processes into fixed internal powers, just as similar accounts of rationality do. And a properly formulated conception of responsible agency can restore proper awareness of human sociability in both respects.

Reading source

Barnes, 2000, pp. 64–9

Barnes outlines a way to avoid choosing between analysing social worlds either as being made out of individuals and their choice, or as a social world that makes individuals and determines their choices. Instead, he argues that we need to see how our social worlds create notions of the 'individual', which then play a part in further creating and maintaining those social worlds. The ultimate point of his analysis is that the individual and the social should not be separated but need to be analysed together.

5 Conclusion

Security affects us all in different ways: in our sense of personal security as we walk down the street; in our sense of national security when wars break out; in our inner emotions about health or our person; and in so many other ways. As this book unfolds you will explore security in relation to the home, in international arenas, in epidemics and health and in the city. Across these different understandings of security, you will pursue the overall aim of understanding how our social worlds are made and unmade.

This chapter has explored two case studies. One of these dug in the dirt to find insecurity in our food. The other read into the Harry Potter stories for ways in which inner emotional security is developed and mined for profit. Three sociological concerns in the construction of social worlds and security were also explored through these case studies, and these will recur throughout this book: matter, mediation and the individual. None of these concerns is taken uncritically but they provide ways of understanding the social in security. This chapter has focused on an extended notion of security in the social, making it clear that security plays a role in the largest and the smallest moments that make up our social worlds.

References

Barnes, B. (2000) *Understanding Agency: Social Theory and Responsible Action*, London, Sage.

Blake, A. (2002) *The Irresistible Rise of Harry Potter*, London, Verso.

Brown, S. (2005) *Wizard!: Harry Potter's Branding Magic*, London, Cyan.

Callon, M. and Latour, B. (1981) 'Unscrewing the big Leviathan: how actors macro-structure reality and how sociologists help them to do so' in Knorr-Cetina, K. and Cicourel, A.V. (eds) *Advances in Social Theory and Methodology: Towards an Integration of Micro- and Macro-Sociologies*, London, Routledge & Kegan Paul, pp. 277–303.

Environment Agency (EA) (2005) *'Science Update on the Use of Bioaccessibility Testing in Risk Assessment of Land Contamination'* [online pdf, 172k], http://www.environment-agency.gov.uk/commondata/acrobat/bioacc_update_v2_970501.pdf (accessed 31 January 2007).

Ground Investigation Limited (undated) *'Arsenic Contaminated Soil: Estimating the True Risk to Human Health'* [online pdf, 2.2 MB], http://www.grc.cf.ac.uk/lrn/resources/casestudies/file/LRNCSE05.pdf (accessed 31 January 2007).

Klein, N. (2000) *No Logo: Taking Aim at the Brand Bullies*, London, Flamingo.

London Borough of Hackney (LBH) (2005) 'Letter of 21st September, 2005'.

Lury, C. (2004) *Brands: The Logos of the Capitalist Economy*, London, Routledge.

Rowling, J.K. (1997) *Harry Potter and the Philosopher's Stone*, London, Bloomsbury.

Rowling, J.K. (1998) *Harry Potter and the Chamber of Secrets*, London, Bloomsbury.

Rowling, J.K. (1999) *Harry Potter and the Prisoner of Azkaban*, London, Bloomsbury.

Rowling, J.K. (2000) *Harry Potter and the Goblet of Fire*, London, Bloomsbury.

Rowling, J.K. (2003) *Harry Potter and the Order of the Phoenix*, London, Bloomsbury.

Rowling, J.K. (2005) *Harry Potter and the Half-Blood Prince*, London, Bloomsbury.

Ruby, M.V., Davis, A., Schoof, R., Eberle, S. and Sellstone, C.M. (1996) 'Estimation of lead and arsenic bioavailability using a physiologically based extraction test', *Environmental Science and Technology*, vol. 30 no. 2, pp. 422–30.

Rustin, M. and Rustin, M. (2001) *Narratives of Love and Loss: Studies in Modern Children's Fiction* (rev. edn), London, Karnac.

Simmons, J. (2005) 'Harry Potter, marketing magician', *The Observer*, 26 June.

Wynne, B. (1996) 'May the sheep safely graze?' in Lash, S., Szerszynski, B. and Wynne, B. (eds) *Risk, Environment and Modernity*, London, Sage.

Chapter 2
Global security after 11 September 2001

Matt McDonald

Contents

1	**Introduction**	**48**
	1.1 Teaching aims	50
2	**Asylum seekers**	**51**
3	**Global climate change**	**63**
4	**Conclusion: security policies in international politics**	**75**
References		**77**

1 Introduction

During the Cold War, when the world was effectively split between rival superpower camps and the fear of nuclear annihilation was pervasive, we in the West knew what 'security' in international politics meant. From the end of the Second World War to the fall of the Berlin wall, our understanding of security was dominated by the Cold War context, one characterised by uncertainty and fear. The key protagonists did not often talk to each other, but rather communicated through signals such as missile build-ups and troop deployment, with their rivalry played out in the race for prestige in outer space or (more violently) in proxy wars throughout Africa, Latin America and Asia. Security was synonymous with a fear of military attack or even annihilation, and it was to be protected or advanced through militarised vigilance – whether on the part of western political leaders and intelligence agencies and directed at political developments in distant and newly decolonised regimes, or on the part of concerned and patriotic citizens of western states and directed at their own neighbours. This conception of security was constantly reiterated by political leaders and communicated through media outlets. So strong was the articulation of the threat posed by the Communist 'other' in western states such as the United States of America and the United Kingdom that it served to define who we were, arguably circumscribing the types of political action that individuals within such states could feasibly engage in without fear of being designated as unpatriotic, or even as a traitor. This is particularly applicable to what is widely known as the McCarthyism era in the USA from the late 1940s to the mid-1950s: this was a period of intense suspicion (even paranoia) about communist espionage and subversion of political institutions, most readily associated with Senator Joseph McCarthy and the House Committee on Un-American Activities.

In this chapter, I want to suggest that this historically specific conception of the reality of international politics and security continues to dominate the way that most states and security intellectuals think about this topic. I also want to point to some of the choices inherent in accepting such a conception of security as it applies to international politics, and the ways in which particular articulations of security can *create* particular types of relationships between individuals and broader political communities, mediating the ways in which people view and respond to a range of developments and actors in global politics.

In international relations literature and arguably in the day-to-day practice of world politics, security is generally understood as referring to the preservation of state sovereignty and territorial integrity, usually from external military threat (Walt, 1991). But there is nothing inevitable about such an understanding of security. Aside from being related to the particular experience of the cold war period, it should also be remembered that states themselves – the central institutions in this schema – are quite new, and nation-states even newer. For others, though, the limitations of this focus on the preservation of the state in a dangerous international environment are more fundamental.

First, threats to the lives of individuals in contemporary global politics are less likely to be through interstate war than overwhelming global problems such as hunger, poverty, disease and environmental change. A range of voices in international relations (from international institutions such as the United Nations and critical academics to non-governmental organisations) have argued in this context that security needs to be redefined in such a way as to reflect these 'new' global realities (UNDP, 1995; Booth, 2005).

Second, many states are not only increasingly unable to provide for the well-being and safety of their citizens, they may in fact be a direct threat to the welfare and survival of individuals within. This failure of the 'social contract' is manifested in human rights abuses and in the problem of refugees and asylum seekers, who point directly to the limitations of a conception of security underpinned by the assumption that states are the best or indeed the only agents capable of providing for individual well-being. For some, such as Ken Booth (1991), this situation necessitates changing our understanding of security, from one associated with the preservation of state sovereignty to an approach that prioritises the rights and needs of individuals in a global society.

Reflecting on and interrogating the assumptions and limitations of traditional conceptions of security in international relations in this way is important for at least two reasons. First, it serves to remind us that when political leaders or strategic analysts talk about 'security' or 'national security', they are often talking about the protection of a particular political regime or a territorial space, not necessarily (or arguably even usually) the people who live within the state itself. Second, as the cases below illustrate, security is not just an analytical category; it carries certain baggage with it, and the invocation of 'security' *does* things. Specifically, and at least since its association with the nation-state in the early years of the cold war, security has come to be viewed as that political goal which makes all other objectives possible, with the provision of security the most important task that a state's political leader is obliged to perform.

Defining an issue as a security issue therefore has important practical implications, and may be seen as **performative** rather than simply descriptive. Representations of security and threat can be performative in potentially allowing for (or enabling) a level of funding and importance that may not otherwise be the case and even (for some analysts) allowing emergency measures to deal with those issues (Buzan et al., 1998). For theorists like David Campbell (1998), definitions of security are also performative in that they serve to construct national identities: representations of security and discourses of threat tell us who we are, what we value, and of what (or more accurately of whom) we should be afraid. These definitions, for Campbell, therefore mediate between individuals and broader political communities, creating particular types of relationships and defining what it means to be a citizen of a particular nation-state, for example. It is for this reason – the power of 'security' in defining political priority and constructing relationships between individuals and broader political communities – that the debate about the meaning of security in international relations is more than just a case of academic navel-gazing. Rather, it comes to the heart of questions about belonging, values, and the boundaries of ethical responsibility in global politics.

While arguably gaining ground in the climate of hope immediately following the end of the Cold War, the post-2001 global context of the 'war on terrorism' means that alternative security conceptions have once again been marginalised as many states (most notably the USA, the world's only remaining superpower) are choosing to prioritise the military fight against terrorism above global campaigns against hunger, poverty, disease or environmental change. In this context, recognising the choices inherent in defining security and understanding the means through which particular security discourses and policies are enabled and legitimated is clearly important. The case studies outlined in this chapter illuminate some of these choices and processes, particularly pointing to the implications of the 'war on terrorism' for the way security is understood and practised in global politics.

1.1 Teaching aims

The aims of this chapter are to:

- outline key debates about the meaning of security in international relations before and after 11 September 2001
- illustrate the socially constructed nature of security and security threats in global politics by analysing the issues of asylum and global climate change
- identify the political implications of defining security, and the basis of security definitions in sets of ethical assumptions
- illustrate the performative nature of language about security and threat: the ways in which the designation of security and threat *does* things

- identify the ways in which representations of security and threat mediate relationships between individuals and broader political communities.

2 Asylum seekers

The case study below examines the issue of asylum seekers through the concept of **securitisation**. This concept was first elaborated by Ole Wæver (1995), and has since been taken up more systematically by Wæver and a group of colleagues whose approach to security studies has become known as the Copenhagen School. Securitisation refers to the process whereby issues *become* security issues: not by fitting an objectively defined set of criteria, but by being constructed as such by relevant actors. More specifically, this approach focuses on the role of 'speech acts' (usually by political leaders) in designating an issue or a particular group of people as an existential threat to a political community, usually the nation-state. This framework is particularly applicable to the question of asylum seekers and refugees, who have frequently (particularly after 11 September 2001) been defined as a security threat to a number of western, liberal democratic nation-states. In this case study, I will look specifically at the Australian government's 'securitisation' of asylum, in particular its approach to 433 asylum seekers during a stand-off on the high seas in 2001.

An asylum seeker is a type of refugee who seeks political asylum under the terms of international law: the 1951 UN Convention Relating to the Status of Refugees and the 1967 Protocol Relating to the Status of Refugees. To achieve refugee status, an asylum seeker must be able to establish that s/he has:

> [A] well-founded fear of persecution because of his/her race, religion, nationality, membership in a particular social group or political opinion; and is unable or unwilling to avail himself/herself of the protection of that country, or to return there, for fear of persecution.
>
> (UN, 1951, Article 1)

Claims for asylum are decided either by officials in the country of arrival (in immigration departments, for example), or by the United Nations High Commission for Refugees (UNHCR), the central agency for dealing with refugees and asylum seekers, with offices throughout the world. The states that offer political asylum have signed up to and ratified the 1951 Convention and 1967 Protocol.

At the end of 2005, some 20.7 million people were defined as 'persons of concern' to the UNHCR (2006): refugees, asylum seekers, internally displaced persons (IDPs), returned refugees, returned IDPs, and other stateless persons. Of these, 8.4 million could be defined as refugees, while 773,500 could be defined as asylum seekers, that is people who applied for political asylum in UNHCR offices or to governments.

Two important questions emerge from the above: where are refugees and asylum seekers coming from, and where are they going to? It may not surprise you to learn that, according to the UNHCR (2006, pp. 15–19), the main originating states of refugees in 2005 were those experiencing ongoing conflict: Afghanistan, Sudan and Burundi were the largest 'producers' of refugees. The 'recipient' states may be more of a surprise. According to many opinion polls and media outlets, people in the developed world tend to believe that refugees overwhelmingly target and arrive in developed states (Refugee Council, 2004). But as UNHCR (2006) figures show, the world's largest receiving state for refugees in 2005 was Iran, followed by Pakistan. Between them, these states hosted almost two million of the world's 8.4 million refugees, dwarfing for example the number arriving in the UK by a figure of around six to one. The most common 'push' factor for refugees is armed conflict and the most common recipient states are those immediately bordering states in conflict (such as Afghanistan). This certainly challenges the popular notion that asylum seekers and refugees are motivated primarily by a desire to improve their quality of life by seeking to exploit the goodwill

Figure 2.1
Refugee processing centres in states such as Pakistan and Iran hosted one in four of the world's refugees in 2005, often providing little more than makeshift tents

of developed states. So why is it that so many people in the UK and other developed states hold this view? The crucial question here is: where do prevailing perceptions about refugees and asylum seekers come from? As we explore the relationship between asylum seekers and security, the importance of this question will become even clearer.

While some analysts rightly point out that security could be defined in such a way as to *prioritise* the needs of asylum seekers as among the world's most vulnerable people (Doty, 1998/9), I am particularly concerned here with the issue of why asylum seekers are included in traditional understandings and approaches to security. How is it that asylum seekers come to be viewed as threatening to the security of a particularly political community (for example, a nation-state)? At what level *could* such an argument be made? We might define security broadly enough to encompass health or economic concerns, in which broader concerns about asylum seekers bringing and spreading disease or exploiting the welfare system of a particular country could be considered threatening. Both of these (and particularly fears of economic exploitation) are common misperceptions in the developed world, in spite of significant evidence that refugees (and immigrants generally) contribute to economic vitality in recipient states by engaging in work that many 'locals' are unwilling to do, and by offsetting ageing populations (Williams, 1995).

We might argue that asylum seekers pose a direct security threat in more traditional terms: that some within their number might seek to violently overthrow the state or engage in terrorist activity. The latter has been increasingly invoked since 11 September 2001, although arguably more to justify hardline approaches to asylum seekers than because these were genuine concerns. Related to this is the argument that asylum seekers pose a threat to state sovereignty, usually defined as the right of a particular state to determine who enters the country. It is important to note here that states which are signatories to the 1951 Convention and 1967 Protocol are effectively *compelled* to process the claims of asylum seekers who reach their country. If they are found to be refugees, these states are also compelled to allow them to remain. Finally, we might argue that asylum seekers constitute a threat to a particular political community because they undermine the core values and societal integrity of a particular group. Such representations of security and threat are often just as important in communicating a particular image of 'our national values' to domestic populations, again serving to mediate between individuals and broader political communities, creating particular ideas about citizenship. Along with the arguments about 'sovereignty', the imperative of preserving 'our values' is one of the most common arguments against accepting asylum seekers, and is defined by the Copenhagen School as a concern with preserving 'societal security' (Buzan et al., 1998). In general, when asylum seekers are viewed and constructed as a security threat, combinations of the above arguments are used.

In late August 2001, a matter of weeks before an Australian national election and the 11 September attacks in the USA, a boat full of asylum seekers off the west coast of Australia briefly captured international attention. The boat, a Norwegian freighter called the *Tampa,* had responded to a distress call and rescued more than four hundred asylum seekers whose own vessel – launched from Indonesia – was sinking in international waters. After rescue, the asylum seekers indicated to the ship's captain that they wanted to land on Christmas Island, several hundred kilometres from the Australian mainland but part of Australia's migration zone. Here, their claims for refugee status could be heard and if successful, they would be allowed to remain in Australia. The Australian government refused to allow the *Tampa* to reach Australia's migration zone. The captain held firm and a stand-off on the high seas

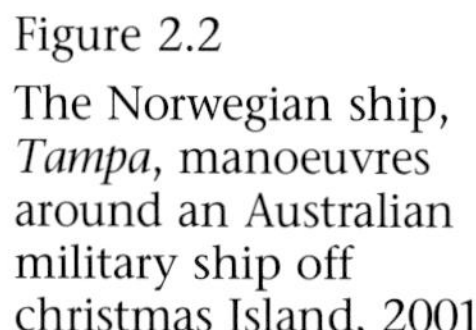
Figure 2.2
The Norwegian ship, *Tampa,* manoeuvres around an Australian military ship off christmas Island, 2001

ensued, with the *Tampa* blockaded by Australian naval forces which eventually boarded the ship after several days and sent the asylum seekers to Pacific island nations for the processing of their claims. The international media was scathing of the Australian government's position, particularly when reports surfaced of the increasingly difficult conditions that the asylum seekers faced on the vessel itself (inadequate food, water and medical treatment). Crucially, however, the Australian government's position received widespread support from its electorate, with up to seventy per cent approving the government's position. A significant part of this support, it could be argued, was achieved through convincing the Australian population that the 433 asylum seekers on board the *Tampa* constituted a threat to Australian security.

From the outset, conservative Prime Minister John Howard argued that Australia's position was about protecting Australian sovereignty and security. In what would become the government's mantra on this issue, he argued that it was in Australia's national interests that the government alone had the 'right to decide who comes into this country and the circumstances in which they come' (McDonald, 2005, pp. 304–8; see also Burke, 2001, pp. 322–31; McMaster, 2002; Maley, 2003). Foreign Minister Alexander Downer noted that 'at the heart of [the *Tampa* issue] is the protection of our territorial integrity', while Defence Minister Peter Reith noted that 'if you can't control who comes into your country, that is a security issue'. Immigration Minister Phillip Ruddock echoed the concerns underpinning the formation of the racist Immigration Restriction Act (known popularly as the White Australia Policy) at the start of the twentieth century in arguing that Australia could be 'overrun with large numbers of asylum seekers'. The leading figure in the push for the establishment of a federal Australian state, Henry Parkes, spoke in the late 1880s of the threat posed by 'the countless millions of inferior members of the human family who are within easy sail of these shores' (Burke, 2001, p. 15).

These representations positioned asylum seekers as violating Australian sovereignty and undermining the security of the Australian state. The government also invoked the strategic language of deterrence in arguing that its approach to the issue would send a message to would-be people-smugglers and asylum seekers that Australia was not a 'soft touch'. The asylum seekers on board the *Tampa* had paid people-smugglers to take them from Indonesia to Australia, after most had reached Indonesia from their home countries (including Afghanistan and Iraq). This led to claims in the Australian media that asylum seekers were not 'genuine refugees' because they were wealthy enough to pay the high prices that people-smugglers demand for a berth. As the UNHCR definition of a refugee outlined earlier indicates, however, economic wealth or privation is not a relevant factor for adjudicating on asylum seekers' claims.

The representation of asylum seekers as a threat to security (to Australian sovereignty, economic well-being and values) reached fever pitch after the events of 11 September. The Defence Minister argued that the open entry of asylum seekers could allow for a 'pipeline for terrorists to come in and use [the] country as a staging post for terrorist activities'. He also linked 11 September with asylum seekers in arguing that the events of that day made him 'determined to have an immigration program which the government is able to conduct with integrity'. Australian Member of Parliament, Peter Slipper, went further in stating that there was:

> An undeniable link between illegals and terrorists ... Many of these illegals come from Afghanistan [and] it is not beyond the realms of possibility that some people gaining illegal entry into Australia this way are people who have been involved in terrorism or who do represent a threat to this country.
>
> (Peter Slipper, cited in McDonald, 2005, p. 306)

Prime Minister Howard also noted that in the wake of 11 September, Australia had a redoubled obligation to check who was entering the country. Given the extent of public concern about the threat of terrorism after 11 September, such a representation may be seen as particularly significant in both enabling the Government to pursue its policy on asylum seekers with widespread public support, and furthering a particular conception of security in which Australia needed to be protected from the threat posed by asylum seekers. Again, in this context, representations of security and threat may be seen as important political acts, mediating relationships between individuals and nation-states, telling those individuals what their core values are and from what (or whom) they need protecting.

In Reading 2.1, below, Wæver outlines his conception of how security is constituted in particular political communities; of how security *works*. For Wæver, security is not an objective condition that can be quantified based on how many missiles a country has, on how many other countries have, for example. Such an approach doesn't allow us to see why the UK Government, for example, viewed the possibility that Saddam Hussein *might* have been developing a nuclear weapons programme in 2002–03 as far more of a threat to British security than the thousands of confirmed nuclear missiles of Russia or the USA. In short, what matters in security politics and understanding how issues, events or actors become *threats* is not material reality but rather the meaning we give to these issues, events or actors: what intentions we ascribe to other actors and how we choose to interpret particular developments or events. A central part of this interpretation, indeed for Wæver the most important part, is language.

Read the following extract by Ole Wæver. He argues that *speech acts* construct security and in particular designate particular events, actors or issues as threats. The usual form of these acts involves a state's political leader – or someone who occupies a position of authority within a political community – depicting an issue as an existential threat to the group itself. Through this process threats are designated and, for the Copenhagen School, extraordinary responses to them are legitimated. Certainly, representations of security and threat are, for Wæver, a means by which individuals are tied to particular conceptions of political community and designations of 'our' core values. And language is not simply about depicting external reality but is performative, both constructing that reality and enabling political responses to it. Language, in short, does things.

Reading 2.1 Ole Wæver, 'Securitization and desecuritization'

Reading the theoretical literature on security, one is often left without a good answer to a simple question: What really makes something a security problem? ... [S]ecurity problems are developments that threaten the sovereignty or independence of a state in a particularly rapid or dramatic fashion, and deprive it of the capacity to manage by itself. This, in turn, undercuts the political order. Such a threat must therefore be met with the mobilization of the maximum effort.

Operationally, however, this means: *In naming a certain development a security problem, the 'state' can claim a special right,* one that will, in the final instance, always be defined by the state and its elites. Trying to press the kind of unwanted fundamental political change on a ruling elite is similar to playing a game in which one's opponent can change the rules at any time s/he likes. Power holders can always try to use the instrument of *securitization* of an issue to gain control over it. By definition, something is a security problem when the elites declare it to be so:

> And because the End of this Institution [the Leviathan, the Sovereign], is the Peace and Defense of them all; and whosoever has right to the End, has right to the Means; it belongeth of Right, to whatsoever Man, or Assembly that hath the Soveraignty, to be Judge both of the meanes of Peace and Defense; and also of the hindrances, and disturbances of the same; and to do whatsoever he shall think necessary to be done, both before hand, for the

> preserving of Peace and Security, by prevention of Discord at home and Hostility from abroad; and, when Peace and Security are lost, for the recovery of the same.
>
> (Hobbes, 1968 [1651], p. 232)

Thus, that those who administer this order can easily use it for specific, self-serving purposes is something that cannot easily be avoided.

What then *is* security? With the help of language theory, we can regard 'security' as a *speech act*. In this usage, security is not of interest as a sign that refers to something more real; the utterance *itself* is the act. By saying it, something is done (as in betting, giving a promise, naming a ship).[1] By uttering 'security,' a state-representative moves a particular development into a specific area, and thereby claims a special right to use whatever means are necessary to block it.[2]

The clearest illustration of this phenomenon – on which I will elaborate below – occurred in Central and Eastern Europe during the Cold War, where 'order' was clearly, systematically, and institutionally linked to the survival of the system and its elites. Thinking about change in East–West relations and/or in Eastern Europe throughout this period meant, therefore, trying to bring about change without generating a 'securitization' response by elites, which would have provided the pretext for acting against those who had overstepped the boundaries of the permitted.

Consequently, to ensure that this mechanism would not be triggered, actors had to keep their challenges below a certain threshold and/or through the political process – whether national or international – have the threshold negotiated upward. As Egbert Jahn put it, the task was to turn threats into challenges; to move developments from the sphere of existential fear to one where they could be handled by ordinary means, as politics, economy, culture, and so on. As part of this exercise, a crucial political and theoretical issue became the definition of 'intervention' or 'interference in domestic affairs', whereby change-oriented agents tried, through international law, diplomacy, and various kinds of politics, to raise the threshold and make more interaction possible.

Through this process, two things became very clear. First, the *word* 'security' is the *act*; the utterance is the primary reality. Second, the most radical and transformational perspective – which nonetheless remained realist – was one of minimizing 'security' by narrowing the field to which the security act was applied (as with the European détente policies of the 1970s and 1980s). After a certain point, the process took a different form and the aim became to create a speech act *failure* (as in Eastern Europe in 1989). Thus, the trick was and is to move from a positive to a negative meaning: Security *is* the conservative mechanism – but we want less security!

Under the circumstances then existing in Eastern Europe, the power holders had among their instruments the speech act 'security'. The use of this speech act had the effect of raising a specific challenge to a principled level, thereby implying that all necessary means would be used to block that challenge. And, because such a threat would be defined as existential and a challenge to sovereignty, the state would not be limited in what it could or might do. Under these circumstances, a problem would become a *security* issue whenever so defined by the power holders. Unless or until this operation were to be brought to the point of failure – which nuclear conditions made rather difficult to imagine[3] – available avenues of change would take the form of *negotiated limitations* on the use of the 'speech act security'. Improved conditions would, consequently, hinge on a process implying 'less security, more politics!'

To put this point another way, *security* and *insecurity* do not constitute a binary opposition. 'Security' signifies a situation marked by the presence of a security problem *and* some measure taken in response. Insecurity is a situation with a security problem and *no* response. Both conditions share the security problematique. When there is no security problem, we do not conceptualize our situation in terms of security; instead, security is simply an irrelevant concern. The statement, then, that security is always relative, and one never lives in complete security, has the additional meaning that, if one has such complete security, one does not label it 'security.' It therefore never appears. Consequently, transcending a security problem by politicizing it cannot happen *through* thematization in security terms, only *away* from such terms.

An agenda of *minimizing* security in this sense cannot be based on a classical critical approach to security, whereby the concept is critiqued and then thrown away or redefined according to the wishes of the analyst. The essential operation can only be touched by faithfully working *with* the classical meaning of the concept and what is already inherent in it. The language game of security is, in other words, a *jus necessitatis* for threatened elites, and this it must remain.

Such an affirmative reading, not at all aimed at rejecting the concept, may be a more serious challenge to the established discourse than a critical one, for it recognizes that a conservative approach to security is an intrinsic element in the logic of both our national and international political organizing principles. By taking seriously this 'unfounded' concept of security, it is possible to raise a new agenda of security and politics. This further implies moving from a positive to a negative agenda, in the sense that the dynamics of securitization and desecuritization can never be captured so long as we proceed along the normal critical track assumes security to be a positive value to be maximized.

That elites frequently present their interest in 'national security' dress is, of course, often pointed out by observers, usually accompanied by a denial of elites' right to do so. Their actions are then labelled something else, for example, 'class interests,' which seems to imply that authentic security is, somehow, definable independent of elites, by direct reference to the 'people.' This is, in a word, wrong. All such attempts to define people's 'objective interests' have failed. Security is articulated only from a specific place, in an institutional voice, by elites. All of this can be analyzed, if we simply give up the assumption that security is, necessarily, a *positive* phenomenon.

Critics normally address the *what* or *who* that threatens, or the *whom* to be secured; they never ask whether a phenomenon *should* be treated in terms of security because they do not look into 'securityness' as such, asking what is particular to security, in contrast to non-security, modes of dealing with particular issues. By working with the assumption that security is a goal to be maximized, critics eliminate other, potentially more useful ways of conceptualizing the problems being addressed. This is, as I suggested above, because security:insecurity are not binary opposites. As soon as a more nominalist approach is adapted, the absurdity of working toward maximizing 'security' becomes clear.

Viewing the security debate at present, one often gets the impression of the object playing around with the subjects, the field toying with the researchers. The problematique itself locks people into talking in terms of 'security,' and this reinforces the hold of security on our thinking, even if our approach is a critical one. We do not find much work aimed at *desecuritizing* politics which, I suspect, would be more effective than securitizing problems.

Notes

1 More precisely, in the theory of speech acts, 'security' would be seen as an *illocutionary* act; this is elaborated at length in my 'Security, the speech act.' See also J.L. Austin, *How to do Things with Words* (Oxford, Oxford University Press, 1975, 2nd edn.), pp. 97ff.

2 A point to which we will return: the other side of the move will, in most cases, be at least the price of some loss of prestige as a result of needing to use this special resort ('National security was threatened') or, in the case of failure, the act backfires and raises questions about the

viability and reputation of the regime. In this sense the move is similar to raising a bet – staking more on the specific issue, giving it principled importance and thereby investing it with basic order questions.

3 The strongest case for the theoretical status of speech act failure being equal to success is given by Jacques Derrida, 'Signature event context,' *Glyph* 1 (1977), pp. 172–97 (originally presented in 1971). The article was reprinted, in a different translation, in Jacques Derrida, *Margins of Philosophy* (Chicago, IL, University of Chicago Press, 1982).

Reference

Hobbes, T. (1968 [1651]) Leviathan, *Harmondsworth, Penguin.*

Reading source

Wæver, 1995, pp. 54–7

The usefulness of the concept of securitisation to understanding Australia's approach to and depiction of asylum seekers is quite apparent. Here we have political leaders using 'speech acts' to articulate very clearly their view that these asylum seekers constitute a security threat: they threaten Australian sovereignty; they might be terrorists; they're looking to exploit the goodwill of Australia and Australians. What matters here is not whether these things are true. Certainly, there has been no evidence of asylum seekers or refugees being responsible for terrorist activity in Australia since 2001, and many of the asylum seekers onboard the *Tampa* were *escaping* the Taliban regime in Afghanistan, a regime the Australian government was about to declare enemy number one in the war on terrorism. Asylum seekers might challenge sovereignty defined as total control over a country's geographical area, but the idea of sovereignty as complete autonomy is an illusion; sovereignty defined in such terms is already undermined profoundly by global economic interaction and interdependence, as well as by Australia's own commitment to international rules and norms that are precisely designed to compel states to act in particular ways, including towards asylum seekers (Maley, 2003). For the securitisation approach, these inconsistencies and misrepresentations don't matter. What does matter is that these representations are articulated by those within a position of power and authority, and that these representations are believed by, and resonate with, the relevant constituency. When that happens, we have a security threat.

However, understanding the processes through which threats are constructed – while a progression from the relatively static traditional security approaches – raises a further and arguably more fundamental question: *why* are issues presented as threats? In simple terms, we might argue that the Australian political leadership genuinely believed that asylum seekers constituted a threat: that Australia had to preserve its sovereignty and territorial integrity, particularly in the context of the developing threat of global terrorism. Of course, this explanation is not necessarily charitable in terms of its ethical implications since it ultimately involves denying responsibility for asylum seekers, among the most vulnerable people in the world. The real concern here is that it has contributed to a range of developed states engaging in something approaching a 'race to the bottom' when it comes to refugee policy, in which states have attempted to make their immigration restrictions as strict as or stricter than others to avoid being faced with an ever-increasing proportion of the world's stateless people. In his application of securitisation to asylum and immigration in Europe, Jef Huysmans (2006) warned that this certainly became more prominent in European Union states after 2001.

Yet the argument that the Australian government may have believed Australia to be genuinely threatened by asylum seekers has two other problems. First, the government went 'above and beyond' articulating genuine concern by actually fabricating stories and events in such a way as to portray asylum seekers in the worst possible light. Just days before the federal election in 2001, Defence Minister Reith argued that asylum seekers had thrown their children from another vessel into the open ocean to prompt rescue by Australian naval forces. Prime Minister Howard responded by arguing that these people clearly had different values from other Australians and concluded that 'I don't want people like that in Australia'. It later emerged that the story had been fabricated: their vessel was in fact sinking (see Marr and Wilkinson, 2003). This revelation, and the resignation of Defence Minister Reith, occurred only after the conservative (National Party/Liberal coalition) government was re-elected.

The second problem with the argument of genuine concern is that it is abstracted from the context in which these 'concerns' were articulated. As Copenhagen School theorists argue, designating an issue as an existential threat allows for extraordinary measures in dealing with that threat. For these theorists, it allows for normal procedures and approaches to be suspended at times of crisis, a dynamic that others have applied frequently to a range of state justifications for the suspension of human rights concerns in the face of the terrorist threat (see, for example, Bigo and Walker, 2006). And crucially, defining a threat and then 'responding' to it can also contribute to perceptions of political legitimacy within the constituency; perceptions that the government is 'doing the job' of providing security. With a cynical interpretation, the timing and form of representations of asylum seekers in the Australian context does point to a broader recognition that designating threats and threatening 'others' can serve to legitimise particular types of responses and those actors can be deemed capable of protecting political communities from those threats. Security, in this sense, *does* things.

3 Global climate change

The previous case study introduced the idea that security is not only an analytical category but also a political one. The following case study of global climate change takes up this theme, but rather than focusing on the processes through which security is constructed and the implications that such constructions have, it focuses on the ethical choices made in the process of defining security in certain ways: whose interests are prioritised, and whose are neglected? Environmental issues generally throw up complex questions of ethical responsibility, but climate change in particular is worth addressing in detail here, given that the debate on how to respond to it – particularly through international institutions and agreements – has been underpinned by ethical debates about rights, responsibilities and obligations. Of course, for traditional security academics, global environmental change does not fit with ideas about what security means in international politics. With global climate change there is no inherent 'violence', no threat to the territorial integrity of the state, no external 'enemy' against whom to rally troops or maintain vigilance. Such differences to the usual scope of security studies and practices have often been invoked to question the relevance of environmental change to security (Buzan, 1983; Deudney, 1990; Levy, 1995). And yet thinking about and exploring this relationship is important, particularly if representations of security are understood as articulations of a group's core values.

For some, the relationship between security and global climate change is strong simply because it has the potential to fundamentally undermine the survival of humanity, not to mention other living beings (Mathews, 1989; Renner, 1996). While uncertainty remains over the impacts and timescale involved in climate change, there is now almost universal recognition in scientific circles that global climate change caused by humans is indeed occurring. The leading scientific body on climate change, the Intergovernmental Panel on Climate Change (IPCC), has suggested that if patterns of greenhouse gas emissions continue at 2001 levels, the earth's average temperature will increase by between 1.8 and 6.4 degrees Celsius by 2100 (IPCC, 2007). Such an increase would not only be without precedent in recorded history, but would lead to displacement through sea-level rises; an increase in the number and intensity of extreme weather events such as droughts, floods and cyclones; the spread of vector-borne diseases such as malaria; changed weather patterns with implications for delicate ecosystems and agricultural production; widespread species extinction; and economic downturn associated with changes in agricultural capacity as well as the cost of responding to manifestations of environmental change. A widely publicised 2006 British report into the potential economic implications of climate change concluded that it had the potential to shrink the global economy by up to twenty per cent (Stern, 2006). And linking with the previous case study, some experts have even warned that up to 150 million people may be displaced by the effects of climate change by 2050 (Houghton, 1999).

Figure 2.3
Global warming threatens species' habitats, such as that of the polar bear

This threat to survival is precisely what has motivated some state representatives and international bodies to argue that climate change constituted as significant a security threat as any other (UNDP, 1995; CNN, 2004). In 2004 the UK's chief scientific advisor, Sir David King, argued that global warming was a far greater threat to the world than international terrorism (BBC News, 2004). And while crude comparisons are not always particularly helpful, consider that approximately 3300 people were killed in the 2001 terrorist attacks in the USA compared with about 30,000 deaths from 1999 floods in Venezuela or up to 200,000 deaths from the 2004 Asian tsunami. For many, the scale of the climate change threat and the limited attention and funding it receives relative to concerns of large-scale violence warrants its consideration as a security issue.

But does the scale of the threat to life make environmental change a security issue? For critical security theorists in international relations such as Booth, whose work we will look at more closely in a moment, this is self-evident: for security to make any sense in international relations it has to be defined in such a way as to prioritise that which threatens people. In fact, for theorists such as Booth, nothing points to the problems of traditional approaches to security more starkly than their inability to make their theory of security relevant to the experience of 'real people in real places'. But the gap between traditional approaches to security that prioritise the protection of state sovereignty and those that prioritise individual welfare or emancipation provides an important rationale for exploring the relationship between environmental change and security. Simply, issues such as climate change raise fundamental questions about who needs protection, from whom or what, and who is able to provide security. Environmental issues – particularly transnational ones in which we as individuals may be simultaneously those 'threatened by' the problem and those causing it (through driving cars or eating meat, for example) – complicate and destabilise assumptions about what security means. In short, environmental issues challenge the 'common sense' of associating security with states, sovereignty and violence.

Given the particular challenges posed by environmental change, it is worth focusing on the types of choices that political communities make in defining security and prioritising particular concerns and groups over others in responding to it. Nowhere are these choices more stark or more important when it comes to the issue of climate change than in the policies and practices of the USA. In 2006 the USA was not only the world's largest contributor to global climate change (contributing up to twenty-five per cent of all greenhouse emissions), but it was also among the most resistant to global cooperation on climate change. At the same time, as a global superpower, the USA was particularly able to influence global security politics and dynamics, and since the onset of the 'war on terror' it has consistently spent more on military resources than the several of the next-largest countries combined. So how and why did the USA make these choices, and what, if anything, do they tell us about the way security is understood in this context?

Since the Bush administration took office in 2001, it argued against the central dimensions of the global climate change regime and, within months of his election, President George W. Bush pulled out of the Kyoto Protocol, the key international agreement on climate change.

Previous US President Bill Clinton had signed the protocol while still in office, but Bush not only refused to ratify it, he also revoked Clinton's signature. The protocol, which was signed in 1997 and came into force in early 2005, constituted an international agreement committing signatory states in the developed world to binding greenhouse emissions targets. At the time, signatory states committed themselves to an average reduction in greenhouse emissions from 1990 levels of 5.2 per cent between 2008 and 2012.

The cornerstone of Bush's rejection of the Kyoto Protocol was his argument that it was unacceptable because it exempted 'eighty per cent of the world, including major population centres such as China and India, from compliance, and would cause serious harm to the US economy' (Bush, 2001). There are two important choices or 'moves' made in this argument, both of which may be considered relevant to the construction of security.

The first concerns Bush's comment on the exemption of China and India from the terms of the Kyoto Protocol. All developing states were exempted from making binding emissions commitments under the terms of the protocol, based on a series of ethical considerations including: that they were least responsible for the problem of climate change; and that they were least able to respond effectively to climate change, given their limited economic and infrastructural capacity. Developing states were therefore exempted from emissions targets, at least until those most responsible for and able to respond to climate change – developed states such as the USA – had begun to address the problem. In rejecting the protocol on this basis, the Bush administration's criticism of the protocol amounted to a critique and even a rejection of these ethical principles, giving us a crucial insight into how ethical obligation and even 'security' was conceived by the Bush administration.

The second dimension of President Bush's position is his argument that committing the USA to binding emissions targets would hurt his country's economy. While many certainly held this view within the USA, the uncertainty associated with the long-term impact of climate change, and the cost of adapting to it, means that this is far from an uncontestable argument. Consider that Hurricane Katrina is estimated to have cost the US government at least $200 billion in reconstructive efforts: a staggering sum that represents only half the US defence budget for the same year. More importantly, however, the argument for rejecting the protocol on these grounds ultimately defines a global problem only in terms of how it affects the USA. As noted, the USA is historically more responsible for the causes of climate change, and has a far greater capacity to respond to it than impoverished states.

Furthermore, developing areas around the equator will be more affected by climate change than states such as the USA; defining rejection along *state* terms gives us little hope of responding effectively to a *global* problem.

I want to suggest that there is nothing inevitable about drawing these conclusions and using them as a basis for policy, and still less of conceiving of (unsustainable) domestic lifestyles as those in need of being protected from the threat of efforts to redress climate change. Rather, these policies must be viewed as a series of choices on the part of the Bush administration, choices about what values were in need of being protected, from what threats and through what means. Rather than a policy based ultimately on the argument that 'lifestyles within my country need to be protected from an international agreement that will potentially threaten those lifestyles', it is more than possible to imagine a policy based on the argument that 'people throughout the world – particularly future generations and those in the developing world – need to be protected from the threat that global climate change poses to the long-term survival of life on the planet'. In essence, these arguments provide different conceptions of security: of those in need of being protected (from my population to the most vulnerable in the world); of the types of threats to that security (from military threats like terrorism to environmental change); and of the actors capable of providing it (from the state to global cooperation and institutions). In short, a particular political community in this position might argue that for the sake of the most vulnerable – for example, future generations and those in the developing world who will be most affected by climate change and least able to respond to manifestations of it – a change in perspective and policy is needed, even in the face of economic sacrifice. But such an interpretation involves an alternative ethical framework, and such a change in perspective is radically inconsistent with traditional approaches to security, which focus exclusively on the preservation of the state from threats that are usually external and military.

In Reading 2.2, below, Booth argues that security should be conceived as **emancipation**: as the freeing of people from structural impediments that prevent them carrying out what they would otherwise choose to do. He points to some of the limitations and implications of thinking of security in traditional 'realist' terms, particularly the tendency for this approach to focus our attention less on people than on states. For Booth, this emphasis on states is inherently problematic: it involves a focus on the means rather than the ends of security, while states themselves might often be a threat to – rather than the protector of – individuals. Booth implicitly points to the failure of the state to live up to its end of the bargain of the 'social contract'. The social contract, as elaborated by Thomas Hobbes in particular (see Reading 2.1), is a situation in which individuals cede some individual autonomy and rights to the state – the Leviathan in Hobbes's terms – in exchange for its protection in a violent state of nature. For Booth, this distinction between a safe world within and a violent world without is at the heart of traditional security approaches, but one that appears fundamentally inconsistent with the experience of millions of people throughout the world (including refugees and asylum seekers in particular) who are victims of their own state's brutality and oppression. At the very least the belief in the inherent good of states, for theorists such as Booth, needs to be questioned rather than taken for granted. We need to ask whether states are actually providing for the welfare of people within them, and in doing so break the inherent relational link established between individuals and nation-states at the heart of both academic thought and international practice. Further, we need to avoid situations in which one group's security is purchased at the expense of others. This, for Booth, can never be understood as true or stable security.

Read the following extract by Ken Booth, with the above concerns in mind.

Reading 2.2 Ken Booth, 'Security and emancipation'

Traditional security thinking, which has dominated the subject for half a century, has been associated with the intellectual hegemony of realism. This traditional approach has been characterized by three elements: it has emphasized military threats and the need for strong counters; it has been status quo oriented; and it has centred on states. The epitome of this approach was a book published some years ago by Edward Luttwak, in which he said that 'strategy is not a neutral pursuit and its only purpose is to strengthen one's own side in the contention of the nations' [1985]. These words represent the perfect expression of strategy as ethnocentrism writ large: the argument which follows is diametrically opposed to such an outlook. While no security concept should dismiss the danger of war, the importance of military power or the role of states, the Luttwak Simplifier is neither appropriate for academics nor is it a rational way to see the world community through the interregnum.

The pressures to broaden and update the concept of security have come from two sources. First, the problems with the traditionally narrow military focus of security have become increasingly apparent. It is only necessary here to mention the greater awareness of the pressures of the security dilemma, the growing appreciation of security interdependence, the widespread recognition that the arms race has produced higher levels of destructive power but not a commensurate growth of security, and the realization of the heavy burden on economies of extravagant defence spending. The second set of pressures has come from the strengthening claim of other issue areas for inclusion on the security agenda. The daily threat to the lives and well-being of most people and most nations is different from that suggested by the traditional military perspective. Old-fashioned territorial threats still exist in some parts of the world. Obviously much on the minds of everybody is Kuwait, which in August 1990 was occupied and then annexed by Saddam Hussein's forces. For the most part, however, the threats to the well-being of individuals and the interests of nations across the world derive primarily not from a neighbour's army but from other challenges, such as economic collapse, political oppression, scarcity, overpopulation, ethnic rivalry, the destruction of nature, terrorism, crime and disease. In most of the respects just mentioned people are more threatened by the policies and inadequacies of their own government than by the Napoleonic ambitions of their neighbour's. To countless millions of people in the world it is their own state, and not 'The Enemy' that is the primary security threat. In addition, the security threat to the regimes running states is often internal rather than external. It is almost certainly true that more governments around the world at this moment are more likely to be toppled by their own armed forces than by those of their neighbours. In the last few weeks alone there have been problems from the military in Argentina, and there are constant rumours of the military challenge even to the traditionally civilian-dominated Kremlin.

The broader security problems just mentioned are obviously not as cosmically threatening as was the Cold War. But there are problems of profound significance. They already cost many lives and they could have grave consequences if left untreated. The repression of human rights, ethnic and religious rivalry, economic breakdown and so on can create dangerous instability at the domestic level which in turn can exacerbate the tensions that lead to violence, refugees and possibly inter-state conflict. The Lebanon and Kashmir are only two examples of 'domestic' problems with international implications which have been attracting attention through 1990.

Communities which are wealthy and have a significant level of social justice do not seem to fight each other. There has not been a war since 1945 between the 44 richest countries [Naisbitt and Aburdene, 1996]. 'Security communities' – islands of what Kenneth Boulding [1979] called 'stable peace' – have developed in several parts of the world.

For whatever reason there does seem to be a correlation between democracy and freedom on the one hand and warlessness (within security communities) on the other. As a result even relatively conservative thinkers about international politics seem increasingly to accept that order in world affairs depends on at least minimal levels of political and social justice. This is where, finally, emancipation comes in.

Emancipation versus power and order

Emancipation should logically be given precedence in our thinking about security over the mainstream themes of power and order. The trouble with privileging power and order is that they are at somebody else's expense (and are therefore potentially unstable). This was illustrated by the Sonnenfeldt doctrine for Eastern Europe. During the Cold War of the 1960s and 1970s there was military stability in Europe (hot war would not pay for either side) but there was no political stability (because millions were oppressed). In the end the vaunted 'order' created by dividing Europe into the two most heavily armed camps in history proved so unstable that it collapsed like a house of cards (and miraculously almost without violence). True (stable) security can only be achieved by people and groups if they do not deprive others of it.

'Security' means the absence of threats [Buzan, 1991, pp. 16–18]. Emancipation is the freeing of people (as individuals and groups) from those physical and human constraints which stop them carrying out what they would freely choose to do. War and the threat of war is one of those constraints, together with poverty, poor education, political oppression and so on. Security and emancipation are two sides of the same coin. Emancipation, not power or order, produces true security. Emancipation, theoretically, is security.

Implicit in the preceding argument is the Kantian idea that we should treat people as ends and not means. States, however, should be treated as means and not ends. It is on the position of the state where the conception of security as a process of emancipation parts company with the neo-realist conception as elaborated in *People, States and Fear*. The litmus test concerns the primary referent object: is it states, or is it people? Whose security comes first? I want to argue, following the World Society School, buttressed on this point by Hedley Bull, that individual humans are the ultimate referent. Given all the attention he paid to order between states, it is often overlooked that Bull considered 'world order' – between people – to be 'more fundamental and primordial' than international order: 'the ultimate units of the great society of all mankind', he wrote 'are not states ... but individual human beings, which are permanent and indestructible in a sense in which groupings of them of this or that sort are not' [Bull, 1977].

Those entities called 'states' are obviously important features of world politics, but they are unreliable, illogical and too diverse in their character to use as the primary referent objects for a comprehensive theory of security:

- States are unreliable as primary referents because whereas some are in the business of security (internal and external) some are not. It cannot serve the theory and practice of security to privilege Al Capone regimes. The traditional (national) security paradigm is invariably based upon a text-book notion of 'the state', but the evidence suggests that many do not even approximate it. Can 'security' be furthered by including the regimes of such as Hitler, Stalin or Saddam Hussein among the primary referents of theory or practice?
- It is illogical to place states at the centre of our thinking about security because even those which are producers of security (internal and external) represent the means and not the ends. It is illogical to privilege the security of the means as opposed to the security of the ends. An analogy can be drawn with a house and its inhabitants. A house requires upkeep, but it is illogical to spend excessive amounts of money and effort to protect the house against flood, dry rot and burglars if this is at the cost of the well-being of the inhabitants. There is obviously a relationship between the well-being of the sheltered and the state of the shelter, but can there be any question as to whose security is primary?
- States are too diverse in their character to serve as the basis for a comprehensive theory of security because, as many have argued over the years, the historical variety of states, and relations between them, force us to ask whether a theory of the state is misplaced [see, for example, Held, 1983]. Can a class of political entities from the United States to Tuvalu, and Ancient Rome to the Lebanon, be the foundation for a sturdy concept of security?

When we move from theory to practice, the difference between the neo-realist and the utopian realist perspective on the primary referent should become clearer. It was personified in the early 1980s by the confrontation between the women of Greenham Common and Margaret Thatcher on the issue of nuclear weapons. Thatcher demanded Cruise and Trident as guarantors of British sovereignty. In the opinion of the prime minister and her supporters the main threat was believed to be a Soviet occupation of Britain and the overthrow of the Westminster model of democracy. It was believed that British 'sovereignty' and its traditional institutions safeguarded the interests of the British people. Thatcher spoke for the state perspective. The

Greenham women sought denuclearization. The main threat, they and anti-nuclear opinion believed, was not the Soviet Union, but the nuclear arms build-up. They pinned tokens of family life, such as photographs and teddy bears, on the perimeter fence of the Greenham missile base, to indicate what was ultimately being threatened by nuclear war. People could survive occupation by a foreign power, they argued, but could not survive a nuclear war, let alone nuclear winter. By criticizing nuclearism, and pointing to the dangers of proliferation and ecological disaster, the women of Greenham Common were acting as a home counties chapter of the world community.

The confrontation between the Greenham women and the Grantham woman sparked interesting arguments about principle and policy. I thought the Greenham women right at the time, and still do. But the path to nuclear abolition cannot be quick or easy; nor is it guaranteed. The hope of some anti-nuclear opinion for a grand abolition treaty (a sort of Hobbes today, Kant tomorrow) is not feasible [Schell, 1984]. But it is rational to act as though abolition is possible. Indeed, to do otherwise is to perpetuate the belief that there is ultimately no stronger basis for human coexistence than genocidal fear. Over a long period such minimalist thinking seems to be a recipe for disaster. The search for nuclear abolition has value as part of a process of extending the idea of moral and political community (which even realists like Carr saw as the ultimate foundation of security). Kant would have seen the search for total global abolition as a 'guiding ideal'; he might have called it a 'practical impracticality'.

References

Boulding, K. (1979) Stable Peace, *Austin, TX, University of Texas Press.*

Bull, H. (1977) The Anarchical Society: A Study of Order in World Politics, *London, Macmillan, p. 22.*

Buzan, B. (1991) People, States and Fear *(2nd edn), Boulder, CO, Lynne Rienner.*

Held, D. (1983) 'Central perspectives on the modern state' in Held, D. (ed.) States and Societies, *Oxford, Blackwell, pp. 1–55.*

Luttwak, E. (1985) Strategy and History: Collected Essays, Volume Two, *New Brunswick, NJ, Transactions Publishers, p. xiii.*

Naisbitt, J. and Aburdene, P. (1996) Megatrends 2000: Ten New Directions for the 1990s, *London, Avon Books, p. 29.*

Schell, J. (1984) The Abolition, *London, Avon Books.*

Reading source

Booth, 1991, pp. 318–21

For some, the choices in the US government's approach to security, and particularly the ethical dimensions of those choices, are illustrated clearly in its response to Hurricane Katrina. When this hurricane hit the US Gulf Coast in mid-2005, it caused widespread damage and flooding in the city of New Orleans, leaving hundreds of thousands of people without shelter, food or water. In the days that followed, these conditions led to civilian deaths and lawlessness, with people struggling to stay alive in increasingly dangerous conditions. As the days passed, critics argued that the government was doing too little, too slowly. Indeed, it took agencies over a week to reach some stranded residents, and several days to evacuate the New Orleans Convention Centre, despite reports of overcrowding, criminality and unsanitary conditions. The slow nature of the official response to this situation, in which over 1500 people eventually died, was in part created by wrangling over jurisdiction, but some have also linked it to different 'security' priorities on the part of the Bush administration.

For commentators such as Stephen Zunes (2005), the capacity to respond effectively to human suffering caused by Hurricane Katrina was undermined by the pursuit of security in Iraq, evident in the fact that critical infrastructure and National Guard forces (traditionally the front-line of hurricane relief) had been committed to the ongoing conflict in Iraq. These different priorities could be viewed as manifestations of different understandings or conceptions of security, with the US government defining security in terms of the protection of the state from military threat (i.e. against terrorism or Saddam Hussein's ultimately unproved weapons of mass destruction (WMD) programme), rather than as the emancipation of the most-vulnerable, in Booth's terms.

Is it unfair to characterise the US position in such terms? Of course we might argue (as the US government did at times) that responsibility belonged to lower-level agencies, and we could certainly point out that the government could not have predicted that Hurricane Katrina would happen when it did, nor have the impact that it did. But we should also bear in mind that this unpredictability, and the need for prevention and precaution, is precisely that which underpins security policy. Indeed, the need for prevention in the face of potential threats was the argument used by the Bush administration in articulating the need for a radical departure from traditional security policy and international law in responding to the threat of Saddam Hussein's WMD programme 'before it was fully formed'. Had this way of approaching future threats been applied to environmental concerns (as has been suggested by numerous analysts and political practitioners in the form of the 'precautionary principle'), we would arguably have seen a radically different approach

Figure 2.4
The victims of Hurricane Katrina endured overcrowding and unsanitary conditions

to climate change and a different approach to natural disasters such as Hurricane Katrina.

Katrina serves to remind us that states may not, as Booth suggests, always be operating in the best interests of their citizens. This gap between the state and individuals is certainly not inevitable – some states, as Booth argues, are better at providing for individual welfare than others – but is more likely if we continue to view the state as the necessary answer to the core question of security: whose security? Perhaps more fundamentally, the tendency to focus on states – and state boundaries as the limits of ethical responsibility in global politics – means that it becomes particularly difficult to effectively address transnational problems such as global climate change, which arguably necessitates a broader conception of ethical responsibility in both time (i.e. future generations) and space (i.e. those outside the state). While the USA was the most prominent and important actor arguing along these lines regarding the Kyoto Protocol, the fact that some of the narrower concerns expressed by the USA were echoed by a range of other states – including some eventual signatories – suggests that this 'mindset' continues to dominate the way in which ethical obligation is viewed in global politics. If security can be viewed as the preservation or protection of a group's core values, the important questions become: how is that group defined (narrowly or broadly); and how are these values defined (exclusively or inclusively)? Booth's questions are: how is it possible for communities to be defined in ways that recognise membership in a broader global society; and how can values be defined in such a way as to prioritise the needs of the most vulnerable?

4 Conclusion: security policies in international politics

The world, we are told, changed on 11 September 2001. Traditional calculations of security threats were less relevant, the ambit of security policy required fundamental rethinking, while the way we make sense of security politics similarly needed total re-examination. But why should this be the case? 11 September was certainly a tragic event, but the number of those killed in the attacks is dwarfed by annual deaths from hunger or preventable disease. And while the scale of political violence was certainly horrific, it was significantly outnumbered by the hundreds of thousands killed in genocide in Rwanda in the 1990s, for example. But perhaps this is to miss the point: what has changed is the resonance of traditional ways of thinking or feeling about what makes us secure. We might expect death and destruction in the 'wild zones' of the developing world, but traditional security approaches would position those with the greatest military power, such as the USA, as those most secure in the world. 11 September seemed to undermine this argument, even invert it, by suggesting that a global superpower such as the USA might in fact be targeted by some in the 'wild zones' who choose to respond to a perceived unequal order and marginalisation through violence against the state (and its people) deemed most responsible for that order and most able to change it. Whatever the rights and wrongs of this argument – and it is certainly difficult to justify mass violence generally, much less against civilians – it arguably poses fundamental challenges for the way we think about what makes a political community secure.

And yet the US government's immediate response to this potentially profound question about security was increased military spending, an increased willingness to intervene, and arguably a broader commitment to tame these 'wild zones' through threats and violence. This of course raises a second core question about security after 11 September: while claims that 'everything has changed' are still ringing in our ears, and have been used to justify new doctrines of preventative military intervention and the suspension of human rights (for asylum seekers and domestic populations through restrictive anti-terror legislation, for example), have we in fact seen more *re-affirmation* of traditional security thinking than *re-examination*? Do we still see the answer to problems posed by post-11 September security defined in terms of the need for more guns, more bombs, more military personnel and an increased willingness to use violence? And most fundamentally for our purposes, is security still defined in traditional terms: as the preservation of the state from military threat? The focus of our attention in discussions of global security still seems to be the state, and in the face of global problems and challenges such as climate change, ethical responsibility to vulnerable outsiders continues to be denied. For all the discussion about change in security frameworks, dynamics and practices, on core questions such as 'security for whom?', 'by what means?' and 'from what threats?', the dominant answers continue to be (respectively): the state; through force; and from violence and threats to sovereignty. This would suggest that, after 11 September, the global security context is characterised more by continuity than change.

The critical approaches to security articulated by Ole Wæver and Ken Booth challenge such security politics in different ways, and give us new insights into the way security works in international relations. Wæver's concept of securitisation, while criticised on the basis that it focuses on representations by state elites and fails to provide an alternative vision for security politics, destabilises the idea of rational actors responding to objective threats. By pointing to the construction of these threats and the political implications of this construction, Wæver points to the often-ignored role of choice when it comes to security politics: the choice of political leaders and others to perceive and articulate visions of threat, and the choice that relevant audiences ultimately make in believing and accepting these visions. Acknowledging this allows for the possibility of challenging threat constructions, particularly those that position the world's most vulnerable people – asylum seekers and refugees, for example – as a threat to the sovereignty, identity and security of a particular political community.

Booth's critique is even more fundamental. He shares with Wæver the view that it is important to engage with security as a political category because of the unique capacity of issues on security agenda to command political attention and funding, and to construct particular types of relationships between individuals and nation-states. But Booth does not simply point to these implications or to the arbitrary choices made in ignoring some forms of human suffering and prioritising others in the name of security. He goes on to provide us with philosophical anchorage for redressing the suffering of the most vulnerable: emancipation. As a critique of traditional approaches, Booth's work begins by refusing to accept what is so often taken for granted: that security should be about physical violence, that the answer to the question of 'security for whom' should be states, that states are necessarily the best means of achieving individual welfare. The brief example of Hurricane Katrina reminds us that states can sometimes fail to adequately provide for individual well-being (even while pursuing 'national security'), while the broader example of climate change reminds us that some issues have no respect for bounded communities, and responding effectively to such issues requires a change in where boundaries of ethical responsibility are drawn.

As an articulation of an alternative security vision, Booth's equation of security with emancipation is more controversial. Some see in it a universalising strategy that privileges a western conception of 'progress', while others see little in the concept itself that gives us an insight into how it might be applied or 'operationalised' in different contexts. But part of challenging traditional security approaches and practices must be articulating new visions for where we want to go, and articulating alternative answers to questions that we take for granted such as 'security for whom?', 'from what threats?' and 'by what means?'. Such a move involves questioning the solution mentality or problem-solving approach that permeates the way many policy-makers and intellectuals consider problems of security and violence, and adopting a critical perspective aimed at asking how the contemporary order itself came about (see Cox, 1981). In this chapter I have tried to draw your attention to the importance of these questions: it's up to you to decide how they might be answered in different contexts.

References

BBC News (2004) 'Global warming "biggest threat"' [online], BBC, London, http://news.bbc.co.uk/1/hi/sci/tech/3381425.stm (accessed 22 February 2007).

Bigo, D. and Walker, R.B.J. (2006) 'Theorising the liberty–security relation: sovereignty, liberalism and exceptionalism', *Security Dialogue*, special section, vol. 37, no. 1, pp. 1–82.

Booth, K. (1991) 'Security and emancipation', *Review of International Studies*, vol. 17, no. 3, pp. 313–26.

Booth, K. (2005) *Critical Security Studies and World Politics*, Boulder, CO, Lynne Rienner.

Burke, A. (2001) *In Fear of Security: Australia's Invasion Anxiety*, Sydney, Pluto.

Bush, G.W. (2001) 'Text of a letter from the President to Senators Hagel, Craig, and Roberts' [online], www.whitehouse.gov/news/releases/2001/03/20010314.html (accessed 22 February 2007).

Buzan, B. (1983) *People, States and Fear*, Hemel Hempstead, Harvester Wheatsheaf.

Buzan, B., Wæver, O. and de Wilde, J. (1998) *Security: A New Framework for Analysis*, Boulder, CO, Lynne Rienner.

Campbell, D. (1998) *Writing Security: United States Foreign Policy and the Politics of Identity (2nd edn)*, Minneapolis, MN, University of Minnesota Press.

CNN (2004) 'Official: global warming bigger threat than terrorism' [online], http://edition.cnn.com/2004/WORLD/americas/02/05/canada.environment.reut/ (accessed 22 February 2007).

Cox, R. (1981) 'Social forces, states and world orders: beyond international relations theory', *Millennium*, vol. 10, no. 2, pp. 126–55.

Deudney, D. (1990) 'The case against linking environmental degradation and national security', *Millennium*, vol. 19, no. 3, pp. 461–73.

Doty, R.L. (1998/9) 'Immigration and the politics of security', *Security Studies*, vol. 8, no. 2–3, pp. 71–93.

Houghton, J. (1999) 'As things hot up', *The Economist*, special issue, 'The world in 2000', p. 146.

Huysmans, J. (2006) *The Politics of Insecurity: Fear, Migration and Asylum in the EU*, London, Routledge.

Intergovernmental Panel on Climate Change (IPCC) (2007) *Climate Change 2007: The Physical Scientific Basis*, Geneva, United Nations Environment Programme.

Levy, M.A. (1995) 'Is the environment a national security issue?', *International Security*, vol. 20, no. 2, pp. 35–62.

Maley, W. (2003) 'Asylum-seekers in Australia's international relations', *Australian Journal of International Affairs*, vol. 57, no. 1, pp. 187–202.

Marr, D. and Wilkinson, M. (2003) *Dark Victory*, Sydney, Allen and Unwin.

Mathews, J.T. (1989) 'Redefining security', *Foreign Affairs*, vol. 68, no. 2, pp. 162–77.

McDonald, M. (2005) 'Constructing insecurity: Australian security discourse and policy post-2001', *International Relations*, vol. 19, no. 3, pp. 297–320.

McMaster, D. (2002) 'Asylum-seekers and the insecurity of a nation', *Australian Journal of International Affairs*, vol. 56, no. 2, pp. 279–90.

Refugee Council (2004), 'Nailing press myths about refugees' [online], http://www.refugee-action.org.uk/information/challengingthemyths.aspx (accessed 13 April 2007).

Renner, M. (1996) *Fighting for Survival*, New York, NY, W.W. Norton.

Stern, N. (2006) *The Economics of Climate Change: The Stern Review*, Cambridge, Cambridge University Press.

United Nations (UN) (1951) *Convention Relating to the Status of Refugees* [online], http://www.unhcr.org/protect/3c0762ea4.html (accessed 22 February 2007).

United Nations Development Programme (UNDP) (1995) *Human Development Report, 1994*, New York, NY, Oxford University Press.

United Nations High Commissioner for Refugees (UNHCR) (2006) *2005 Global Refugee Trends*, Geneva, UNHCR; also available online at http://www.unhcr.org/cgi-bin/texis/vtx/statistics/opendoc.pdf?tbl=STATISTICS&id=4486ceb12 (accessed 13 April 2007).

Wæver, O. (1995) 'Securitization and desecuritization' in Lipschutz, R.D. (ed.) *On Security*, pp. 46–86 New York, NY, Columbia.

Walt, S.M. (1991) 'The renaissance of security studies', *International Studies Quarterly*, vol. 35, pp. 211–39.

Williams, L. (1995) *Understanding the Economics of Immigration*, Canberra, Commonwealth of Australia.

Zunes, S. (2005) 'Hurricane Katrina and the war in Iraq', *Foreign Policy in Focus* [online], http://www.fpif.org/fpiftxt/491 (accessed 22 February 2007).

Chapter 3
Security, the self and the home

Elizabeth B. Silva

Contents

1	**Introduction**	**82**
	1.1 Teaching aims	83
2	**Routines and 'the normal' in home life**	**83**
	2.1 A study of contemporary home-life routines	85
3	**The individual, the home and materiality**	**94**
	3.1 Security in the individual and the social	94
	3.2 Materiality and security in the home	98
4	**Ontological security in the home**	**102**
	4.1 *The Truman Show*	102
5	**Conclusion**	**105**
References		**107**

1 Introduction

In the western industrialised world the most common associations people make with the word 'security' relate to risks originating from changes in the outside world, such as global warming, surveillance, health epidemics, terrorism and war. Yet our everyday lives are also sites of risk. In this chapter we explore some of the ways in which 'security' is not just a concern that is external to the individual but also depends on what goes on in everyday personal life and in the more private spaces of the home. We consider security as senses of being 'held' (practically and figuratively) and as feelings of connection with the environment. To explore these aspects of security in the making of social worlds, this chapter addresses two key concerns: the individual and the social, and materiality.

We often perceive change in our social world as a risk, even though change is a constant feature of life. Just as we as individuals can be uncomfortable with change, so too can societal changes be a source of unease, for example household composition has changed dramatically in Britain over the last forty years. Household size has declined from an average of 2.9 people in 1971 to 2.4 in 2005. In the same period the proportion of one-person households has grown from 18 per cent to 29 per cent, the biggest increase being among those aged 25 to 44. The proportion of households containing a married or cohabiting couple with dependent children declined from 35 per cent of all households in 1971 to 22 per cent in 2005. Lone-parent households with dependent children showed the reverse trend, rising from 3 per cent in 1971 to 7 per cent in 2005 (Office for National Statistics, 2006). But what do these changes in household structures mean? These are material manifestations of the changing ways in which individuals are living their private lives. For example, households are constructed in many different ways, marriage may not be a lifetime commitment, people have changing patterns for work, and individual priorities shift over a lifetime. These trends reflect changes in attitudes regarding partnerships, family life and gender relationships, as well as a myriad of changes in the British welfare system and labour market (Silva and Smart, 1999). How do these changes affect us and our home lives? Do the changes have any bearing on our senses of security?

The British sociologist Anthony Giddens (1991) argues that social events affect self-identity and that a connection exists between a person's lifestyle and the way they understand who they are. He also claims that in situations of change we persist in following an ordered pattern, seeking 'normality' and providing a certain unity to particular clusters of habits in our social world. These habits create feelings of security. I will critically explore these arguments in this chapter by introducing a number of authors who have engaged with issues relevant to the exploration of security of **the self** in everyday circumstances.

1.1 Teaching aims

The aims of this chapter are to demonstrate that:

- the making of social worlds includes security concerns that are related to the dynamics of everyday life and to the internal life of individuals
- security encompasses the individual and the social through the ways that senses of security are connected to a subtle process of coordination of routines, order and predictability in the self and in the behaviour of others
- security can be disrupted when change is introduced in personal or family life or in the material basis of everyday life in the social world.

2 Routines and 'the normal' in home life

> **Home** (noun) **1** the place where one lives; **2** an institution for people needing professional care; **3** a place where something flourishes or from which it originated; **4** (in games) the place where a player is free from attack.
>
> (*Pocket English Oxford Dictionary*, 2002, p. 432)

In the week before writing this chapter my house was affected by a twenty-four-hour power cut. I could not work with my computer, the heating system stopped, and I reverted to the pre-industrial state of candle lights, piles of blankets, lack of communication with no television or telephone, having to get creative about what to eat and how to amuse myself. When electricity was restored, further disruption ensued with the alarm system screaming, various electric clocks needing resetting, and much of my food in the fridge and freezer spoiled. Dependence on all of these technologies is **routine** nowadays, part of the way of life in many people's social world.

Routines vary at an individual level and at the level of culture, and yet they make life normal and predictable. Routines make the world feel secure. The sociologist Erving Goffman remarked that we move in a world of normalcy that often deflects thoughts of danger connected with the everyday (Goffman, 1972). There is a great sense of security to be found in many routinised aspects of everyday life. But there is also great vulnerability as we depend on technologies and systems that are out of our control, as the experience of my power cut shows.

The water we consume has to be delivered by a supplier. Our money is in the bank, not with us. Our increasingly essential mobile communication is provided by companies that are dependent on satellite systems controlled by agencies over which we, and even our governments, have little control (Collins, 2006). There is a lot that escapes our control, even when such risks do not threaten our survival.

We live our everyday lives against this background of considerable dependence on the external world. Sociologists such as Giddens have examined and analysed some of these dependencies. He argues that in this world of dependence and vulnerability, individual paths of transition through our lives are also open to change and chance. While Giddens (1991) speaks of relevant contemporary social trends, it is important to qualify the limits of his claims. For example, his ideal model of the individual currently negotiating the pressures of the changing world is a financially independent, childless adult. But not every one of us is this sort of individual. This has implications for his analysis of the role of routines in individuals' search for security in the world. For the independent, childless individual, routines appear as social events continuously open to change. They are 'ephemeral routines', reliant on happenings of various sorts. My research on family routines, which we will examine closely, suggests that 'routines of care' are not independent from unknown events or circumstances (Silva, 2004). Moreover, the argument about the freedom of affluent adult individuals needs to be countered by the fact that the liberty and power to choose, together with individual responsibility for choices made, are socially quite dissimilar because liberty, power and choices are dependent on patterns of social inequality that are prevalent in our social world. For example, I may want to take a job that offers me a chance of promotion but is three hours away from my home, and the option to take this job may be restricted because my child is still young or because my parents are old. If I could find substitute care for my child or parents, I might not be able to afford housing costs, even with the salary rise offered by the new job. Social patterns ensure that, even though routines may vary to fit different life circumstances, broad patterns still exist. The micro-patterns of everyday life that constitute the mainstay of security at the individual level are linked to broad patterns of cultural arrangements. These include links of partnership, parenting, school hours, employment, working hours, friendship, shopping hours, and so on.

We can move on now to explore the constitution of these patterns in the context of changing home life in the contemporary British world.

2.1 A study of contemporary home-life routines

From 1998 to 2004 I carried out an ethnographic study of twenty-three families (originally Economic and Social Research Council award no. LI132251048) profiling their home life and routines. I found that they exhibited different lifestyles. The patterns of time spent in the home are particularly significant. From these families, six women and five men stay at home all day. All of the men who stayed at home worked, except one (a civil servant on disability benefit doing an Open University degree). In contrast, only one woman works from home, although two others also carry out some minor earning activities at home. The people who work from home have very similar daily patterns and their routines are more fragmented than either the men who work away from home, or the women who are based at home full-time. There is no traditional gendered pattern related to these home routines, and this is a reflection of one of the major social changes in the twentieth century in home life: women's increased labour market participation. But there are also signs of what may become a major social pattern in the twenty-first century way of living: an increasing number of homeworkers. Individuals and households show fragmented and diverse patterns of everyday home routines. But there are two key structuring elements to routine: school hours (and the school calendar), and hours and patterns of paid work.

In the research process of data collection and analysis, I was concerned with getting people to talk about what they do in the home, when they do things during the course of the day and about what happens as they do things. I wanted to record in-depth multiple narratives of people's everyday home lives. Here I want to concentrate on and discuss the everyday routines of two families – the Chambers family in London, and the Wells family in Lancashire (these are not their real names). You should remember that these are cases from an affluent European country and that home life in other parts of the world can be extremely different from these ones.

The Chambers family

Rose Chambers is Canadian, forty-one years old and works as a school management systems officer, five minutes' drive from home. Ronald Chambers is forty-three, British, and works as a radio music programme producer, thirty minutes away from home by motorbike. Their two children, ten-year-old Susie and six-year-old Steve, go to the local state school. They have lived in the same house for more than fifteen years, during which time they have refurbished most of it. It is a terraced house in north London, with distinctive external features. It lies opposite a common, and is near a major shopping area. It has three bedrooms, a large lounge and dining room, a loft in the process of being converted, and a small back garden. There are cluttered shelves and piles of things – books, CDs, bags, clothing – which they describe as 'waiting to be put in their places'.

Figure 3.1
A typical north London terraced house, similar to the one lived in by the Chambers family

Figure 3.2
A typical kitchen in a north London terraced house

Rose's daily routine

Rose *OK, yeah. My husband looks after the children in the morning. I don't do anything for the children apart from say hello and good morning and things. I get up, I have a shower ...*

Elizabeth *At what time?*

Rose *Oh, I get up about, normally this is, I get up about six fifteen, six thirty, I have a shower, I get dressed and I go to work. And you want to know what I do?*

Elizabeth *How far is work?*

Rose *Oh, it's only five minutes up the road.*

Elizabeth *By car?*

Rose *By car because I travel round to schools. And then I, I go to work, then I come home very often at lunchtime I come home, I take the dog out or I – just potter about for half an hour, if I can – very often I can't come home but I try. And then I go ...*

Elizabeth *What time do you come home?*

Rose *Oh, any time, I mean sometimes it can be – any time I get a break after sort of eleven o'clock so sometimes it's not till three, if I'm working till six sometimes I don't get a chance to get here till about three but I feel I have to come home for the dog really. And then I come and then I get home you know, again I have varied hours so it can be six o'clock, I pick up the children from the childminder at six, four thirty, four fifteen, six fifteen or – I pick them up from school at three fifteen on the days I work ...*

Elizabeth *Is the childminder near?*

Rose *Yeah, she's – right across from school which again is just round the corner.*

Elizabeth *So then you are at home various times but you are at home with the children ... and how do things develop then?*

Rose *Well – usually I just, I come home, oh – I do – do lots of things I don't really think about. I potter about in the kitchen, get dinner, and I get the children, sometimes I get them to do their homework, sometimes I sit down with them and watch a bit of, a bit of telly with them or chat to them but usually – I dunno, all of a sudden it's seven o'clock! And Ronald gets home about seven and then, and then it's serious homework time for Susie ...*

Elizabeth *Does she have homework every day?*

Rose *Yeah. And then it's bath.*

Elizabeth *What time?*

Rose *Steve's bath starts about seven thirty and he's in the bath and then it's getting him ready for bed. By then I'm getting dinner for Ronald so he's taking over the children again and he's putting them, he's giving them a story and putting them to bed and he's very often the one looking over their homework as well. He helps Susie quite a lot with her homework. Once the children are in bed about eight thirty, Susie goes at nine, then we just sort of collapse! And sometimes – yeah, I mean we might sort of – you know, I suppose we sometimes chat, sometimes we read a book but it's usually just sort of collapse on the settee and then go to bed.*

Elizabeth *Watch TV?*

Rose *Yeah. Yes.*

Elizabeth *What time do you go to bed?*

Rose *Sometimes not till twelve or one. Usually not before, usually not before eleven thirty.*

Elizabeth *You don't sleep very much.*

Rose *No, not enough!*

Ronald's daily routine

Ronald *Well I get up at about seven, well I get up ... 'cos Steve wakes me up at seven 'cos ...*

Elizabeth *[He's] your alarm clock ... my daughter does that ...*

Ronald *Steve comes in and wakes me up and I come down with him and make his lunch for school and get his clothes ready ... go back to bed until ... I set my alarm for twenty to eight and then I get up then and have a shave and a shower and get dressed and then – give the children their breakfast and then take them to school. Susie goes by herself nowadays to school just before we go and I take Steve to school which is ...*

Elizabeth *What time do you leave home?*

Ronald *About ten to nine or quarter to nine. And then I come back, hop into my motorbike clothes and ... and then – I'm very sort of ye know, intensely busy during the day, it's very, quite pressurised, although I enjoy the work tremendously and ... can be quite stressful but I do enjoy it. As I say, I usually finish about six o'clock and come home and ... very much what we're doing, what ye know – what tonight's like really, coming home and spending a little time with the children, I actually give the children their bath – well really Steve and get him ready for bed and ... and then we – collapse usually about nine o'clock you know because we're usually sort of ... I practise with Susie and – ye know – homework and things like that. So yeah, we're busy till about half past eight which is when the children go to bed and – and then we usually watch television at nine o'clock, we watch the news and then – after that, sometimes I've got things to do, I might be working on the computer, on the household accounts or ... a little bit of work to do but that's rare, sometimes ... the church 'cos we go to church and it's a lay church where everybody is expected to contribute, all the men anyway are expected to contribute to speaking and so very often, well sometimes ... talks ... ye know ... something worth watching on television we'll watch that, we don't go out very much and – that's it really.*

Elizabeth *What time do you go to bed?*

Ronald *Oh, about half past eleven I suppose. That's what we try ...*

Rose and Ronald seemed to become increasingly aware of their routine through the invitation to talk. Elsewhere, Rose explicitly said she doesn't think about it. It is clear that many activities (practical or mental, for example) overlap and some things happen simultaneously. Everyone has a place, an activity and a time to do things. This doesn't mean that life is regimented. There is order, continuity and expectation. We see in the conversation the building of material and relational life, the association of individuals and objects (and even pets), mediated by each other's roles in the home environment.

The Wells family

The Wells family lives in a detached house in a small 1980s estate in Rochdale, Lancashire. It is well located with a supermarket nearby. Ray Wells, forty-five, is a plumber by trade and owns his own building maintenance firm which he runs from home, having converted a front room into an office. Lindsay, aged forty, works as a manager of an online retail sales shop. They have both been married before, and have five children between them. Lindsay's children are twenty-year-old Geof and fourteen-year-old Cathy. Ray has a fourteen-year-old daughter, Caroline. They are joint parents to eleven-year-old Vicky and eight-year-old Marcia. All of them live in the house, though Caroline is not there all the time and shares a bedroom with Cathy. Lindsay's first husband is a neighbour and their houses share a back garden gate. He is remarried, has a four-year-old son, Jack, and he is 'always around'. There is also Sam, a ten-year-old boy who has been looked after by the family since he was three. On weekday mornings he arrives at the house at eight, is taken to school with the Wells' children and returns with them, staying until six in the evening. There is no payment involved; it is just a friendship arrangement. Sam also goes on holidays with the Wells

Figure 3.3
A typical 1980s detached house in a cul de sac, similar to the one lived in by the Wells family

family. The children's schools are a ten-minute walk away, but they travel by car. Lindsay's job is also within walking distance.

This household works as an extended family with various kinds of relationships taking place. Lindsay in particular appears to take pleasure in having quite an 'unconventional' lifestyle.

Ray's daily routine

Ray *Well I wake up at six because the alarm's on my side so I wake Lindsay up and I stay awake until she finally gets out of bed. Then, I nod back off again and I wake up usually about half past seven and – I wake Cathy up and then get Geof up about half past seven, quarter to eight, I get Vicky and Marcia up at eight o'clock, quite often I have two or three phone calls then between eight and half past ... If the work's in this area, the lads who work for me come up here for about half past eight and then I send them off on their jobs. I get the kids ready for school, for their breakfast and things like that, drop them off at school at ten to nine, then I either go out on to the sites where the lads are working or I come back here and I get other phone calls 'cos the other people I do work for don't start till nine you see. Then it varies. I'm usually out roughly till lunch time-ish.*

Elizabeth *What is lunch time?*

Ray *Well say between twelve and one. If Lindsay's coming home I pick her up and we have lunch, if not I come back to sort out ... at the moment, because me work's local I then go and pick the kids up at quarter past three. Come back home, and I either do some work at home or help make the tea or whatever. I do the kids 'cos they want their stuff and I like to have the sport on in the background.*

Elizabeth *And ...*

Ray *After tea it varies.*

Elizabeth *You usually have tea at what time?*

Ray *Between five and six, one day a week I play cricket in the summer, outdoor ... I would play at least twice a week tennis, or tennis or badminton and – weekend, well – I, unless there's a football match on, we don't go out during the week normally. If there's a football match on and Lindsay wants to watch it, if it's on telly or the kids – she'll ... to t'club to watch it or whatever.*

Elizabeth *And then? Do you spend most of your evenings at home?*

Ray *Yeah.*

Elizabeth *How many hours of TV do you watch?*

Ray *It varies, she doesn't like going to bed on her own, so – go and watch a bit of telly or whatever and when she's ready to go to sleep, if I'm not tired, I'll come down and watch television. I quite like the peace between say half past ten and midnight when there's nobody here and I can flick through or ye know ...*

Lindsay's daily routine

[This conversation happened with other members of the family around and Ray is invited to join in.]

Lindsay *We never seem to have a routine, I think that's the trouble in our house! ... I'm not a very good housewife ... she's asking me what is a routine, we never have a routine day do we?*

Ray *No, we don't ...*

Lindsay *That's the trouble, we just do not have a routine but when I'm working, I get up at six and – I always have a shower every morning, I've got very curly hair so I always have to have a shower and comb my hair straight and – I have a cup of tea by myself, put my make-up on 'cos I don't go anywhere without my make-up on, and then I walk across to work, it only takes me six minutes. And then ...*

Elizabeth *What time do you leave home to go to work, quarter to seven?*

Lindsay *Ten to seven. And then – quite often Ray works locally, so if he does, he picks me up and I come home at lunchtime for an hour and I usually ...*

Elizabeth *What time is that, lunchtime?*

Lindsay *Twelve o'clock. I usually put the washing in and tidy up a bit or I go to the swimming baths which is just across the road from work, I go swimming in my lunch hour ... and then when I get home, we go across to [ex-husband's house] – Ray usually meets me at work or if he's working ...*

Elizabeth *What time is that?*

Lindsay *Quarter past three I finish work and the children finish school at quarter past three, so by the time I get there it's about twenty past and they're just coming out of school then. Then we come home and – I don't know, if Ray's at home sometimes I have an hour in bed so that I can stay up later at night.*

Elizabeth *Are you able to sleep then or are you just ...*

Lindsay *Yeah, sometimes I just ... I just have to go and have an hour ... and – or if he's not – I usually – I don't know – just potter about really, put some washing in the tumble dryer, make the tea,* *sometimes go shopping. It varies and we do a lot of things in the evenings. We ... sports and social club ...*

Elizabeth *And what time do the children go to bed?*

Ray *Too late!*

Lindsay *Yeah, too late. We find more and more, we used to have, we used to get everybody in bed for half past eight and we used to have time to ourselves didn't we and now – oh, we can't rid of them any more ...*

Elizabeth *And what time do you go to bed?*

Ray *Depends on ...*

Lindsay *I have half an hour in bed when I get home – well usually we don't get to bed before eleven-ish, it's usually half ten, eleven but if I'm not working the next day it wouldn't bother us what time we went, would it really?*

Ray *Doesn't bother me anyway does it?*

Lindsay *No, it doesn't bother you but it bothers me.*

Elizabeth *You need more sleep?*

Lindsay *But we don't like – yeah, but – I don't like going to bed on my own, I won't go on my own, not that I'm frightened or anything but we just – I don't – I don't know what I'm supposed to say – I don't ... we have quite a set routine at weekends. We always – I have to work every other Saturday but we always meet our friends in [the] pub 'cos they do nice lunches and we both take the children there so we know ... at lunchtime and have our lunch out. Saturday evening we usually always go out or ...*

Elizabeth *Just the two of you or everybody?*

Lindsay *Just the two, we have a lot of friends and we usually go out with friends.*

You can see in these two families many of the traces of the statistics and references to social change that we noted in the introduction and which have been prominent in Giddens' analysis of the links between self-identity and the changing contemporary social world. For instance, all the adults have jobs and both parents or partners have roles in looking after the needs of the children. You can also see some of the elements of my critique about the limits of freedom to choose how to live everyday life when individuals have care responsibilities. Ray's daily routine interweaves work activities and childcare. Rose and Ronald Chambers, by comparison, do childcare shifts in combination with their complementary working hours. Ray, working from home, intersperses work with domestic life. His narrative contains a strong emphasis on work routine. Like the Chambers, members of the Wells family do not get up at the same time, and they also have different bedtimes. One or two generations ago, married people of similar social strata tended to have more standard patterns of everyday routines, as inferred by historical analysis (Roberts, 1995) and time-use diaries (Gershuny, 2000). These four adults structure their days quite differently, but in both families the fathers sort out the children in the morning and take them to school, while the mothers appear to be the most constant presence after school. The families are generally together for evening activities. Activities are very interdependent, as we can see from Ray's mention that 'if Lindsay sleeps ...', or from Lindsay saying 'if Ray's at home ...'.

The home lives of both families, and also those of the other families in my study, appeared to conform to a pattern marked by their working lives and by the school life of their children. Only four partners in the twenty-three households I studied mentioned the same getting up time. The morning routines were quite separate for people living together. Children's affairs were prominent in home-life routines, and working patterns of partners tended to accommodate their childcare needs. But to what extent were these routine patterns consistent with 'free choice'? The subject of autonomous choice in everyday life, as noted in the discussion of Giddens, includes complex explorations of the boundaries between the public and the private in people's lives. It was apparent in my study that patterns of home life, routines and habits need to be well coordinated for the effective conduct of daily affairs. This is not to say, however, that this is equally important for everyone. There are many different sorts of home life and the presence of children in the home may constrain lifestyles and the use of home space more than other factors. The pattern of order and continuity required for the development of a sense of security in home life relates to the extent and relevance of the home in the daily life of the individual concerned. Home does not mean the same thing for everyone and meanings of home vary over a lifetime, as well as in different historical and cultural circumstances. As we noted above, the cases we looked at here are specific to a western industrialised country in the early twenty-first century. Despite the particular contours of these family cases and the variations that the idea of 'home' entails, the ways in which individuals go about everyday life in predictable ways provide a sense of security in relationships. Routines enable the coordination of conduct and individual access to shared realities. It is, then, important to think about what happens when disruption occurs to routines.

3 The individual, the home and materiality

Home is often associated with the private, but we have also seen that the home is embedded in the wider context of various social systems. Most individuals are not split between a 'home self' and a 'work self'. Personal, subjective and intimate aspects of living are not closed off and isolated from the public. As Joe Bailey (2000) remarks, the workplace could be classified as private as much as the family could be classified as public. Yet following a tendency to identify private and public with physical location, some analyses of home life appear particularly important for reflection about security and the ways the boundaries between 'public' and 'private' are sometimes perceived to operate. The concept of **ontological security** provides a productive way of addressing these connections.

3.1 Security in the individual and the social

> [Ontological security]: A sense of continuity and order in events, including those not directly within the perceptual environment of the individual.
>
> (Giddens, 1991, p. 243)

Order and continuity – the crucial ingredients of routines – are integral components of the concept of ontological security, seen by many as essential for fulfilling an individual life and achieving the relational life that constitutes 'a social world'. The discussion of the role of ontological security in the social, linked to the house, first appeared in the mid-1970s in an article by Clare Cooper (1976). It has since become a prominent concern in sociology, also drawing on the earlier existential psychology of Ronald D. Laing (1960) and Erik Erikson (1950). The sociologist Giddens (1991) proposed that a sound self-identity of social agents depends on ontological security, which sustains the ability to construct a coherent narrative of selfhood. A narrative of selfhood is a personal account that encompasses the roles of social institutions, and how the individual is, or was, able to rely on these institutions and the continuity of self-identity over time:

> A man [*sic*] may have a sense of his presence in the world as a real, alive, whole, and, in a temporal sense, a continuous person. As such, he can live out into the world and meet others: a world and others experienced as equally real, alive, whole, and continuous. Such a basically *ontologically* secure person will encounter all the hazards of life ... from a centrally firm sense of his own and other people's reality and identity.
>
> (Laing, 1960, p. 39)

These authors often argue that ontological security can best be achieved from developments in early life (see Chapter 1 in this book), through mothering practices and care in the family home in early life. *Home is Where We Start From* is a collection of essays by the British psychoanalyst Donald W. Winnicott (1986). This collection is useful for thinking further about security, the self and the home, but, because of the psychoanalytic direction of Winnicott's thinking, it is necessary to re-conceive some of his ideas from a sociological perspective. What follows is thus a sociological interpretation of his work.

The early experience of the infant, argues Winnicott, provides the acquisition of trust that anchors reality at an existential level. This 'basic trust' is developed from early life connections, established through habit and routine. Early experiences will therefore play a fundamental role in feelings of ontological security in later life. Basic trust is developed in the 'potential space' that relates and separates infant and mother, or mother-substitute. This process of separation means that the maintenance of habits and routines, while protecting against anxiety, is also fraught with tension. Winnicott stresses that the infant is 'all the time *on the brink of unthinkable anxiety*' (Winnicott, 1962, p. 57).

A framework of routine cultivates a sense of 'being' that is separate from 'non-being' (where the infant feels that he or she does not exist), which is crucial to ontological security. Routines that are external to the person function like 'not me' objects ('transitional objects', for example, a furry toy or a soft cloth/blanket) connecting infant and carer, defending against anxiety and linking emerging experiences to a stabilised, and thus reliable (well-known) world of objects and people. Trust protects against threats and dangers, sustaining hope and courage in face of whatever difficult circumstances one might confront. Basic trust is, to use Giddens' words (1991, p. 38), a 'defensive carapace', allowing individuals to get on with the affairs of day-to-day life. This 'defensive carapace' offers a conviction of security regardless of its 'reality'. It is a practice that fends off threats to bodily and psychological integrity. For instance, when you realise that the home is the place where accidents are most likely to occur (RoSPA, undated; Department of Health, 1997; BBC News, 2001), it seems odd that a feeling of relative invulnerability tends to be associated with the comfort of being at home. For example, the high incidence of domestic violence in homes stresses the fragility of this strong association. A 2006 Home Office British Crime Survey of 22,463 people showed that 26 per cent of women and 17 per cent of men have experienced at least one incident of domestic violence since they were sixteen years old (Walker et al., 2006). Researchers also say these numbers would be even greater if the many sexual assaults that take place within the home were included, but some victims are hesitant to report these assaults as they are often seen as private family matters.

The habits that make life normal and predictable organise the social world in imperceptible ways. Routines are thus the 'un-event' (that is, an event so obvious as not to demand attention), characteristic of much of everyday life. As such, routines only become significant when they are broken. Housework is a case of major significance in post-1970s' feminist writing about women's oppression: it's never done and it's always invisible (Oakley, 1974), yet piles of dirty laundry and stinking toilets remind one of the significance of doing housework.

Read the following extract by Donald W.Winnicott, which is based on a talk he gave in 1967. He considers the relationship between a healthy individual and a good-enough environment.

Reading 3.1 D.W. Winnicott, 'The concept of a healthy individual'

Preliminaries

We use the words 'normal' and 'healthy' when we talk about people, and we probably know what we mean. ...

...

I hope that I shall not fall into the error of thinking that an individual can be assessed apart from his or her place in society. Individual maturity implies a movement towards independence, but there is no such thing as independence. It would be unhealthy for an individual to be so withdrawn as to feel independent and invulnerable. If such a person is alive, then there is dependence indeed! Dependence on mental nurse or family.

Nevertheless I shall study the concept of the health of the *individual*, because social health is dependent on individual health, society being but a massive reduplication of persons. Society cannot get further than the common denominator of individual health, and indeed cannot get so far, since society needs must carry its unhealthy members.

Maturity at age

... The tendency towards maturation is part of that which is inherited. ... A good-enough environment can be said to be that which facilitates the various individual inherited tendencies so that development takes place according to these inherited tendencies. Inheritance and the environment are each external factors if we speak in terms of the emotional development of the individual person ...

It can usefully be postulated that the good-enough environment starts with a high degree of adaptation to individual infant needs. Usually the mother is able to provide this because of the special state she is in, which I have called primary maternal preoccupation. Other names have been given to this state, but I am using my own descriptive term. Adaptation decreases according to the baby's growing need to experience reactions to frustration. In health the mother is able to delay her function of failing to adapt, till the baby has become able to react with anger rather than be traumatized by her failures. Trauma means the breaking of the continuity of the line of the individual's existence. It is only on a continuity of existing that the sense of self, of feeling real, and of being, can eventually be established as a feature of the individual personality.

...

The individual and society

...

... The life of a healthy individual is characterized by fears, conflicting feelings, doubts, frustrations, as much as by the positive features. The main thing is that the man or woman feels he or she *is living his or her own life*, taking responsibility for action or inaction, and able to take credit for success and blame for failure. In one language it can be said that the individual has emerged from dependence to independence, or to autonomy.

...

At this point I tend to think in terms of HOLDING. This goes for the physical holding of the intra-uterine life, and gradually widens in scope to mean the whole of the adaptive care of the infant, including handling. In the end this concept can be extended to include the function of the family, and it leads on to the idea of the casework that is at the basis of social work. Holding can be done well by someone who has no intellectual knowledge of what is going on in the individual; what is needed is a capacity to identify, to know what the baby is feeling like.

In an environment that holds the baby well enough, the baby is able to make *personal development according to the inherited tendencies*. The result is a continuity of existence that becomes a sense of existing, a sense of self, and eventually results in autonomy.

...

Culture and separation

In this way health can be shown to have a relationship with living, with inner wealth, and, in a different way, with the capacity to have cultural experience.

In other words, in health there is no separation, because in the space–time area between the child and the mother, the child (and so the adult) lives creatively, making use of the materials that are available – a piece of wood or a late Beethoven quartet.

This is a development of the concept of transitional phenomena.

...

It is human beings who are likely to destroy the world. If so, we can perhaps die in the last atomic explosion knowing that this is not health but fear; it is part of the failure of healthy people and healthy society to carry its ill members.

Reading source

Winnicott, 1986, pp. 21–2, 27–8, 36–7

You can see that, while Winnicott is concerned with the uniqueness of a human being and the movement that the individual development process makes towards independence and autonomy, he stresses that it is dependence that makes the social, and that makes healthy individuals. Yet this presupposes a 'good-enough environment' – which is nothing but the 'social world' – to facilitate the development of individual inherited tendencies. One inherits not only genes but also an environment that provides effortless 'holding' through processes of identification at the personal and social levels.

Routines are implicated in the coordination of everyday lives and they create senses of security in individuals and in social environments. We can now move on to introduce further complexity regarding the role of materiality in security.

3.2 Materiality and security in the home

Technology is a relevant matter for the exploration of materiality and security in the home, as it impinges concretely on relations between 'private' and 'public', which bring about the concerns with 'ontological security' already discussed.

Read the following extract by Roger Silverstone, Eric Hirsch and David Morley. Do any of their points enlighten our discussion?

Reading 3.2 Roger Silverstone, Eric Hirsch and David Morley, 'Information and communication technologies and the moral economy of the household'

Objects and meanings, technologies and media, which cross the diffuse and shifting boundary between the public sphere where they are produced and distributed, and the private sphere where they are appropriated into a personal economy of meaning (Miller, 1987), mark the site of the crucial work of social reproduction which takes place within the household's moral economy. Information and communication technologies are, of course, crucially implicated in this work of social reproduction, not just as commodities and appropriated objects, but as mediators of the social knowledges and cultural pleasures which facilitate the activities of consumption as well as being consumables in their own right.

... In the continuous work of reproduction – and via the mesh of class position, ethnicity, geography and the rest – the household engages in a process of value creation in its various daily practices: practices that are firmly grounded in, but also constitutive of, its position in space and time and which provide the bases for the achievement of what Anthony Giddens defines as 'ontological security' – a sense of confidence or trust in the world as it appears to be (Giddens, 1989, p. 278). At stake too – and this is particularly true in an advanced capitalist society – is the family/household's ability to display, both to itself and to others, through the objectification of those practices, its competence and its status as a participant in a complex public economy (Douglas and Isherwood, 1980; Bourdieu, 1984; Miller, 1987). Different families will draw on different cultural resources, based on religious beliefs, personal biography, or the culture of a network of family and friends, and as a result construct a (more or less permeable, more or less defended) bounded environment – the home. Their success or failure is also, of course, a matter of political and economic resources.

... And while mediated and non-mediated meanings, commodities and objects are formed and transformed as they pass across the boundary that separates the private from the public spheres, it is the quality of the achievement of 'home-ness' – that which turns space into place, that which supports the temporal routines of daily life – which expresses the project which Giddens sees as particular, and particularly problematic, in modern society (cf. Giddens, 1984, p. 119; 1990).

Objects and meanings, in their objectification and incorporation within the spaces and practices of domestic life, define a particular semantic universe for the household in relation to that offered in the public world of commodities and ephemeral and instrumental relationships. But they do so through an evaluative – a moral – project, which in turn results in the creation of a spatially and temporally bounded sense of security and trust, a sense of security and trust without which domestic (indeed any) life would become impossible.

Information and communication technologies make the project of creating ontological security particularly problematic, for media disengage the location of action and meaning from experience, and at the same time (and through the same displaced spaces) claim action and meaning for the modern world system of capitalist social and economic (and moral) relations. Indeed, the media pose a whole set of control problems for the household, problems of regulation and of boundary maintenance. These are expressed generally in the regular cycle of moral panics around new media or new media content, but on an everyday level, in individual households, they are expressed through decisions to include and exclude media content and to regulate within the household who watches what and who listens to and plays with and uses what. Similarly, and in relation to media other than television or the video, for example in relation to the telephone, access to incoming [as] well as outgoing calls is both constitutive of individual identity (the adolescent constructs her or his identity and social network through it; the mother of the family takes responsibility for the maintenance of the conjugal kin or friendship network through it) and the subject of regulation (the costs of calling, but also anxieties about unwelcome calls).

The computer, too, in its problematic status as games machine, as educator, or as work-facilitator, potentially and actually extends and transforms the boundaries around the home (both homework and the games exchange culture, as well as possible links with school in reality – and the magical potential ascribed to the technology in fantasy) and can threaten to shift or undermine what is taken for granted in the routines of domestic life. In fact, of course, this challenge is often thoroughly dealt with by the technology's incorporation into the moral economy of the household: it is the computer which is, as often as not, transformed by this incorporation, much more than the routines of the household.

References

Bourdieu, P. (1984) Distinction: A Social Critique of the Judgement of Taste, *London, Routledge.*

Douglas, M. and Isherwood, B. (1980) The World of Goods: Towards an Anthropology of Consumption, *Harmondsworth, Penguin.*

Giddens, A. (1984) The Constitution of Society, *Cambridge, Polity.*

Giddens, A. (1989) 'A reply to my critics' in Held, D. and Thompson, J.B. (eds) Social Theory in Modern Societies: Anthony Giddens and His Critics, *Cambridge, Cambridge University Press.*

Giddens, A. (1990) The Consequences of Modernity, *Cambridge, Polity.*

Miller, D. (1987) Material Culture and Mass Consumption, *Oxford, Blackwell.*

Reading source

Silverstone et al., 1992, pp. 18–20

Although Silverstone et al. present an important analysis of the mediation of matter and relationships in the home, one problem is that they conceive of the household as consensual and homogeneous. In the case of the Chambers and Wells families, we saw that differences exist between partners in routines and roles. We know that conflict and unequal power relations are part of home living (Chapman, 2004) and these can be highly significant in terms of 'ontological security'. Reading 3.2 is also slightly outdated, not just in terms of how the authors discuss partnering and family life, but also in terms of technological development and uses of ICT (information and communication technology). Nowadays the storage capacity of most of these technologies has changed the patterns of use and the supposedly converging cohesion effect on family life. Ways of exercising the individualisation of tastes increases as personal times, desires and tastes can be catered for.

The 'smart house' (Spigel, 2005), together with emerging practices deriving from this concept, has already changed the direction of the connections between private and public, and has dislocated the home boundaries: from the outside world (called public) individuals can communicate with their homes (called private) while away at work or travel. In catering for the needs of its occupants, the house becomes more 'human': a mobile phone signal triggers curtains to close, lights to switch on, microwave ovens to start 'cooking', and so on. In this process of technological and social change – where we can manage the 'mobile home' remotely, and where the 'mobile person' can be 'at home' in a variety of contexts – we are still left to consider the habitual connections that bind us together, as individuals in the early twenty-first century, in the social world of Europe and similar places.

4 Ontological security in the home

So far in this chapter we have seen that social circumstances are neither separate from personal life nor are they external. As anxieties, dangers and opportunities are everywhere (as argued by Giddens), how do people function amid the social transformations around them?

Assessing the current pace of social change, Giddens (1991) argues that present everyday life is no riskier than in previous times, but that for ordinary individuals and experts alike, thinking in terms of risk and risk assessment is a more or less ever-present exercise. We are all lay people in respect of most 'expert systems' that intrude in our daily lives. For example, many of us do not know how to fix small computer problems that hamper our communications with others or affect our work. We tend to depend on health experts for advice on how to treat minor physical problems. This is why no-one escapes the current risk climate and when crises occur the sense of ontological security is put under strain.

Ontological security is connected to the ability to construct a coherent narrative of selfhood. It encompasses the reliability of social institutions and some continuity of self-identity over time. For stable and continuous social relations to exist, as argued by Winnicott and Giddens, there must be a basis of trust between individuals, and between individuals and institutions, and this trust springs directly from the ontological security experienced by individuals. Because the ways we perform in the social world involve decisions that are dependent on context, and therefore risk, the need to take decisions generates anxiety. This anxiety can only be managed and overcome with a sense of shared trust in the relationship. Security is connected to these subtle processes of coordinating patterns of behaviour in the self and in others, and diverse levels of social change may disrupt senses of security. An example will help here.

4.1 *The Truman Show*

It is day 10,909. Truman Burbank is an insurance executive, an ordinary guy, happily married to a nurse named Meryl, living in a small American seaside town called Seahaven, where nothing really happens. Everything is clean and apparently perfect. What Truman doesn't know is that he is the central character in a soap opera and that his whole life is a fiction. This is the set-up for the world's 'most popular' television show, as depicted in the film, *The Truman Show*. Miniscule cameras watch every moment of Truman's life as 'artists' act out the roles of his family and friends. Hundreds of technicians constantly adjust every detail of his world, from the weather to the lighting, in the masterwork of proclaimed entertainment genius, Christof. The show is phenomenally popular.

For thirty years Truman has accepted his world unquestioningly, but now he sees significant 'incidents', like a light falling from the sky, the reappearance of his 'father' who was supposed to have drowned in a boating accident when he was a boy, strange messages picked up on his car radio (actually the director's cues to actors), and he begins to anticipate events and predict the movement of people about town. Although members of the cast make strenuous attempts to dissuade him, he decides to try and explore the world outside Seahaven. He wants to travel to Fiji where he has been told that his former girlfriend Sylvia now lives. However, he's enclosed on the island by a manufactured fear of water since seeing his father 'die'. Truman realises that something is wrong, but he cannot find out what it is.

There are no life-altering events in this film, only subtle changes. What makes it gripping is the contrast between the naive, trusting Truman and the behaviour of those around him, all living a lie and desperately trying to prevent him from discovering the truth. The tension in the film comes from the audience knowing what Truman doesn't, and in waiting for him to find out.

The 1998 film predates the emergence of 'reality television' shows such as *Big Brother* and is an inversion of them (see **Redman and Whitehouse-Hart, 2008**). Whereas 'reality TV' shows often potentially 'distort' behaviour because those being watched are aware of being watched, *The Truman Show* explores what happens in a reality programme about a person who has absolutely no idea that he is appearing on television. This reveals the full naturalisation of everyday life. It manufactures reality in ways that may seem unreal to us, but, as Christof says in the film: 'we accept the reality we are presented with'.

The film has many layers of meaning that could be analysed. A range of readings and identifications certainly exists, but the one I offer here is that the film demonstrates a lifestyle where there is supposedly no distinction between private and public life. This is a totally 'real' show that has no boundaries except the walls of the enormous set. The Truman character is an illustration of celebrity as a creation. His very ordinariness is a construction. What does he represent? What are the particular social values that he embodies in the world that uses and creates him as celebrity? Is Truman an example of how to conduct oneself in everyday life?

The character of Truman encompasses the person, the environment and the way of living, all of which appear 'easy' to identify with. Truman, his story and his lifestyle are universalised and even the most intimate details of his life are up for discussion. His house is typical in its furnishings, gadgets and design. His home life features set life rhythms of biological and social time. Yet it seems that Truman has not properly grown up. Everything in the story is a construction. The medium of television used in the film is crafted to be closer to the real and the everyday (Hesmondhalgh, 2005). The television programme within the film is constructed to fit the rituals of everyday life with the regular schedules of presentation. The contrasts of the world pictured and that of the audience, presumably our own world, bring about identifications between Truman and the audience (Stevenson, 2005): we fear for his 'fate'.

Figure 3.4
Poster for the film, The Truman Show (1998)

The Truman Show serves as a 'symbolic token' (Giddens, 1991, p. 18) for its audience because it symbolises the existence of a shared value as a 'standard', which is used for comparison with the individual lives and circumstances of the audience. It presents in its story a sort of 'expert system', where everything is artificial, conclusive and external to Truman himself. This penetrates all aspects of his social life: food, medicine, work, friendship, partnership, family history, buildings, landscape and transport. For example, his wife often shows off new gadgets; Truman is unaware that she is marketing products to the viewing public. The whole system on which the story is based depends on trust, which is directly connected to the psychological security of Truman himself, and of the audience. But this security is fragile, and ultimately breaks down, bringing in a different kind of security, this time linked to the unknown: the possibility of the autonomous development of Truman as an individual. It potentially reinforces the safety of the real world as lived, when Truman escapes. At the end of the film Truman stands at a crossroads. The world he took for granted has been shattered. Taking charge of his own life involves risk, but he goes on to confront the possibilities, even if we may wonder how adequately prepared he is to confront this unknown world, but that's another story for another film. He breaks with the setting that made his private life public and the film asserts the values of a social world that preserves the integrity of the individual.

In the contemporary world, the range of potential courses of action open to individuals are supposedly very large. *The Truman Show* narrows all possibilities to very predictable daily sequences. The setting is traditional, but the sense of security is fake. Like Truman, we normally take a lot for granted in our lives. We know who we are, where we live, how things are supposed to carry on, the different things to expect as the day goes by from morning to night, the weather and the seasons change, the course of our lives progresses. Yet chaos constantly threatens to break everyday conventions and when it does, or when we become aware of this possibility, overwhelming anxiety may erupt.

5 Conclusion

In this chapter we have seen that security is not external to the individual, but also depends on what goes on in the self, in the home and in everyday life. The overarching concept of ontological security shows the connection between an abstract notion of security and concrete senses of being held and feeling connected with the environment. I have established the importance of ontological security for individual maturity and social cohesion, and have also discussed some of the threats the contemporary world brings to prevailing senses of ontological security.

Section 2 explored the significance of routines and the idea of normality, as related to senses of security, in the self and in home life. The families displayed the ordinariness of the connections between everyday life and security. We saw how different conceptions of the individual have a bearing on conceptions of routines. Giddens (1991) conceives the individual as childless and financially independent, for whom routines are accordingly ephemeral and circumstantial. But the ways that the individuals I studied understood and operated their routines showed interdependent lives that drew on their 'social world' differently. Connections between individualised routines revealed patterns in family and home life that constitute a basis for the order and continuity in events that create 'ontological security'.

Section 3 explored the issue of security and the home and its relation to the boundaries and connections between the private and the public, with a theoretical focus on the themes of the individual and the social and on materiality in the home. It related the discussion of routines to the concerns raised in the work of Winnicott regarding the development of the individual in society and the senses of security emerging from the provision of a 'good-enough environment'. From Winnicott we saw that change is continuous with life, and that to tolerate and welcome change, a framework of routine is essential. Such a framework separates anxiety, creating trust. As we remarked earlier, often the sense of trust is fictional. The prevalence of home accidents and levels of violence in domestic space testify to this. I introduced the concept of 'ontological security' (compare Giddens, 1991) which informs our sociological understanding of security as internal processes related to everyday living. This was expanded with a reflection on the work of Silverstone et al. (1992) about the effects of rapidly changing ICT on domestic life, chiefly about how this affects the sense of security in the family. I discussed the limits of the 'threats' that ICT poses in relation to the pace of technological and social change.

In Section 4 I expanded the discussion of 'ontological security' in connection to social changes, drawing again from the work of Giddens (1991) to outline the development of the contemporary contours of ontological security on a wider scale. Because individuals cannot escape a climate of change, the need to change increases at the individual level. I illustrated the implications of the sense of ontological security for the individual in a changing world with a discussion of *The Truman Show*. In the film, an individual living in a domestic environment modelled on the 1950s captures an audience's identification with the ever-present possibility of a breakdown in ontological security.

This chapter demonstrates that security and the home make a strong imaginary 'pair', but it has also showed that the claims of threats in the world out there and those of security in the home are unstable. Vulnerability and security coexist, not only in the home but also within the self and in the everyday. Issues of security and insecurity have to be qualified as belonging to practices of instability that are characteristic of the contemporary cultural context. Current processes for achieving ontological security rely on social worlds where individual autonomy and conformity to rules are often challenged. A myriad of issues constitutes 'threats', ranging from the breakdown of 'expert systems' to the effects of information and communication technologies. Similarly important are examples such as family changes, ordinary accidents in the home, personal breakdowns, domestic violence or death.

This chapter argues that senses of ontological security are linked to how changes in our social worlds are perceived and experienced. The ambivalence of normality in home life today is evident in changes in British household composition over the last thirty years, as outlined in the Introduction. Changes in personal life are intimately linked to changes in the wider sociocultural context. This is not to say that individuals and families are passively subject to change. On the contrary, it is very much because people want to live in different ways that change takes place. In this process ontological security is not negatively affected by social changes but is constantly remade in the context of continuing change.

References

Bailey, J. (2000) 'Some meanings of "the private" in sociological thought', *Sociology*, vol. 34, no. 3, pp. 381–401.

BBC News (2001) 'Talking point' [online], BBC, London, http://news.bbc.co.uk/1/hi/talking_point/1231354.stm (Accessed 8 February 2007).

Chapman, A. (2004) *Gender and Domestic Life: Changing Practices in Families and Households*, New York, Palgrave.

Collins, R. (2006) 'Networks, market and hierarchies: governance and regulation of the UK internet', *Parliamentary Affairs*, 10 February.

Cooper, C. (1976) 'The house as a symbol of the self' in Proshansky, H.M., Ittelson, W.H. and Rivlin, L.G. (eds) *Environmental Psychology: People and their Physical Settings*, (2nd edn), New York, Holt, Rinehart and Winston.

Department of Health (1997) *Safe as Houses: Handy Tips to Prevent Accidents in the Home*, London, The Stationery Office.

Erikson, E.H. (1950) *Childhood and Society*, New York, NY, Norton.

Evans, J. and Hesmondhalgh, D. (eds) (2005) *Understanding Media: Inside Celebrity*, Maidenhead, Open University Press/Milton Keynes, The Open University.

Gershuny, J. (2000) *Changing Times: Work and Leisure in Postindustrial Society*, Oxford, Oxford University Press.

Giddens, A. (1991) *Modernity and Self-identity*, Cambridge, Polity.

Goffman, E. (1971) *Relations in Public*, London, Allen Lane.

Goffman, E. (1972) *Interaction Ritual*, London, Allen Lane.

Hesmondhalgh, D. (2005) 'Producing celebrity' in Evans, J. and Hesmondhalgh, D. (eds) pp. 97–134.

Laing, R.D. (1960) *The Divided Self: An Existential Study in Sanity and Madness*, London, Tavistock.

Oakley, A. (1974) *The Sociology of Housework*, London, Martin Robertson.

Office for National Statistics (2006) *Social Trends*, vol. 36, London, The Stationery Office; also available online at www.statistics.gov.uk/socialtrends36 (accessed 9 February 2007).

Pocket English Oxford Dictionary (2002) (9th edn), Oxford, Oxford University Press.

Redman, P. and Whitehouse-Hart, J. (2008) '"I just wanted her out": attachment, the psycho-social and media texts' in Redman, P. (ed) *Attachment*, Manchester, Manchester University Press/Milton Keynes, The Open University.

Roberts, E. (1995) *Women and Families: An Oral History, 1940–1970*, Oxford, Blackwell.

Royal Society for the Prevention of Accidents (undated) 'The home safety book' ref: HS 178, Birmingham, RoSPA; also available online at http://www.rospa.com/homesafety/advice/general/preventing_accidents.htm (accessed 8 February 2007).

Silva, E.B. (2004) 'Materials and morals: families and technologies in everyday life' in Silva, E.B. and Bennett T. (eds) *Contemporary Culture and Everyday Life*, Durham, Sociologypress.

Silva, E.B. and Smart, C. (1999) 'The new practices and politics of family life' in Silva, E.B. and Smart, C. (eds) (1999) *The 'New' Family?*, London, Sage.

Silverstone, R., Hirsch, E. and Morley, D. (1992) 'Information and communication technologies and the moral economy of the household' in Silverstone, R. and Hirsch, E. (eds) *Consuming Technologies: Media and Information in Domestic Spaces*, pp. 15–31, London/New York, Routledge.

Spigel, L. (2005) 'Designing the smart house: posthuman domesticity and conspicuous production', *Cultural Studies*, vol. 8, no. 4, pp. 404–26.

Stevenson, N. (2005) 'Audiences and celebrity' in Evans, J. and Hesmondhalgh, D. (eds) pp. 135–71.

Walker, A., Kershaw, C. and Nicholas, S. (2006) *Crime in England and Wales 2005/2006*, fifth report of the British Crime Survey, Home Office; also available online at http://www.homeoffice.gov.uk/rds/crimeew0506.html (Accessed 9 February 2007).

Winnicott, D.W. (1962) 'Ego integration in child development' in Winnicott, D.W., *The Maturational Processes and the Facilitating Environment*, London, The Hogarth Press.

Winnicott, D.W. (1986) 'The concept of a healthy individual' in Winnicott, C., Shepherd, R. and Davis, M. (eds) *Home is Where We Start From: Essays by a Psychoanalyst*, Harmondsworth, Penguin.

Chapter 4
Security in the city

Sophie Watson

Contents

1 Introduction **112**

1.1 Teaching aims 115

2 The making of contemporary urban fear **115**

3 The subjects of fear **116**

3.1 Urban divisions 119

3.2 Psycho-social accounts of fear in the city 121

3.3 Gated communities 124

3.4 Sports utility vehicles 130

3.5 CCTV and surveillance 133

3.6 A local case study: north London 136

4 Conclusion **140**

End-note **141**

References **141**

1 Introduction

Pro-urban and anti-urban discourses have articulated the **city** variously as a site of intermingling, difference and heterogeneity, of heightened sensibility and excitement, of the potential for social interaction and democratic civic life on the one hand, or as sites of threat, contamination, unruly forces, alienation, dangerous others and chaos. In *The Country and the City* (1973) Raymond Williams strove to depart from these binary representations of the city. While exploring the contrasts between rural and urban life, Williams was intent on challenging the pejorative views of rural life, and on revealing the complexity of both urban and rural experience and the interconnections between them. These tensions between negative and positive imaginaries of the city have been played out in the way that cities have been planned and made. Fears of those perceived as threatening or different from the dominant cultural norms and social forces have underpinned decisions to build cities in this way or that (Watson, 2006). In other words, the very matter of the city is implicated in dominant urban imaginaries[1] and in the social life enacted in urban spaces.

In the early nineteenth century, industrialisation developed in tandem with urbanisation across large parts of the western world, bringing in its wake poor living conditions, in particular slum dwellings, ill health and disease, and social unrest in many cities. Engels (1968 [1844]) graphically described the urban deprivation, poor housing and health in *The Condition of the Working Class in England*, which finds its literary counterpart in Charles Dickens' descriptions of London:

> It's a black, dilapidated street avoided by all decent people; where the crazy houses were seized upon, when their decay was far advanced, by some bold vagrants, who, after establishing their own possession, took to letting them out in lodgings. Now, these tumbling tenements contain, by night, a swarm of misery. As on the ruined human wretch, vermin parasites appear, so, these ruined shelters have bred a crowd of foul existence that crawls in and out of gaps in walls and boards; and coils itself to sleep, in maggot numbers where the rain drips in; and comes and goes, fetching and carrying fever, and showing more evil in its every footprint than Lord Coodle and Sir Thomas Doodle, and the Duke of Foodle, and all the fine gentlemen in office, down to Zoodle, shall set right in five hundred years – though born expressly to do it.
>
> (Dickens, 2003 [1853], pp. 256–7)

> A dirtier or more wretched place he had never seen. The street was very narrow and muddy, and the air was impregnated with filthy odours ... covered ways and yards, which here and there diverged

> from the main street, disclosed little knots of houses, where drunken men and women were positively wallowing in filth.
>
> (Dickens, 1985 [1837–9], p. 103)

The social consequences of urbanisation were a preoccupation of a great deal of late nineteenth- and early twentieth-century western writing on cities. In a famous essay 'The metropolis and mental life' (1948 [1903]), the German sociologist Georg Simmel suggested that urban subjects have to develop a sense of reserve – a 'blasé attitude' – as a response to the over-stimulation and unceasing contact with strangers in the modern city. Tönnies (1957 [1887]) argued that cities separated out the multiple social ties of community (*Gemeinschaft*) and made exchanges specialised and one-dimensional in forms of association (*Gessellschaft*). The city was increasingly defined as the antithesis of the country – urban life is characterised by anonymity, superficiality, indifference and segregation, and rural life is imagined as cohesive, connected and organic (Wirth, 1938).

The origins of city planning in the late nineteenth century thus lay in the perceived disorder, pollution, ill health and immorality that characterised the industrial city. In this context the notions of progress, rationality and order that were embedded in the project of modernity were translated into planning ideas and the desire to organise social and economic activities in cities in a rational, predictable and safe way. Planning in Britain was centrally concerned with clearing slum dwellings, and public health initiatives, on the one hand to assuage fears that overcrowded cities were hotbeds of germs and disease (you will encounter the contagionist accounts of disease in Chapter 5) and, on the other hand, to mitigate the growing dissatisfaction of the poorer classes, who were feared to be on the verge of revolt, following their European counterparts. There was a further gendered dimension to these interventions. The mid-Victorian social investigators of London represented the urban topography of the time as bifurcated between high and low life – the west and east ends. The prostitute was positioned as the quintessential figure of the urban, herself endangered and a source of danger to men who congregated in the streets (Walkowitz, 1992, pp. 413–15). She too had to be controlled and segregated at a distance from the secure suburbs of the Victorian bourgeois family. Urban policy intervention was thus concerned with making social worlds where the threat of 'contaminating others' – the poor working classes, or the street prostitute – was kept at bay, where the idea of a secure social world was core.

Race and ethnicity represent another category of difference in the city. Minorities have experienced a long history of subjection to various forms of intervention and management in cities, legitimated by powerful sections of society as a strategy for making safer social worlds. According to Anthony King (1990) the central social fact of colonial planning was segregation. Marguerite Duras (1952), in her novel *The Sea Wall*, described the transport system in colonial Saigon in the 1930s:

> It was only from these crowded trolleys and beyond that you could have any idea of the other city, that one in which no white people lived. White with dust and under an implacable sky they lumbered along with a moribund slowness of clanking metal. Old cast offs of the metropolis. Naturally, no white person worthy of the name would ever have ventured to use these trolley cars; to be seen in one would be to lose face – Colonial face.
>
> (quoted in Bridge and Watson, 2002, p. 91)

Ethnicity or racial difference in cities is not simply socioculturally defined, it is also inscribed in the very bodies that are marked as culturally and racially different. We could argue that, at the level of the individual, the very materiality of particular bodies, and the fear that they bring contamination, has further shaped the way in which cities have been planned and made. This is graphically illustrated in the early Venetian Ghetto of the Renaissance, where difference – the difference of the Jews from the Christians – was a powerful force in the Venetian imaginary. Richard Sennett (1994) explains that when the Christians shut the Jews behind the walls of the Ghetto, they believed they were: 'isolating a disease that had infected the Christian community, for they identified Jews in particular with corrupting bodily vices. Christians were afraid of touching Jew: Jewish bodies were thought to carry venereal diseases as well as to contain more polluting powers. The Jewish body was unclean' (quoted in Bridge and Watson, 2002, p. 317). Sennett goes on to argue that the fear of touching Jews represented the frontier to the conception of the common body of the medieval era – the body in the imitation of Christ – where 'beyond the frontier lay a threat – a threat redoubled because the impurity of the alien body was associated with the sensuality, with the lure of the Oriental, a body cut free from Christian constraints'.

Cities and individuals who are able to exercise only limited power within them have long been subject to management and segregation, in attempts to make safer social worlds for those who imagine themselves to be a danger. Interventions into the city by urban planners and policy makers, it could thus be argued, have always been motivated in part by an attempt to manage fear and risk. As Leonie Sandercock (2003, p. 108) puts it: 'planning and urban management discourses are, and always have been, saturated with fear. The history of planning could be rewritten as an attempt to manage fear in the city'.

1.1 Teaching aims

The aims of this chapter are to:

- explore the role of security in the making of urban social worlds
- illustrate how the fear of different others in the city, in particular contexts, underpins social–spatial segregation and division
- explore the role of the media in mediating a sense of ontological insecurity in the city
- show how fears are translated (mediated) into new built forms (matter)
- show how new material artefacts are promoted on a security/safety platform
- explore the contribution of psycho-social and sociological accounts to understanding the fear of others in the city.

2 The making of contemporary urban fear

> As she walked down the empty street, she glanced repeatedly over her shoulder, her eyes darting this way and that. Hearing steps behind her she crossed and increased her pace while trying surreptitiously to catch a glimpse of the person behind and assess the distance to the more crowded thoroughfare before her.
>
> He jumped on to the tube as the doors closed. Settling down into his seat he noticed a young man across the aisle, shifting nervously in his seat, his face hooded and a rucksack on his knee. The hairs began to prickle along his spine.
>
> Stepping out of her office, she waved her card at the electronic button to open the door, wished the security guard good night as he desultorily watched her movements on a screen, drove off at a pace, oblivious through daily exposure to the cameras flashing in her rear-view mirror.

Many of us would recognise moments such as these in our daily lives either as residents of, or visitors to, cities. In the aftermath of the 11 September 2001 attacks in the USA, and the 7 July 2005 bomb attacks on the London transport system, security has become a major national, local and personal issue as governments and individuals seek to minimise threat and danger in city spaces. Fears and insecurities – real and imagined – are increasingly played out in the city. Where cities once protected themselves against the invading hordes with city walls, now we build walls between ourselves and others within the city itself.

We have seen that discourses of fear and risk in the city are not simply a contemporary phenomenon. Fears have been attached to different social and cultural objects over time, and deployed within a complex web of different interests and power relations in the city. Terrorist attacks on cities across the globe have mobilised a new climate of fear in the city and heightened a new and pessimistic discourse of the city as a dangerous place. The searching of bags in museums, airports and on public transport has become so normal as to not warrant comment.

Global cities are sites of an exacerbated sense of fear and risk. Their significance as locations for the head offices of large corporations and financial institutions heightens their vulnerability to terrorist attack as symbolic sites of global capitalism (Sassen, 2001). Manuel Castells (1996, pp. 384–5) emphasised the role of cities as hubs of information exchange and 'nodes' of strategic importance within global networks, attracting the cosmopolitan and powerful elites who run these networks. For many urban citizens, their sense of security in going to work via public transport, or even being in the office, was shattered following the bomb attacks in New York, London and Madrid, mobilising new strategies for self-protection and safety. Images of the 11 September 2001 attack on New York in particular saturated the media immediately after the first attack, and no individual was left untouched, changing for many their presumption of relative security in the city. As Derek Gregory wrote soon after the event:

> [T]he confusion of raw, immediate, and unedited images, through the replays, jump-cuts and freeze-frames, through the jumbling of amateur and professional clips, through the juxtaposition of shots from multiple points of view, and through the agonising, juddering close-ups, this was a cinematic gaze that replaced optical detachment with something closer to the embodied gaze. It was by this means – through this medium – that the horror of September 11 reached out to touch virtually everyone who saw it.
>
> (Gregory, 2004, p. 26)

3 The subjects of fear

The fear of **others** is an inherent part of city life. What changes are the subjects to whom such fear is attached, together with how it is mediated. Over the latter part of the twentieth century and into the twenty-first century, rapidly increasing levels of migration have accounted for the most radical sociocultural shifts in many global cities like London, New York and Sydney, and other large cities such as Manchester, San Diego, Johannesburg, Islamabad and Berlin. As a result, urban citizens and visitors to cities are increasingly exposed to people who are different from themselves. Increased migration represents one of the most visible impacts of globalisation in cities across the globe. Ulf Hannerz (1993, quoted in Short, 2004, p. 115), describes the four main groups who constitute these transnational communities in cities: business-people, including highly skilled managerial and entrepreneurial elites usually associated with finance and business services; Third World populations comprising low-waged immigrants who occupy insecure, unskilled or semi-skilled low-paid sectors of the urban service economy; expressive specialists who participate in the arts and cultural scene; and tourists. John Rennie Short (2004, p. 116) points to the divide between the cosmopolitans, who dwell in an international world of flows, and the rest – mainly the second group outlined here who dwell in a world of places, with little opportunity for movement. These are the migrants who are more likely to be visibly different – ethnically, racially – and thus more vulnerable to hostilities expressed by the dominant cultural group.

In Reading 4.1 below, Zygmunt Bauman (2003) links the anxieties mobilised in a fast-changing world – where old certainties have broken down – to the fear of outsiders. This fear crystallises around the idea of crime and the need for security.

Read the following extract by Zygmunt Bauman. Consider how the individual and social are inextricably bound up in a rapidly changing socio-economic context that produces new political consequences – policies that aim to be tough on crime, which are forcefully linked with migration and asylum. You will see how the electorate's fear and desire for personal safety were exploited by both parties in the fight for the French presidency in 2002, with Jacques Chirac and Lionel Jospin vying with each other to produce increasingly strong commitments to security measures. Note also how youth is singled out as particularly threatening.

Reading 4.1 Zygmunt Bauman, 'Togetherness dismantled'

A spectre hovers over the planet: the spectre of xenophobia. Old and new, never extinguished and freshly defrosted and warmed up tribal suspicions and animosities have mixed and blended with the brand-new fear for safety distilled from the uncertainties and insecurities of liquid modern existence.

People worn out and dead tired as a result of forever inconclusive tests of adequacy, and frightened to the raw by the mysterious, inexplicable precariousness of their fortunes and by the global mists hiding their prospects from view, desperately seek culprits for their trials and tribulations. They find them, unsurprisingly, under the nearest lamp-post – in the only spot obligingly illuminated by the forces of law and order: 'It is the criminals who make us insecure, and it is the outsiders who cause crime'; and so 'it is rounding up, incarcerating and deporting the outsiders that will restore our lost or stolen security.'

To his summary of the most recent shifts in the European political spectrum Donald G. McNeil Jr gave the title 'Politicians pander to fear of crime'.[1] Indeed, throughout the world ruled by democratically elected governments the sentence 'I'll be tough on crime' has turned out to be the trump card that beats all others, but the winning hand is almost invariably a combination of a promise of 'more prisons, more policemen, longer sentences' with an oath of 'no immigration, no asylum rights, no naturalization'. As McNeil put it, 'Politicians across Europe use the "outsiders cause crime" stereotype to link ethnic hatred, which is unfashionable, to the more palatable fear for one's own safety.'

The Chirac versus Jospin duel for the French presidency in 2002 was only in its preliminary stages when it degenerated into a public auction in which both competitors vied for electoral support by offering even harsher measures against criminals and immigrants, but above all against the immigrants that breed crime and the criminality bred by immigrants.[2] First of all, though, they did their best to refocus the anxiety of electors that stemmed from the ambient sense of *precarité* (an infuriating insecurity of social position intertwined with an acute uncertainty about the future of the means of livelihood) onto a fear for personal safety (integrity of the body, personal possessions, home and neighbourhood). On 14 July 2001 Chirac set the infernal machine in motion, announcing the need to fight 'that growing threat to safety, that rising flood' in view of an almost 10 per cent increase in delinquency in the first half of the year (also announced on that occasion), and declaring that the 'zero tolerance' policy was bound to become law once he was re-elected. The tune of the presidential campaign had been set, and Jospin was quick to join in, elaborating his own variations on the shared motif (though, unexpectedly for the main soloists, but certainly not for sociologically wise observers, it was Le Pen's voice that came out on top as the purest and so the most audible).

On 28 August Jospin proclaimed 'the battle against insecurity', vowing 'no laxity', while on 6 September Daniel Vaillant and Marylise Lebranchu, his ministers of, respectively, internal affairs and justice, swore that they would show no tolerance to delinquency in any form.

Vaillant's immediate reaction to the events of 11 September in America was to increase the powers of the police aimed principally against the juveniles of the 'ethnically alien' *banlieues*, the vast housing estates on the outskirts of cities, where according to the official (convenient to officials) version the devilish concoction of uncertainty and insecurity, poisoning the lives of Frenchmen, was brewed. Jospin himself went on castigating and reviling, in ever more vitriolic terms, the 'angelic school' of the softly-softly approach, swearing he had never belonged to it in the past and would never join it in the future. The auction went on, and the bids climbed skywards. Chirac promised to create a ministry of internal security, to which Jospin responded with a commitment to a ministry 'charged with public security' and the 'coordination of police operations'. When Chirac brandished the idea of locked centres for confining juvenile delinquents, Jospin echoed the promise with a vision of 'locked structures' for juvenile offenders, outbidding his opponent with the prospect of 'sentencing on the spot'.

Notes

1 D.G. McNeil Jr, 'Politicians pander to fear of crime', *New York Times*, 5–6 May 2002.

2 See Nathaniel Herzberg and Cécile Prieur, 'Lionel Jospin et le "piège" securitaire', *Le Monde*, 5–6 May 2002.

Reading source

Bauman, 2003, pp. 119–21

3.1 Urban divisions

A further effect of globalisation processes on cities has been that the wealth of the world is increasingly unevenly distributed, with a growing divide between the rich and the poor. In the early twenty-first century the top 0.25 per cent of the world's population had as much wealth as the other 99.75 per cent (Short, 2004, p.109). At the urban level, the divisions between rich and poor are mapped onto a social–spatial segregation where different occupational and income groups inhabit different parts of the city. This is particularly marked in the cities of the developing world, where many cities have expanded at such a pace that, according to the United Nations' *State of the World's Cities* report (UNCHS, 2001), urban growth 'will become synonymous with slum formation in some regions' (quoted in Sutherland, 2006, p. 1), while a predicted two billion people will be living in slums by 2030. As in the Victorian period, slums are forcefully linked in public discourse with fears of crime. As Hilson Baptiste, the housing minister for Antigua and

Barbuda, put it: 'We have seen slums move from one area to the next drug pushing, prostitution moves to the new area, and the new area becomes a slum' (quoted in Sutherland, 2006, p. 2). A particularly stark illustration of the ever-growing divide between rich and poor is in the growing numbers of people in cities who are homeless, living on the streets from Bristol to Bombay, as a result of the exponential increase in house prices and the dearth of low-income housing in the latter part of the twentieth and early twenty-first centuries. Dominant representations of the homeless as undeserving and even threatening are also mediated through newspaper stories and government discourses. Homeless people are part of the urban 'others' who inhabit a city's marginal spaces, which are represented in the media as sites of fear.

This representation of the city as containing dangerous 'others' is reinforced by many urban analysts, and US urbanists in particular, who represent the contemporary city in gloomy and pessimistic ways. For Neil Smith (1996), the twentieth-century discourse of urban decline in the USA has now become a material reality in the de-gentrified, revanchist city, where race/class/gender terror is 'felt by middle and ruling class whites who are suddenly stuck in place by a ravaged property market, the threat and reality of unemployment, the decimation of even minimal services, and the emergence of minority and immigrant groups.'

Mike Davis (1990) is another such writer, who paints a picture of Los Angeles as a militarised city, where street benches are constructed to prevent people sleeping on them, where sprinklers in the park deter the homeless at night, where shopping centres and libraries are patrolled to keep out those deemed undesirable, and where the floodlights from police helicopters scan the streets at night. This narrative is further embellished in his more recent apocalyptic account of *Dead Cities* (Davis, 2002), the combat zone of urban America, beset by white flight, de-industrialisation, housing and job segregation, and discrimination. Here we find tales of urban neglect, greed and political scandal, and urban infrastructures collapsing from environmental disasters quite as potent as any terrorist threat. For many of us, images such as these are familiar from films like *Blade Runner* (1982) which allow our image of the city as dangerous to flourish.

As I have argued earlier, fear can be attached to different groups at different times and places. Moreover, difference can be ignored, embraced or resisted depending on the particular socio-economic context. For example, in areas where ethnic diversity is seen to offer the opportunity for varied culinary delights and new restaurants, such diversity might be celebrated. In areas of high unemployment and limited social resources, or where there are established homogeneous communities, new groups or minorities are more likely to be perceived as a threat. Youth – as we saw in the extract from Bauman – has frequently been represented as threatening in films like *Boyz n the Hood* (1991) depicting specifically racialised gang life in US cities, while countless stories in the press draw attention to youth violence in city streets. For older people in particular, young people dressed in baggy clothes, hooded jackets, with unconventional body markings, piercing or hairstyles, congregating on the street, appear threatening (Watson, 2006, p. 119). Media representations combine with and exacerbate imaginary fears that young people represent danger and potential violence, even when such fears are not justified, as in the majority of urban encounters. The figure of the threatening other in cities can thus take many forms – the paedophile lurking at the school gate, the pickpocket or the mugger – and stories of their prevalence litter the local and national press, creating a climate of insecurity and uncertainty.

An evaluation of every encounter in the city in terms of risk profoundly organises the ways in which we conduct ourselves in everyday life:

> The disposition to perceive one's existence as being at risk has had a discernible effect on the conduct of life. It has served to modify action and interaction between people. The disposition to panic, the remarkable dread of strangers and the feebleness of relations of trust have all had important implications for everyday life ... Through the prism of the culture of abuse, people have been rediscovered as sad and damaged individuals in need of professional guidance. From this emerges the diminished subject, ineffective individuals and collectivities with low expectations. Increasingly we feel more comfortable with seeing people as victims of their circumstances rather than as authors of their lives. The outcome of these developments is a world view which equates the good life with self-limitation, and risk aversion.
>
> (Furedi, 1997, p. 147)

3.2 Psycho-social accounts of fear in the city

You have already been introduced to notions of ontological security (in Chapter 3 of this book), and to some psycho-social ways of understanding how social worlds are in part made up. Here I want to build on these notions to argue that the exposure of city dwellers to those who are different from themselves can threaten their sense of ontological security, creating a fear of others, particularly racialised others. **Psycho-social** accounts can provide helpful insights as to how such exposure may create and reinforce strategies of exclusion and segregation. The French psychoanalyst Julia Kristeva gives an insightful archaeology – as she describes it – of attitudes to the foreigner. For her, the place of the foreigner in our psychic life is integral to our sense of self: 'Strangely the foreigner lives within us: he is the hidden face of our identity, the space that wrecks our abode, the time in which understanding and affinity founder ... by recognising him within ourselves, we are spared detesting him in himself' (Kristeva, 1991, p. 1). Thus splitting off the part of our selves that we fear and detest, the foreigner within – a process central to Freudian theory – we avoid the things we cannot face. According to Kristeva, the foreigner can only be defined in a negative fashion (1991, p. 95). This produces in the foreigner a demeanour of indifference and aloofness as a shield and protection against the attacks and rejections that he experiences.

David Sibley (1995) has also drawn on psychoanalytic ideas to understand contemporary practices of exclusion – notably the exclusion of gypsies. In Reading 4.2 below, he enlists object relations theory developed by Melanie Klein – whose work is similarly deployed by other social theorists (see **Redman, 2008**) – to understand the way in which stereotypical views are formed.

Read the following extract by David Sibley. Think about which groups are stereotyped in your locality. What underlies the exclusionary discourses at play – is it age, race or sexuality or another attribute?

Reading 4.2 David Sibley, 'Images of difference'

The determination of a border between the inside and the outside according to 'the simple logic of excluding filth', as Kristeva puts it, or the imperative of 'distancing from disgust' (Constance Perin) translates into several different corporeal or social images which signal imperfection or a low ranking in a hierarchy of being. Exclusionary discourse draws particularly on colour, disease, animals, sexuality and nature, but they all come back to the idea of dirt as a signifier of imperfection and inferiority, the reference point being the white, often male, physically and mentally able person. In this chapter, I will discuss ways in which psychoanalytical theory has been used in the deconstruction of stereotypes, those 'others' from which the subject is distanced, and I will then examine some of the particular cultural sources of stereotyping in western societies. Stereotypes play an important part in the configuration of social space because of the importance of **distanciation** in the behaviour of social groups, that is, distancing from others who are represented negatively, and because of the way in which group images and place images combine to create landscapes of exclusion. The issues I examine concern oppression and denial. I try to show how difference is harnessed in the exercise of power and the subordination of minorities.[1]

Stereotypes

The reception and acceptance of stereotypes, 'images of things we fear and glorify', as Sander Gilman puts it,[2] is a necessary part of coming to terms with the world. In the following passage from his psychoanalytical account of the deep structure of stereotypes, Gilman assigns a central role to stereotyping in the structuring or bounding of the self:

> The child's sense of self splits into a 'good' self which, as the self mirroring the earlier stage of the complete control of the world (the stage of pre-Oedipal unity with the mother) is free from anxiety, and the 'bad' self which is unable to control the environment and is thus exposed to anxieties. The split is but a single stage in the development of the normal personality. In it lies, however, the root of all stereotypical perceptions. For, in the normal course of development, the child's understanding of the world becomes seemingly ever more sophisticated. The child is able to distinguish even finer gradations of 'goodness' and 'badness' so that by the later Oedipal stage an illusion of verisimilitude is cast over the inherent (and irrational) distinction between the 'good' and 'bad' world and self, between control and loss of control, between acquiescence and denial.[3]

Both the self and the world are split into good and bad objects, and the bad self, the self associated with fear and anxiety over the loss of control, is projected onto bad objects. Fear precedes the construction of the bad object, the negative stereotype, but the stereotype – simplified, distorted and at a distance – perpetuates that fear. Most personalities draw on a range of stereotypes, not necessarily wholly good, not necessarily wholly bad, as a means of coping with the instabilities which arise in our perceptions of the world. They make the world seem secure and stable.

Notes

1 Some recent post-modern writing, for example, Iain Chambers' *Migrancy, Culture and Identity* (Routledge, London, 1994), celebrates difference with some enthusiasm. The theme of Chambers' book is that there are fusions, hybrids and new forms of difference that follow from increasing global movement and interconnectedness. I think that it is important not to be carried away by this. Problems defined by thc firm contours of territorially based conflict, associated with race, ethnicity, sexuality and disability, are persistent features of socio-spatial relations. Many people live in one place for a long time and some have difficulty getting along with those who are different from themselves. Unfortunately, the African

musicians whom Chambers admires and who have certainly enriched British culture are still subject to racism outside the sympathetic environment of the club or the music festival.

2 Sander Gilman, *Difference and Pathology: Stereotypes of Sexuality, Race and Madness* (Cornell University Press, Ithaca, NY, 1985). This book, with its emphasis on visual representation, develops object relations theory to incorporate the world as it is perceived.

3 Ibid, p. 17.

Reading source

Sibley, 1995, pp. 14–15

Sibley goes on to elaborate this argument further in suggesting that stereotypical views of people in a conflict situation arise when a community that represents itself as the norm feels threatened by those whom they perceive as different and threatening. The fear and anxiety is translated into a stereotype (Sibley, 1995, pp. 28–9). Though engaging with the threatening other might dissolve some of this fear, as Sibley points out, a limited and superficial engagement with those who are different might be even more problematic than none at all if it produces only limited knowledge and understanding. These are the processes which construct group boundaries to keep those who threaten them at a distance (1995, p. 46).

The next part of this chapter considers three case studies: gated communities, sports utility vehicles and CCTV **surveillance**. As we shall see in the first two case studies, strategies to exclude others represent a crucial element in the making of contemporary social worlds. Psychic security is thus necessarily connected to the realm of the social. In these strategies for enhancing security, new objects and artefacts – matter – are made. The built form of the city is thus implicated in psychic and social processes.

3.3 Gated communities

> The building is divided into three apartment blocks, each characterised by an unusual *vaulted roof* which sails over the apartment balconies below. The division offers *enhanced privacy* with the *secure entrance* to each block serving a maximum of eight apartments. Safety and security are a priority throughout and *Atrium* offers *secure parking* via electric-operated vehicle gates plus a *video-entry phone system*.
>
> (UK estate agency advertisement)

> The Mountain Springs Ranch community offers lifestyle activities for all ages, like swimming or relaxing in the community pool, fishing in the pond with good friends, or strolling on the trail that meanders along the creek in the 85-acre Ranch Preserve park. Mountain Springs Ranch is a paradise for kids – safe and secure, with woods to play in, frogs to catch, and hills to roll down. And it's just as great for grown-ups. That's fun.
>
> You have space to live, to move and breathe. Space to stretch your body.
>
> (Masterworks, 2002)

Figure 4.1
Self-protection in gated communities often means security fencing, even when it's not obvious what the community is being protected from

An increasingly popular trend across the globe is the flight of households from mixed city spaces into self-segregated homogeneous housing enclaves – gated communities and other forms of private and secure housing estates. Sarah Blandy et al. (2003, p. 3) provide this definition of the gated community: 'Walled or fenced housing developments to which public access is restricted, often guarded using CCTV and/or security personnel, and usually characterised by legal agreements (tenancy or leasehold) which tie the residents to a common code of conduct.' This is the new urban architecture of enclosure and self-protection bunker architecture, as Paul Virilio (1994) calls it. Those who are different, and perceived as threatening, are excluded from these estates by invisible or barely visible codes, or by simple economics (the houses are expensive), or by gates, guards or high electrified fences. Here a whole suite of material practices of everyday living are performed, from the showing of identity cards to driving into an electronically controlled private garage, to minimise contact with threatening unknown others, thereby building an imagined sense of security and constructed community.

Figure 4.2
Typical house in US gated community for affluent residents

Gated communities are now so popular in the USA that they account for approximately 11 per cent of all new housing and provide accommodation for about four million people (Blandy et al., 2003, p. 2). There has also been a huge growth in this form of housing in both developed and developing countries. In Mexico City, for example – a sprawling metropolis of nineteen million where 40 per cent of people live below the poverty line – the rich are to be found in a world of gated communities with rooftop swimming pools and commuting by helicopter, creating, according to one commentator, a 'well-structured apartheid system' (Sudjic, 2006).

Figure 4.3
Gated housing in Mexico City

There are now one thousand gated communities in England (Atkinson and Flint, 2004, p. 9), with most clustered in the south-east. The segregation of residential areas represents an attractive commercial venture for developers, who can increase their profits with the promise of safety and security to its residents. For example, house prices on the Quarry Dene estate in Leeds, where the promise of an electronically operated entrance, security fences and CCTV, topped £500,000 in 2004 – much in excess of equivalent houses in the area (Macleod, 2004). According to *Building Balanced Communities* (Minton, 2002) 65 per cent of eighteen- to twenty-four-year-olds, and 44 per cent of those over sixty-five think that gated communities are a ‘good thing’, acting to insulate residents from the perceived risk of living in cities and to provide greater security. In a recent study of gated communities in the UK, local authority officers, national housing organisations and developers attributed security and exclusivity as the two most important aspects driving demand for gated developments (Atkinson and Flint, 2004). While residents in the Royal Institute of Chartered Surveyors (RICS) report cited concern about crime as their main reason for choosing to live in gated communities (Minton, 2002).

Anita Rice describes one such development in East London, Bow Quarter:

> Like most gated communities, the complex of around 700 apartments is walled off from the surrounding area, employs security guards round the clock and is peppered by dozens of infra-red surveillance cameras.

> ...
>
> Bow Quarter is peaceful, quiet, litter and graffiti-free and, of course, feels totally safe. It stands in stark contrast to the noise, bustle and social mix found on the Bow Road at the end of the street.
>
> (Rice, 2004, p. 1)

The new popularity of gated communities is thus profoundly embedded in a climate of fear and the search for greater security that characterises the contemporary city. In Bauman's (2003) terms the attraction of these residential enclaves, as they are sometimes called, represents a spatial shift in the city from 'mixophilia' to 'mixophobia' where city residents are increasingly reluctant to live alongside those who are different from themselves. According to Bauman, mixophobia is a widespread response to the overwhelming variety of lifestyles and differences that people encounter each day in the city streets, and to those 'accumulated anxieties [which] tend to unload against the selected category of "aliens", picked up to epitomise "strangeness as such". In chasing them away from one's homes and shops, the frightening ghost of uncertainty is, for a time, exorcised' (2003, p. 26). Furthermore, he argues: 'It is insecure men and women, uncertain of their place in the world, of their life prospects and the effects of their own actions, who are most vulnerable to the temptation of mixophobia and most likely to fall into its trap' (p. 115). It is mixophobia, he suggests, which drives individuals into self-segregation in walled and fortified enclaves. Like many others, Bauman attributes this drive towards similarity and sameness to the fact that people in cities are overwhelmed and discomforted by the strangeness and unknowability of others who are different from themselves. Recalling Lewis Mumford's (1938) early analysis of smaller communities, he suggests that alien others in villages and rural areas are enfolded into the community through being known and understood, through being domesticated and incorporated. In contrast, strangers in cities are too numerous to be familiarised – 'they are the unknown variable', whose intentions cannot be predicted and whose 'presence inside the fields of action is discomforting' (Bauman, 2003).

Let us return to Bow Quarter, where Mr Nicholls, one of the residents, has this to say:

> It can make you very insular ... we don't need to leave the building at all'.
>
> ...
>
> Many of the women say they love living here but hate having to walk down from the tube because they are afraid of getting mugged, and there have been spates of muggings.

> As soon as they get past the gates you can almost see a weight come off people's shoulders, you can almost see them breathe a sigh of relief.
> (quoted in Rice, 2004)

As sociologists we need to question not just why and how these social worlds are made, but also their effects. We might want to question whether these gated communities make the world safe for their residents. It could be argued that the notion that re-ordering the city can relieve anxieties that come from other sources – a fear of crime, a discomfort at living in proximity with others who are different, the fluidity and fragility of labour markets, more precarious social bonds, and so on – is in part fallacious. Rather, this very response on the part of individuals to make their world safer by living alongside only those who are similar to themselves, actually diminishes their contact with different others, and can lower their tolerance to them when they are encountered. As Bauman points out, the strategy of retreat does not make city life more secure and enjoyable, rather it multiplies the occasions for mixophobic reactions and makes city life look more 'risk-prone'.

Sennett (1996) takes a similar tack in suggesting that neighbourhoods within cities are becoming increasingly homogeneous ethnically as people elect to live close to people like themselves in a drive towards a 'community of similarity' (1994, p. 42). As a result, people lose the art of relating to and interacting with people who do not share the same language or understandings, so that they regard meeting and negotiating with those who are different with misapprehension. This becomes a cycle which is hard to break. These arguments highlight that, in the attempt to make the world safer for themselves, seeking greater security, individuals may actually be made more insecure and fearful than they were before. Here we see how the individual is inextricably bound to the social.

Research on gated communities confirms such an argument. Despite Rowland Atkinson and John Flint's (2004) finding that gated communities were symbolically linked to a fear of crime and dystopian images of the city and social relationships, they are not always successful in providing the imagined comfort that residents seek. For example, their visibility as wealthy residential areas may actually encourage crime by pinpointing rich enclaves while restricting access to the police in an emergency. Even in the political arena there is considerable controversy as to their benefits. In 2004 the then UK Home Secretary David Blunkett suggested that gated communities contributed to security and order (Rice, 2004), but this view was hotly disputed by the Deputy Commissioner of the Metropolitan Police, who was 'entirely opposed to the idea that we should have any kind of gated communities ... because they are invidious for social cohesion' (Rice, 2004), increasing the gap between rich and poor as the rich withdrew from public space.

Representations of people who are different and the city as dangerous provoke individuals to seek new ways of living in the city, creating new forms of residential segregation and division in order to enhance their sense of security. Thus the very fabric of the city is made and remade as a response to individuals' fears, needs and desires, which are themselves constituted through exposure to public discourse and media representation. Our next case study will consider how such fears can influence some urban residents' choice of car.

3.4 Sports utility vehicles

> The sign at the end of my street is big, red, and features only one, straightforward instruction: 'STOP' ...
>
> Because the street is in the Hollywood hills, however, and because the Hollywood hills are populated by rich people who do a lot of drugs, no one stops. ...
>
> I mention this because of a story, causing outrage in California, about a woman who crashed her Chevrolet Blazer SUV into the side of a Toyota Tercel saloon, killing its driver. The Blazer driver suffered only a minor shoulder injury, but was so spooked by the crash that she replaced her dented Blazer with an even bigger, fatter SUV.
>
> The standard dinner-party take on the story, which appears in Keith Bradsher's SUV-bashing book *High and Mighty*, is that the Blazer driver should have felt so destroyed by guilt at her brutish, Bush-loving behaviour, that she should have immediately traded in her Blazer for a Reliant Robin. Perhaps the killer and her children would then be flattened by someone else's Chevy Blazer, and a jolly important lesson would be learnt by all.
>
> This, of course, is a ridiculous argument. It is not the Blazer driver who should change her car-buying habits, but the rest of the non-SUV driving population.
>
> After all, if everyone on the road was behind the wheel of a three-ton monster, a kind of Cold War-style mutually assured destruction would come into effect.
>
> (Ayres, 2004)

One of the most extreme strategies for self-protection and isolation from the vagaries, terrors and dangers – imagined and real – of contemporary city life is the sports utility vehicle (SUV). No vehicle in recent years has caused such vehement reactions from supporters and opponents.

The claims made on the vehicle's behalf and the discourses of resistance are highly mediated by the press and other forms of media. Thus, the SUV represents a potent site for an exploration of how social worlds are mediated.

SUVs are primarily marketed on a platform of safety and security. In 2005, a typical top-of-the-range model cost more than $100,000. Crucial to the promotional material are the safety and security features, which include a plethora of airbags, locking devices, remote sensors and a panic alarm. Referred to pejoratively by their opponents, they are heavily promoted by advertisers in the USA as defensive capsules against the threat of catastrophic terrorism (Graham, 2004). Such has been their success that they now account for 45 per cent of all car sales in the USA, and 10 per cent in Western Europe. Their growth in popularity at the end of the twentieth century can largely be located in the imagined protection that these vehicles are argued to provide for their occupants, against theft and invasion from others and from harm in the event of an accident. Families with children are particularly targeted with details of their armoured structure and greater visibility. Their success exposes the level of insecurity and fear in the population that can be so readily exploited by car manufacturers for profit.

Figure 4.4
A cartoonist's comment on the perverse popularity of the SUV

In the early years of their popularity there were also heated debates about the impact of SUVs on daily life. Opponents contended that their use was making the world more unsafe, and that their fuel consumption exceeded that of all other vehicles – close to triple that of normal cars. In 2004, the average mile per gallon was 13, compared to the US fuel economy guidelines of 27.5 miles per gallon. This level of petrol consumption had clear implications for the level of demand for oil, particularly in the USA. Thus individual demands for fuel were argued to have macro-political effects, as these are embedded in the wider geopolitics of oil. Stephen Graham (2004, pp. 118–19) went further to draw out interdependencies between SUV fuel consumption, US oil companies and the war on Iraq, in arguing that SUVs were designed and marketed after the first Gulf War as quasi-militarised urban assault vehicles. Thus, SUVs provide an illustration of how 'cities and urban everyday life are affected by an interplay of terror and counter-terror' (Wekerle and Jackson, 2005, p. 33).

Powerful actors such as property developers or the car industry are not the only forces shaping cities, as we saw in Chapter 1 of this book. The opponents of SUVs similarly aimed to capture public and media attention through politics of resistance. As Michel Foucault has argued, power and resistance are intertwined: 'there are no relations of power without resistance' (1980, p. 142). The residents of many cities have protested against the use of SUVs through websites and direct political action. Gerda Wekerle and Paul Jackson (2005, p. 38) quote the case of a journalist in the USA who linked suburban experiences of everyday life to terrorist activities overseas in a bumper sticker: 'I helped blow up a Bali nightclub – by driving my SUV to work every day!' In my neighbourhood, campaigners have posted stickers on the windscreens of SUVs alerting their drivers to the damage they cause.

These different views have been highly mediated by the press and different interest groups have vociferously argued their cases. With the looming threat of a decline in sales as environmental arguments gained strength, the industry – notably Lexus – fought to regain ground with the launch in 2005 of a new hybrid-engine version of one of its SUV models which promised to consume the same amount of petrol as a smaller car (Ayres, 2004).

Our first two case studies demonstrated how fear and anxieties in the city shape individual choices for housing and transport, which in turn have wider effects on the material environment of the city. Our final case study will consider how collective fears have mobilised technological solutions in public space, notably the street. Here again a material solution is found to mediate personal and collective disquiet.

3.5 CCTV and surveillance

Figure 4.5
Photographs depicting the capabilities of closed circuit television (CCTV) cameras, day or night

A prime institutional strategy in cities to decrease fears of attack, theft and violence has been the deployment of CCTV cameras throughout urban space. It is estimated that there are twenty-five million CCTV cameras worldwide. In the UK since the 1980s, more than a million CCTV cameras have been put in cities and towns and up to 500 new ones are currently being added every week (Goold, 2004). The presence of the camera is imagined to enhance safety in the surrounding area and to minimise risk. In Johannesburg in South Africa the installation of surveillance technology in the central business district has reversed its decline, with crime rates decreasing by 80 per cent, and 92 per cent of business entrepreneurs, city workers and residents reporting that they would consider relocating or reinvesting in the city centre (Majola, 2003). At the same time the surveillance camera, in this and other instances, can be seen to enrol urban individuals into the management of their own security in their neighbourhoods, homes and places of work. This is the panoptic effect explored by Foucault in his writing on Jeremy Bentham's design for prisons, where prisoners are – or appear to be – watched from a central tower. The mere presence of an all-seeing eye, even when inactive, produces submission and good behaviour in the prisoners who imagine themselves to be constantly under surveillance. As a result, subjects internalise the very authority to which they have been subjected and monitor and regulate their own actions. It can be argued that cameras in city spaces have similar effects, to the extent that, even when there is no film in the camera, or the camera is switched off, people act cautiously and lawfully.

Read the following extract by Michel Foucault. Do you ever find yourself monitoring your behaviour in the presence of surveillance cameras? As you read, you should be able to understand what Foucault means by 'panopticism'. With this in mind, can you think of any spaces in your neighbourhood that function as a panopticon?

Reading 4.3 Michel Foucault, 'Panopticism'

The constant division between the normal and the abnormal, to which every individual is subjected, brings us back to our own time, by applying the binary branding and exile of the leper to quite different objects; the existence of a whole set of techniques and institutions for measuring, supervising and correcting the abnormal brings into play the disciplinary mechanisms to which the fear of the plague gave rise. All the mechanisms of power which, even today, are disposed around the abnormal individual, to brand him and to alter him, are composed of those two forms from which they distantly derive.

Bentham's *Pantopticon* is the architectural figure of this composition. We know the principle on which it was based: at the periphery, an annular building; at the centre, a tower; this tower is pierced with wide windows that open onto the inner side of the ring; the peripheric building is divided into cells, each of which extends the whole width of the building; they have two windows, one on the inside, corresponding to the windows of the tower; the other, on the outside, allows the light to cross the cell from one end to the other. All that is needed, then, is to place a supervisor in a central tower and to shut up in each cell a madman, a patient, a condemned man, a worker or a schoolboy. By the effect of backlighting, one can observe from the tower, standing out precisely against the light, the small captive shadows in the cells of the periphery. They are like so many cages, so many small theatres, in which each actor is alone, perfectly individualized and constantly visible. The panoptic mechanism arranges spatial unities that make it possible to see constantly and to recognize immediately. In short, it reverses the principle of the dungeon; or rather of its three functions – to enclose, to deprive of light and to hide – it preserves only the first and eliminates the other two. Full lighting and the eye of a supervisor capture better than darkness, which ultimately protected. Visibility is a trap.

To begin with, this made it possible – as a negative effect – to avoid those compact, swarming, howling masses that were to be found in places of confinement, those painted by Goya or described by Howard. Each individual, in his place, is securely confined to a cell from which he is seen from the front by the supervisor; but the side walls prevent him from coming into contact with his companions. He is seen, but he does not see; he is the object of information, never a subject in communication. The arrangement of his room, opposite the central tower, imposes on him an axial visibility; but the divisions of the ring, those separated cells, imply a lateral invisibility. And this invisibility is a guarantee of order. If the inmates are convicts, there is no danger of a plot, an attempt at collective escape, the planning of new crimes for the future, bad reciprocal influences; if they are patients, there is no danger of contagion; if they are madmen there is no risk of their committing violence upon one another; if they are schoolchildren, there is no copying, no noise, no chatter, no waste of time; if they are workers, there are no disorders, no theft, no coalitions, none of those distractions that slow down the rate of work, make it less perfect or cause accidents. The crowd, a compact mass, a locus of multiple exchanges, individualities merging together, a collective effect, is abolished and replaced by a collection of separated individualities. From the point of view of the guardian, it is replaced by a multiplicity that can be numbered and supervised; from the point of view of the inmates, by a sequestered and observed solitude ...

Hence the major effect of the Panopticon: to induce in the inmate a state of conscious and permanent visibility that assures the automatic functioning of power. So to arrange things that the surveillance is permanent in its effects, even if it is discontinuous in its action; that the perfection of power should tend to render its actual exercise unnecessary; that this architectural apparatus should be a machine for creating and sustaining a power relation independent of the person who exercises it; in short, that the inmates should be caught up in a power situation of which they are themselves the bearers. To achieve this, it is at once too much and too little that the prisoner should be constantly observed by an inspector: too little, for what matters is that he knows himself to be observed; too much, because he has no need in fact of being so. In view of this, Bentham laid down the principle that power should be visible and unverifiable. Visible: the inmate will constantly have before his eyes the tall outline of the central tower from which he is spied upon. Unverifiable: the inmate must never know whether he is being looked at at any one moment; but he must be sure that he may always be so. In order to make the presence or absence of the inspector unverifiable, so that the prisoners, in their cells, cannot even see a shadow, Bentham envisaged not only venetian blinds on the windows of the central observation hall, but, on the inside, partitions that intersected the hall at right angles and, in order to pass from one quarter to the other, not doors but zigzag openings, for the slightest noise, a gleam of light, a brightness in a half-opened door would betray the presence of the guardian.[1] The Panopticon is a machine for dissociating the see/being seen dyad: in the peripheric ring, one is totally seen, without ever seeing; in the central tower, one sees everything without ever being seen.[2]

It is an important mechanism, for it automizes and disindividualizes power. Power has its principle not so much in a person as in a certain concerted distribution of bodies, surfaces, lights, gazes; in an arrangement whose internal mechanisms produce the relation in which individuals are caught up.

Notes

2 In the *Postscript to the Panopticon*, 1791, Bentham adds dark inspection galleries painted in black around the inspector's lodge, each making it possible to observe two storeys of cells.

3 In his first version of the *Panopticon*, Bentham had also imagined an acoustic surveillance, operated by means of pipes leading from the cells to the central tower. In the *Postscript* he abandoned the idea, perhaps because he could not introduce into it the principle of dissymmetry and prevent the prisoners from hearing the inspector as well as the inspector hearing them.

Reading source

Foucault, 1977, pp. 199–202

Having read this extract from Foucault you should now be able to see why urban sociologists often draw parallels between CCTV cameras and the idea of the panopticon as discussed by Foucault.

3.6 A local case study: north London

The installation of CCTV in city spaces is a common demand by local residents who see themselves as under threat from violence, antisocial behaviour or theft. A study I undertook in my local area (Watson and Wells, 2005) highlights some of the contradictions entailed. This was an inner London borough comprising an established, white, working-class community, the majority of whom live in a very large public housing estate intersected by a traditional street market which provides a focal point for shopping, chatting and meeting neighbours. In the last quarter of the twentieth century this locality underwent dramatic socio-demographic and ethnic/racial change, initially with the arrival of the Afro-Caribbean and African communities, followed by Bengalis, Turkish, Somalis and a wide diversity of refugees from war-torn countries in the Middle East and Africa. This shift in the racial composition of the area mobilised high levels of nostalgia for a community that is remembered and imagined as more cohesive and able to manage its own affairs. The owner of the DIY shop in the market, Larry, expressed it thus:

> Forty years ago it was rough here but they don't shit on their own doorstep. It was honour among thieves. What ever you did, you did outside the manor. Whereas now they're doing their own, they're killing their own, robbing their own. It's all mixed up. You could go to old Sid down the road and he'd say, leave it to me, I'll sort it out. You can't do that now. If you had any trouble and you lived on the manor

Figure 4.6
The street market

you could go to someone and they'd sort it out. You can't do that anymore, because it's all mixed up with idiots, druggies, young kids who don't know what they're doing. And there's no morals. They've gotta get whatever they want and they don't care how they do it, they don't care who they mug, for whatever reason. I knew about four or five families here, and I could turn to any of them families, they'd have a word, and they'd leave them alone. I know the rules. A gospel rule you learn around Poppy Street, it don't seem to apply now because they're doing each other, you do not grass and you do not grass to the old bill.

(Watson and Wells, 2005, p. 24)

It is interesting that, despite the crime statistics indicating otherwise (Watson and Wells, 2005, p.24), the prevailing opinion was that the area had become more dangerous. An Office for Public Management survey in 2002 (quoted in Watson and Wells, 2005, p. 24), for example, found that 46 per cent of the local population saw drugs as a major problem, and only 42 per cent of residents felt safe out alone at night compared to 67 per cent nationally. Sam – the British Kenyan shop owner – put it this way: 'Twenty years ago, England was a "fantastic country".
Now crime, unemployeds, "too many refugees"' (Watson and Wells, 2005, p. 25).

Even the more recently arrived owner of a South East Asian supermarket agreed: 'In the past more people used this area. These days they don't feel safe to come' (Watson and Wells, 2005, p. 25). 'It's just general safety ... It's not like before, the white people took care of the white people. There's a gap in the relationship. Between the whites and Asians.'

And Larry, describing the time when he owned one of the market's five butchers:

> One day I was opening the shutters on the butcher's shop. A little boy about 12 kept pulling the shutter down. I said 'don't keep doing that you're going to break it'. I went back in and I looked he's doing it again. I said 'you f****** c*** you're going to break the thing'. He's standing there he says 'go on f****** hit me'. I thought, shall I? One bash. And he's blackmailing me, this little kid. One of the police says to me 'you alright?' ... I says 'can't you nick him?' ... And I thought that's it, whereas that boy should have been scared of me, I was scared of him.
>
> (Watson and Wells, 2005, p. 25)

Here in this typical inner-London locality, for many people the answer to the perceived increase in crime, violence and lack of safety was the installation of CCTV cameras throughout the street, and considerable hostility was expressed at the ease at which the richer parts of the borough had already managed to have cameras installed. This desire for increased surveillance, and voluntary submission to the panoptic gaze of the camera instilling self-regulation and imagined protection, follow a trend in cities worldwide. By transferring the problem to an unseeing but ever-present eye, local citizens lose any sense of their own empowerment that alternative forms of local crime control might allow; in this London street this is illustrative of the general malaise and sense of powerlessness that the local people articulated.

Here we see how narratives of fear and anxiety circulate around a locality, exaggerated as they are told and re-told, captured in articles in the local press, which seeks out stories of danger and violence. Often minor criminal events are mediated through press reports to further exacerbate the portrayal of the locality as dangerous – stories of ordinary, safe, everyday life don't sell newspapers.

Emmanuel Martinais and Christophe Bétin (2004), in a study of Lyon city centre in France, found a similar use of CCTV by the new socialist local government in a response to the fears of residents and shopkeepers. CCTV in this city space, they argued, was centrally embedded in a strategy to enhance local security which drew on the prevailing social representations of the deviant, the criminal, and negative social encounters. The authors concluded that CCTV 'not only acts to consolidate dominant social representations in the field of security, but the ways in which it is used leads to reformulation of the rules and social norms construing everyday practices and deviant behaviour in public space' (2004, p. 361).

This case study has highlighted how new urban forms and strategies are subject also to resistance, as urban spaces are made, remade and unmade. This urban strategy has also encountered resistance. Many people see this new technology as invasive of privacy. The civil rights organisation Liberty is concerned with how these systems are regulated: 'It is not so much the technology but how it is used that concerns us, and how to keep the balance between protecting safety and protecting privacy' (Wakefield, 2002). We saw in Reading 4.3 how the panopticon distributes bodies in webs of differentiated power, constructing relations of division between normal and abnormal, negatively branding different objects at different times. So, too, cameras are argued to be techniques which serve to racialise those that are surveilled:

> The real burden of the new urban fear – the part that is not hallucinatory or hyperbolized – is borne by those who fit the racial profile of white anxiety. For those caught squarely in the middle of this paranoid gestalt ... there is the threat of violence, but even more, the certainty of surveillance by powers 'vast and cool and unsympathetic'.
>
> (Davis, quoted in Wekerle and Jackson, 2005)

Others argue that CCTV does little to prevent crime, but merely shifts it to areas not covered by the cameras. In the USA such views have motivated a group of protesters – the New York Surveillance Camera Players – to take to the streets and perform specially adapted plays directly in front of the cameras. This group uses their visibility, their public appearances, interviews with the media and their website 'to explode the cynical myth that only those who are "guilty of something" are opposed to being surveilled by unknown eyes' (Surveillance Camera Players, 2001).

Figure 4.7
The New York Surveillance Camera Players

4 Conclusion

This chapter began with a discussion of pro-urban and anti-urban discourses of the city and suggested that negative urban imaginaries in many instances derived from a fear of others who were perceived to differ from dominant social and cultural norms. Such fears of difference and disorder in the city, it was argued, had a long history. In Section 2 we also explored some of the origins of contemporary fears and anxieties in the city, not least the sense of insecurity following some of the terrorist attacks on major cities in the early part of the twenty-first century. It was also argued that the rapid pace of globalisation, and the changes that followed, were equally important in bringing about an increased sense of fear and risk for many in the city. The large increase in different ethnic and racial groups as a result of increased migration patterns arguably provided a fertile ground for hostility to different others, and their stereotypical representation, which could be understood, in part, using psycho-social approaches.

The case studies examined how negative urban imaginaries and their associated fears and anxieties, combined with real material shifts in the global city (in particular the growing divisions between rich and poor), had concrete and visible effects on the built form (matter) of the city. In the pursuit of an imagined greater security we saw how urban residents look for material solutions in their urban environment, to mitigate an everyday sense of fear and insecurity. We chose to explore these processes through three case studies: gated communities, sports utility vehicles and CCTV; you may be able to think of others in places with which you are familiar. The material urban world has been made through social processes, where fears mediated in many different contexts such as newspapers, advertising and film are translated into a range of built and manufactured (material) forms. The contemporary city is thus highly implicated in the individual and collective desire, and search, for a greater sense of security.

End-note

1 The idea of the 'imaginary' is often used as a shorthand for the various meanings that may relate to – and order – a given entity, whether that be a 'social imaginary', referring to a part of society, or some other type of entity. These 'imaginaries' are usually understood to be constructs and in this sense are contingent on the imagination of social subjects.

References

Atkinson, R. and Flint, J. (2004) *Fortress UK? Gated Communities: The Spatial Revolt of the Elites and Time–Space Trajectories of Segregation*, Research Paper 17 Bristol, ESRC Centre for Neighbourhood Research.

Ayres, C. (2004) 'The confessions of an SUV driver: we are not all insecure unhappy brutes' [online], London, Times Online, http://www.timesonline.co.uk/tol/comment/columnists/guest_contributors/article391628.ece (accessed 26 March 2007).

Bauman, Z. (2003) *Liquid Love: On the Frailty of Human Bonds*, Cambridge, Polity.

Blandy, S., Lister, D., Atkinson, R. and Flint, J. (2003) *Gated Communities: A Systematic Review of the Research Evidence*, CNR paper 12, Bristol, ESRC Centre for Neighbourhood Research.

Bridge, G. and Watson, S. (eds) (2002) *The Blackwell City Reader*, Oxford, Blackwell.

Castells, M. (1996) The Rise of the Network Society, *The Information Age: Economy, Society and Culture*, vol.1, Oxford, Blackwell.

Davis, M. (1990) *City of Quartz: Excavating the Future in Los Angeles*, New York, NY, Vintage.

Davis, M. (2002) *Dead Cities: And Other Tales*, London, The New Press.

Dickens, C. (1985 [1837–39]) *Oliver Twist* (ed.) P. Fairclough, Harmondsworth, Penguin.

Dickens, C. (2003 [1853]) *Bleak House* (ed.), N. Bradbury, Harmondsworth, Penguin.

Duras, M. (1952) *The Sea Wall*, London, Faber and Faber.

Engels, F. (1968[1844]) *The Condition of the Working Class in England*, Palo Alto, CA, Stanford University Press.

Foucault, M. (1977) *Discipline and Punish: The Birth of the Prison*, (trans. A. Sheridan), Harmondsworth, Penguin.

Foucault, M. (1980) 'Power strategies' in Gordon, G. (ed.) *Power/Knowledge – Selected Interviews and Other Writings, 1972–1977*, Brighton, Harvester Press.

Furedi, F. (1997) *Culture of Fear: Risk Taking and the Morality of Low Expectations*, New York, NY, Continuum.

Goold, B. (2004) *CCTV and Policing: Public Area Surveillance and Police Practices in Britain*, Oxford, Oxford University Press.

Graham, S. (2004) 'Towards an urban geopolitics', *City*, vol. 8, no. 2, pp. 165–96.

Gregory, D. (2004) *The Colonial Present*, Oxford, Blackwell.

Hannerz, U. (1993) 'The cultural roles of world cities' in Cohen, A.P. and Fukuo, K. (eds) *Humanising the City*, Edinburgh, Edinburgh University Press, pp. 67–84.

King, A. D. (1990) *Urbanism, Colonialism, and the World Economy*, London, Routledge.

Kristeva, J. (1991) *Strangers to Ourselves* (trans. L. Roudiez), New York, NY/London, Harvester Wheatsheaf.

Le Goix, R. (2003) 'The suburban paradise or the parcelling of cities?' [online], Los Angeles, UCLA, http://www.international.ucla.edu/article.asp?parentid=4664 (accessed 26 March 2007).

Macleod, G. (2004) *Privatising the City? The Tentative Push Towards Edge Urban Developments and Gated Communities in the UK*, London, HMSO, Office of the Deputy Prime Minister.

Majola, B. (2003) 'Perceptions of Joburg inner city improve' [online], www.joburg.org.za/2003/june/june19_perceptions (accessed 26 March 2007).

Martinais, E. and Bétin, C. (2004) 'Social aspects of CCTV in France, the case of the city centre of Lyons', *Surveillance and Society*, vol. 2, nos. 2/3, pp. 361–75.

Masterworks (2002) 'Mountain Springs Ranch' [online], Boerne, TX, http://www.mw-homes.com/mountainspringsranch.htm (accessed 26 March 2007).

Minton, A. (2002) *Building Balanced Communities: The US and UK Compared*, London, Royal Institute of Chartered Surveyors.

Mumford, L. (1938) *The Culture of Cities,* New York, NY, Harcourt Brace.

Redman, P. (ed.) (2008) *Attachment: Sociology and Social Worlds*, Manchester, Manchester University Press/Milton Keynes, The Open University (Book 2 in this series).

Rice, A. (2004) 'Gates and ghettoes: a tale of two Britains' [online], London, BBC Current Affairs Interactive, http://news.bbc.co.uk/1/hi/programmes/if/3513980.stm (accessed 26 March 2007).

Sandercock, L. (2003) *Mongrel Cities: Cosmopolis,* 11 New York, NY, Continuum.

Sassen, S. (2001) *The Global City: New York, London, Tokyo*, Princeton, NJ, Princeton University Press.

Sennett, R. (1994) *Flesh and Stone: The Body and the City in Western Civilization*, London, Faber and Faber.

Sennett, R. (1996) *The Uses of Disorder: Personal Identity and City Life*, London, Faber and Faber.

Short, J. (2004) *Global Metropolitan: Globalising Cities in a Capitalist World*, London, Routledge.

Sibley, D. (1995) *Geographies of Exclusion: Society and Difference in the West*, London, Routledge.

Simmel, G. (1948 [1903]) 'The metropolis and mental life' in *Social Sciences* III, *Selections and Readings*, vol. 2, (trans. E. Shils), (14th edn), Chicago, IL, Chicago University Press.

Smith, N. (1996) *The New Urban Frontier: Gentrification and the Revanchist City*, London, Routledge.

Sudjic, D. (2006) 'Making cities work: Mexico City' [online], London, BBC News, http://news.bbc.co.uk/1/low/world/americas/5061626.stm (accessed 26 March 2007).

Surveillance Camera Players (2001) 'Who we are and why we're here' [online], New York, NY, http://www.notbored.org/generic.jpg (accessed 26 March 2007).

Sutherland, B. (2006) 'Slum dwellers "to top 2 billion"' [online], London, BBC News, http://news.bbc.co.uk/1/hi/world/5099038.stm (accessed 26 March 2007).

Tönnies, F. (1957 [1887]) *Community and Society*, East Lancing, MI, Michigan State University.

United Nations Centre for Human Settlement (Habitat) (2001) *State of the World's Cities*, Nairobi, UNCHS.

Virilio, P. (1994) *Bunker Archaeology*, New York, NY, Princeton Architectural Press.

Wakefield, J. (2002) 'Surveillance cameras to predict behaviour' [online], London, BBC News, http://news.bbc.co.uk/1/hi/sci/tech/1953770.stm (accessed 26 March 2007).

Walkowitz, J. (1992) *City of Dreadful Delight*, Chicago, IL, University of Chicago Press.

Watson, S. (2006) *City Publics: The (Dis) Enchantments of Urban Encounters*, London, Routledge.

Watson, S. and Wells, K. (2005) 'Spaces of nostalgia: the hollowing out of a London market', *Social and Cultural Geography*, vol. 6, pp. 31–46.

Wekerle, G. and Jackson, P. (2005) 'Urbanising the security agenda: anti-terrorism, urban sprawl and social movements', *City*, vol. 9, no. 1, pp. 33–49.

Williams, R. (1973) *The Country and the City*, London, Chatto and Windus.

Wirth, L. (1938) 'Urbanism as a way of life', *American Journal of Sociology*, vol. 44, pp. 1–24.

Chapter 5
Health and security

Simon Carter and George Davey Smith

Contents

1 Introduction **146**

1.1 Teaching aims 147

2 Cholera, contagion and anti-contagion **147**

2.1 Symmetry and co-production 155

3 Security, the 'risk factor' and epidemiology **160**

4 Actor-network theory **168**

4.1 ANT, asthma and the metered dose inhaler 169

5 Conclusion **175**

End-notes **176**

References **176**

1 Introduction

Issues concerning health and disease are intimately connected to matters of security. In 1948 the newly formed United Nations (UN) firmly placed health concerns as central to the security of the individual in Article 25 of the Universal Declaration of Human Rights. By contrast, in the latter part of the twentieth century, nations were more often concerned solely with protection from external 'subversion' or military threats by using armies, police forces and the 'security services'. Recently, with the intensification of globalisation processes, this use of security has been called into question by the emergence of new infectious diseases such as HIV and SARS, together with the increased prominence of diseases such as cholera, malaria and tuberculosis, which were previously thought to be in retreat. Turning full circle, we are now witnessing a return to some of the initial links made between security and health at the formation of the UN.

It has now been recognised that when disease has the potential to affect a significant proportion of a population (as has happened with HIV in some parts of Africa), it threatens economic activity, social cohesion, political stability and food production. Consequently, the United Nations General Assembly recently declared diseases such as HIV, cholera and tuberculosis as threats not just to individual nation-states but also to global security (United Nations, 2001). UN General Secretary Kofi Annan observed that, in a globalised world where 'we are connected, wired, and interdependent', hazards such as emergent infections 'show little regard for the niceties of borders. They are problems without passports' (Annan, 2002, p. 30). This represents a move away from a conceptualisation of security as exclusively about threats to the nation-state and towards greater concern with threats to the health and well-being of individuals, populations and communities – about threats to the health of social worlds.

This chapter will describe a number of historical and contemporary case studies concerning health, illness and disease to examine various aspects of security. These are interesting in themselves but we also intend to use them to introduce and develop a number of contemporary sociological issues that can be broadly characterised as those approaches and methods associated with Science and Technology Studies (S&TS) – the study and investigation of the part played by science and technology in society. Over the past few decades, S&TS has grown as an area of social research. It tends to cross traditional disciplinary boundaries by drawing on sociology, philosophy, politics, media studies, law, anthropology and history. This emerging field of study, as Sheila Jasanoff has explained, has adopted as its foundational concern: 'the investigation of knowledge societies in all their complexity: their structures and practices, their ideas and material products, and their trajectories of change' (Jasanoff, 2004).

This chapter will consider how an examination of health, medicine, science and technology can illuminate aspects in the making of social worlds. We broadly follow Anselm L. Strauss's (1978) definition of a social world as a unit of discourse that is not confined by geography or formal membership of organisations or institutions. It is rather an assemblage or association with shared commitments or practices. Thus everyday life may comprise a mosaic of social worlds, with all of us having multiple 'memberships'. Membership may be a complex and contingent process: for example, no one is born a sociologist; one gradually becomes a member by studying certain topics, by obtaining relevant qualifications, by engaging in existing communities of practice, by publishing in certain places, by sharing discourses, and by taking part in a range of other activities.

1.1 Teaching aims

The aims of this chapter are to:

- outline some of the roles that health and security issues play in the making of social worlds
- give an introduction to Science and Technology Studies (S&TS) using examples from, and issues in, health and security
- provide an account of the concept of co-production
- explore the implications of an S&TS approach for our understandings of mediation and materiality.

2 Cholera, contagion and anti-contagion

The association between health, illness and security is not particularly new. Modernity has been characterised by a periodic focusing on the threats that illness and disease may cause to the security of both local and global social worlds. For example, the emergence of new diseases can radically disrupt existing social worlds, such as the appearance of syphilis in the late fifteenth century (see Crosby, 1972) or HIV in the late twentieth century (see Mann, 1995). This was certainly the case with the arrival of cholera in Britain in the early nineteenth century, which we will now consider in more detail.

Today cholera is understood to be caused by the bacterium *Vibrio cholerae* and is spread by ingesting food or water contaminated by this entity. The source of the infection is often the faeces of an infected person which can distribute the disease rapidly when or where there is inadequate treatment of sewage or a lack of clean water. However, this is very much a late twentieth-century understanding of the disease and we should be very cautious about imposing our contemporary understandings of phenomena such as illness and disease on the past. Diseases from the past (or indeed from the present) have an annoying habit of not always fitting into the tidy categories suggested by modern science or medicine, and this makes the job of the sociological historian a little more difficult (as well as much more interesting).

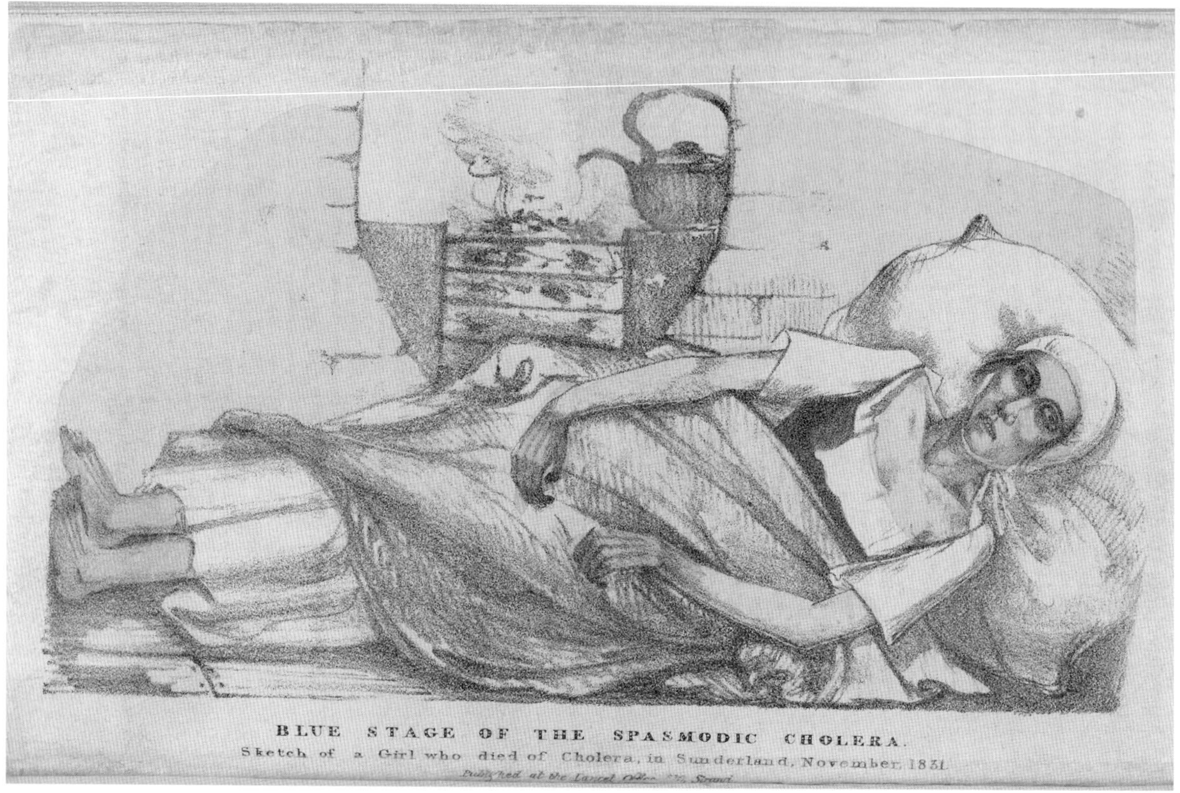

Figure 5.1
Girl dying of cholera in Sunderland *circa* 1831

Cholera first arrived in Britain from continental Europe in October 1831 and in the subsequent year more than 30,000 people died from it and many more were taken ill (Morris, 1976 [1832]). Cholera epidemics periodically reoccurred throughout the rest of the nineteenth century. From the beginning the worlds of science and medicine speculated on the possible origin of this illness. The debates were often acrimonious and it was clear that there was more at stake than simple arguments over the origin of the disease. Like many accounts of illness, the story of cholera intertwines the threads of nature, culture, economics and discourse. One version of the story of cholera reveals a division between holders of 'contagionist' and 'anti-contagionist' views: between those who believed the illness to be spread by something that passed between people and those who considered that something in the environment (such as atmospheric miasmas or 'bad air') to be the principal determination of epidemic illness.

The view that the disease was spread by the passing of some material entity between humans (the contagionist view) was initially supported by the influential medical journal, *The Lancet,* which on 19 November 1831 devoted forty-four pages to the arrival of cholera in Britain. In outlining the contagionist case, *The Lancet* pointed towards several 'proofs of communication of cholera by man':

> We shall classify our proofs of communication under the following heads of:
>
> 1 The coincidence between the irruption of the disease in previously-uninfected places, with the arrival of ships, of caravans of fugitives or pilgrims, of individuals, and with the progress of armies.
>
> 2 Examples of the coincidence between the occurrence of cholera in individuals, and their contact with others actually labouring under the disease.
>
> 3 Examples of immunity afforded by seclusion in the midst of an unhealthy district.
>
> (*The Lancet*, 1831)

This contagionist viewpoint was not widely shared by many in the medical professions, who instead supported non-contagionist theories about the causes of illness, which centred around so-called 'miasma theories'. These theories supposed that diseases were caused by poisonous vapours, characterised by nasty and foul smells, which contained particles from decomposing matter. Inhaling these fumes would either directly lead to illness or predispose the individual to illness. Others suggested that water, rather than air, may contain rotting organic matter and this would make the individual susceptible to illness. Indeed the idea that there were various factors that would weaken or make an individual susceptible to cholera were often folded into the miasma theory of causation. Thus during an outbreak of cholera in 1832 the New York Board of Health circulated the following advice about methods to prevent the spread of the disease, including a wide variety of what today may be taken as (perhaps familiar) lifestyle advice, particularly focusing on avoiding alcohol:

Notice

Be temperate in eating and drinking,
avoid crude *vegetables* and *fruits;*
abstain from *cold water,* when heated;
and above all from *ardent spirits* and if habit have rendered
it indispensable, take much less than usual.
Sleep and clothe warm
Avoid labor in the heat of the day.
Do not sleep or sit in a draught of air when heated.
Avoid getting wet
Take no medicines without advice

(quoted in Rosenberg, 1962)

Throughout the nineteenth century the periodic epidemics of cholera led to a continuation of the debate about the possible causes of this disease in human populations. As already mentioned, these debates were often belligerent and bitter and, as one contemporary commentator observed, 'the opinions which different men entertain upon it seem to bear some relation to their views on other questions' (Budd, 1856). Some medical historians have suggested that the views of those involved in the 'contagion' or 'anti-contagion' debates about cholera in the nineteenth century were in fact reflecting views about the appropriate form of political, economic or social ordering of social worlds at this time.

Read the following extract by Erwin Ackerknecht, which was written in 1948. This influential paper formalises many of the above arguments.

Reading 5.1 Erwin Ackerknecht, 'Anticontagionism between 1821 and 1867'

It is no accident that so many leading anticontagionists were outstanding scientists. To them this was a fight for science, against outdated authorities and medieval mysticism; for observation and research against systems and speculation ...

...

Contagionism was not a mere theoretical or even medical problem. Contagionism had found its material expression in the quarantines and their bureaucracy, and the whole discussion was thus never a discussion on contagion alone, but *always on contagion and quarantines*. Quarantines meant, to the rapidly growing class of merchants and industrialists, a source of losses, a limitation to expansion, a weapon of bureaucratic control that it was no longer willing to tolerate, and this class was quite naturally with its press and deputies, its material, moral, and political resources behind those who showed that the scientific foundations of quarantine were naught, and who anyhow were usually sons of this class. Contagionism would, through its associations with the old bureaucratic powers, be suspect to all liberals, trying to reduce state interference to a minimum. Anticontagionists were thus not simply scientists, they were reformers, fighting for the freedom of the individual and commerce against the shackles of despotism and reaction. This second aspect of anticontagionism contributed probably no less than its scientific aspects to its gaining over the majority of those parts of the medical profession that were independent of the state.

...

In their positive theories the anticontagionists were anything but uniform ... Many followed a more modern and localized 'miasma' theory (poison arising from decaying animal or vegetable matter, 'filth'). From the miasmatic or 'filth' theory to a purely social concept was but a short step.

In our discussions there did exist, like in all such situations, besides the two extremist wings, a large center of 'moderates' that tried to compromise, the so-called 'contingent contagionists,' ... And it is precisely the attitude of this center which decided on the practical applications, and which best illustrates the general orientation of a given period. It is extremely typical for our period that the center, though admitting theoretically contagion in certain limits and as *one* possible factor of many, *practically*, that is in the condemnation and abolition of quarantines, the supreme test of one's convictions, followed the *anticontagionists* ...

...

In examining critically the theoretical foundations of anticontagionism, we should be aware of the fact that certain basic weaknesses were common to *both* parties, anticontagionists and contagionists. Both parties occasionally used unreliable information. Both parties were still obsessed with the Hippocratic idea of the air as primary medium of transmitting the noxious element, whether miasma or contagium, at the expense of any other possibility ... Both parties suffered from the 'fallacy of a single cause.' Both parties were reduced to reasoning by analogy ... Both parties used the animal experiment still very little, and what experimenting they did lacked method and inventiveness. Though the experiments of the next generation did not solve all problems either, they afforded an uncomparably higher degree of certainty than the mere observations on which both parties based their reasoning. Among these observations the contagionists would usually pick a set of more or less true facts that confirmed their theory, leaving out another set of equally true, but incompatible facts, which in their turn the anticontagionists would triumphantly present as proof of their theory. Or, 'facts' and 'observations' being highly complex and ambiguous, both parties would take up the same fact, but succeed in interpreting it in the contrary sense ... 'Observations' depended also to a large extent on the location of the observer ...

I am afraid that, forced to decide ourselves a hundred years ago on the basis of the existing materials, we would have had a very hard time. Intellectually and rationally the two theories balanced each other too evenly. Under such conditions the accident of personal experience and temperament, and especially economic outlook and political loyalties, will determine the decision. These, being liberal and bourgeois in the majority of the physicians of the time brought about the victory of anticontagionism. It is typical that the ascendancy of anticontagionism coincides with the rise of liberalism, its decline with the victory of the reaction. Of course, the latter was not the only factor of the decline of anticontagionism. Was it new discoveries as Bernheim and others declared? Certainly, Snow and Budd made quite an impression. Yet, some doubts are at least allowed, in view of the fact that the change was prior to the decisive discoveries of Pasteur, Koch, etc. ...

...

This strange story of anticontagionism between 1821 and 1867 – of a theory reaching its highest degree of scientific respectability just before its disappearance; of its opponent suffering its worst eclipse just before its triumph; of an eminently 'progressive' and practically sometimes very effective movement based on a wrong scientific theory; of the 'facts,' including a dozen major epidemics, and the social influences shaping this theory – offers so many possible conclusions that I feel at a loss to select one or the other, and would rather leave it to you to make your choice. I am convinced that whatever your conclusions, whether you primarily enjoy the progress in scientific method and knowledge made during the last hundred years, or whether you prefer to ponder those epidemiological problems, unsolved by both parties at the time and unsolved in our own day, all your conclusions will be right and good except for the one, so common in man, but so foreign to the spirit of history: that our not committing the same errors today might be due to an intellectual or moral superiority of ours.

Reading source

Ackerknecht, 1948, pp. 567–9, 588–9

Ackerknecht seeks to explain how the story of cholera reveals a division between holders of 'contagionist' and 'anti-contagionist' views. These broad and differing views on the cause of illness then folded into the political and economic debates of the period. Contagionist theories, by implication, advocated social policies that would have curtailed the movement of people and things that may have spread disease. This included the use of quarantines to restrict the flows of goods and populations. Quarantines were regularly implemented throughout Europe during the nineteenth century in response to the threat of cholera and this often disrupted travel at the first sign of an outbreak. Thus the Reverend Henry Christmas wrote in 1851: 'No one can now eat a few plums too many in Marseilles without alarming sanitary officers of all southern powers' (quoted in Pemble, 1987, p. 35). Quarantines in Britain were regulated by the Quarantine Act 1825 but the powers used to impose restrictions on travel fell into disuse as the anti-contagionist miasmic theory of disease gained ascendancy. These policies ran counter to the economic discourse of free trade favoured by liberal merchants – an important group in the rising industrial bourgeoisie. Conversely, the conservatives of this period viewed agricultural interests as paramount, and they were pro-quarantine in the same way as they supported, for example, the Corn Laws, legislation that imposed import tariffs on grain to protect the landed gentry from competition in the event of cheap foreign imports. The liberal, rising, industrial bourgeoisie was, in this schema, anti-contagionist, and thus opposed the emergence of the new sciences of infection and bacteriology which suggested that infection spread between people.

Ackerknecht's account is a subtle and nuanced account of the political economy of health and security in the nineteenth century, with an admission that his central 'binary' story is an over-simplification of the many theoretical varieties that contained elements of both positions (the 'contingent-contagionism'). However, the important issue is that debates about illness and health were intimately tied to concerns of economic and political security. Views on contagious fevers could influence fiscal policies and vice versa – laws regulating the movement of people and things were intimately tied to the laws of biology describing the trajectory of diseases. Sentiments on cholera transmissibility, the economy and free movement of people and ideas were refracted though each other.

Ackerknecht was also at pains to point out that the idea of contagion (that disease entities could be directly transposed from person to person) received its deepest diminution and anti-contagion its greatest scientific acceptance at the very moment immediately preceding the formulation of modern germ theory by Pasteur and Koch (the idea of a living 'microbe' that transmitted disease). The importance of Ackerknecht's

TO THE INHABITANTS OF THE PARISH OF

CLERKENWELL.

His Majesty's Privy Council having approved of precautions proposed by the Board of Health in London, on the alarming approach

OF THE

INDIAN CHOLERA

It is deemed proper to call the attention of the Inhabitants to some of the Symptoms and Remedies mentioned by them as printed, and now in circulation.

Symptoms of the Disorder;

Giddiness, sickness, nervous agitation, slow pulse, cramp beginning at the fingers and toes and rapidly approaching the trunk, change of colour to a leaden blue, purple, black or brown; the skin dreadfully cold, and often damp, the tongue moist and loaded but flabby and chilly, the voice much affected, and respiration quick and irregular.

All means tending to restore circulation and to maintain the warmth of the body should be had recourse to without the least delay.

The patient should be immediately put to bed, wrapped up in hot blankets, and warmth should be sustained by other external applications, such as repeated frictions with flannels and camphorated spirits, poultices of mustard and linseed (equal parts) to the stomach, particularly where pain and vomiting exist, and similar poultices to the feet and legs to restore their warmth. The returning heat of the body may be promoted by bags containing hot salt or bran applied to different parts, and for the same purpose of restoring and sustaining the circulation white wine wey with spice, hot brandy and water, or salvolatile in a dose of a tea spoon full in hot water, frequently repeated; or from 5 to 20 drops of some of the essential oils, as peppermint, cloves or cajeput, in a wine glass of water may be administered with the same view. Where the stomach will bear it, warm broth with spice may be employed. In every severe case or where medical aid is difficult to be obtained, from 20 to 40 drops of laudanum may be given in any of the warm drinks previously recommended.

These simple means are proposed as resources in the incipient stages of the Disease, until Medical aid can be had.

THOS. KEY,
GEO. TINDALL, } ***Churchwardens.***

Sir Gilbert Blane, Bart. in a pamphlet written by him on the subject of this Disease, recommends persons to guard against its approach by moderate and temperate living, and to have in readiness, the prescribed remedies; and in case of attack to resort thereto *immediately* but the great preventative he states, is found to consist in a *due regard to Cleanliness and Ventilation.*

N.B It is particularly requested that this Paper may be preserved, and that the Inmates generally, in the House where it is left may be made acquainted with its contents.

NOV. 1st, 1831.

T. GOODE, PRINTER, CROSS STREET, WILDERNESS ROW.

analysis of the medical disputes in the nineteenth century is that it showed a debate about health security that was largely conducted by reference to the protagonists' respective social worlds and social interests. In other words, the political and economic interests of both the contagionists and anti-contagionists shaped their beliefs about illness causation and their preferred interventions. In this respect Ackerknecht was probably several decades ahead of his time in his political economic approach to the understanding of a medical issue. Yet as Roger Cooter (1982) has pointed out, this is also the flaw in his argument, and to understand this more clearly we must consider his accounting for anti-contagionism's sudden decline in the last part of the nineteenth century (see also Pelling, 1978).

For Ackerknecht the successes of the anti-contagionists can be almost fully explained by recourse to social explanations: the medical profession typically came from a particular social class – bourgeois liberals. This class had economic and social interests that favoured the 'free' trade of goods and the 'free' movement of people; and contagion theories demanded that the movement of people and things were restricted by quarantines in order to maintain health security, which to the liberal bourgeoisie meant loss and a limit to economic expansion. It was these social factors that pushed the balance of evidence in the nineteenth century in favour of the anti-contagionist position.

Yet a close reading of the Ackerknecht extract also reveals his reasoning about the eventual decline of anti-contagionism. We are not presented with a social explanation at all but rather an account that 'held that disbelief in anticontagionism ... was the result of the inevitable triumph of "real" truth-bearing medical knowledge' (Cooter, 1982, p. 91). Cooter argued that we must be wary of accounts that see social factors as only explaining 'false' and 'erroneous' knowledge whereas 'the truth' is left to emerge through some almost magical process.

2.1 Symmetry and co-production

Within S&TS, this type of account – where an appeal to social factors exists only when the 'truth' has been 'distorted' – has been called the principle of asymmetry. The idea of asymmetry and symmetry, as suggested by the sociologist David Bloor (1976), has become one of the most important organising principles underlying many of the contemporary perspectives in S&TS. The idea of symmetry is a critique of 'weak' sociological explanations of science that could only explain 'mistakes'. In other words, in these 'weak' and asymmetrical sociological accounts 'false' science is explained in terms of social factors, whereas 'true' science needs no explanation as it is merely 'nature' revealing herself to an inquisitive science. In contrast, a symmetrical approach

Figure 5.2 (on facing page)
Broadsheet warning about cholera symptoms and recommending remedies *circa* 1831. Cholera was referred to as Indian to reflect its believed point of origin

argues that any historical or sociological analysis of what comes to be accepted as 'true' or what comes to be accepted as 'false' in science must use the same form of explanation rather than taking an asymmetrical position of only explaining people's beliefs that history proves to be erroneous. An asymmetrical explanation could easily be offered of why the theory of plate tectonics (a theory of geology which holds that the earth's crust is divided into a number of large plates which are in constant motion) was initially rejected by the geology community, possibly as a result of cultural or political factors. But such an explanation could have little to say about how plate tectonics later became a mainstream orthodoxy in geology as this was simply geologists discovering the 'true' nature of the world. Rather than continue this 'weak' sociology, Bloor argued for a 'strong programme' in sociology, in which what had come to be accepted as 'truth' or 'facts' would be treated and analysed in an identical way as what came to be accepted as 'mistakes' or 'errors'. To do otherwise would risk sociologists putting themselves where their critics would, no doubt, like to see them, 'lurking amongst the discarded refuse in science's back yard' (Bloor, 1976, p. 25).

The principle of symmetry taken to its logical conclusion has led to some controversial but productive developments in sociology. At stake in the contagionist/anti-contagionist debate was being able to account for some aspect of the 'natural' world – in this case the spread of disease-causing entities as a threat to security. Ackerknecht's narrative certainly exposed the fallacy of the anti-contagionists, whose scientific beliefs were shown to be influenced by their social interests. Yet a symmetrical approach would in addition contemplate how the natural and social orders may be produced in unison or **co-produced**:

> Co-production is shorthand for the proposition that the ways in which we know and represent the world (both nature and society) are inseparable from the ways in which we choose to live in it. Knowledge and its material embodiments are at once products of social work and constitutive of forms of social life ... Scientific knowledge ... is not a transcendent mirror of reality. It both embeds and is embedded in social practices, identities, norms, conventions, discourses, instruments and institutions – in short in all the building blocks of what we term the social.
>
> (Jasanoff, 2004, pp. 2–3)

The anti-contagionist account of the 'natural' did not simply wither in the face of the 'true' scientific knowledge of modern germ theory and the 'discovery' of microbes. Ackerknecht's account omitted the fact that modern germ theory did not spring fully formed to be accepted as 'truth' into a vacuum of ignorance. Rather it depended on a myriad of social and material practices: of laboratories peopled with skilled scientists; of institutions and bureaucracies able to fund research; of Petri dishes, growth mediums and animals in research; and of experiments and public demonstrations (Pelling, 1978; Latour, 1988; Tomes, 2001). In addition, as germ theory emerged in the late nineteenth century, the social was itself mediated and transformed by the idea of the new microbes, together with the implications that these new entities had for security and health. The notion of a contagion caused by the new microbes as the origin of illness produced a social world made up of new groups (Latour, 1987): contagious people who were sick; healthy people who were dangerous 'carriers'; new laws to regulate and define populations and public health; new experts (hygienists, microbiologists, urban planners/civil engineers) who could radically alter the growing industrial cities by building sewers and demolishing slums in order to secure a safe and healthy social world.

Co-productionist accounts thus attempt to avoid falling into either a material or social determinist position. Science, technology and knowledge production are seen as neither revealing 'the truth' about nature nor a secondary phenomenon that results from some hidden social or political interest. Rather co-production takes a symmetrical approach by drawing attention to the material relations involved in social worlds while also attending to the ways in which the social mediates the production of knowledge. Put simply, the idea of co-production is used in opposition to the notion that the categories of science, nature, technology, society, culture, the social or the material can be neatly separated. These categories are so intertwined and dependent on each other that changes in any one area will have a synergistic effect in all the others.

Read the following extract by Sheila Jasanoff, which explores these issues in more detail. You may come across some concepts or terms that will be unfamiliar to you – some of the key ones will be explained after the article – but for now the important point to note is the way in which analysis of categories like science, nature and society has to take account of their interwoven existence.

Reading 5.2 Sheila Jasanoff, 'Ordering knowledge, ordering society'

Since scientific knowledge first came to be seen as constituted by social practices ... S&TS researchers have realized that the fruits of their labors are at best imperfectly captured by the dictum that scientific knowledge is socially constructed. This formulation gives rise to two unresolvable problems, one theoretical and the other pragmatic. The first is that it confers a kind of causal primacy upon the 'social' that careful work in S&TS, broadly conceived, has consistently denied ... Constructivism does not imply that social reality is ontologically prior to natural reality, nor that social factors alone determine the workings of nature; yet the rubric 'social construction' carries just such connotations (Hacking, 1999). The second and more practical difficulty is that the discourse of social construction tends to inhibit the symmetrical probing of the constitutive elements of both society and science that forms the essence of the S&TS research agenda. One or another aspect of the 'social' – be it 'interests', 'capital', 'gender', 'state' or 'the market' – risks being black-boxed, treated as fundamental, granted agency, and so exempted from further analysis. The suspicion that social constructivists are arrogating to themselves an Archimedean point from which to deconstruct science has provoked criticism of S&TS as insufficiently reflexive (Woolgar, 1988). ...

With greater maturity, science studies as a field has moved to show that what counts as 'social' about science is itself a subject of unsuspected depth and complexity. For example, early efforts to explain how controversies end, in both science and technology ... often represented closure as a negotiated sorting out of competing social interests. Such work assumed, along with mainstream scholarship in economics and political science, that society can be unproblematically conceptualized as composed of interest groups with clearly articulated (exogenous) positions and preferences. These interests, or stakes, were then invoked to explain the positions taken by different actors concerning knowledge claims and their technological embodiments. Newer work recognizes the inadequacy of interests as a primary explanatory category. Interests themselves have a social history: how they arise and are sustained are matters to be investigated, not taken for granted. ...

Perhaps the most important by-product of all this inquiry is the recognition that the production of order in nature and society has to be discussed in an idiom that does not, even accidentally and without intent, give primacy to either. The term *co-production* reflects this self-conscious desire to avoid both social and technoscientific determinism in S&TS accounts of the world. The concept has by now acquired a respectable ancestry within the field, although there are varying schools of thought on exactly how to define and employ it. ...

Pursuing this line of thought, some S&TS scholars see co-production as a process that is as foundational as constitution-making or state-making in political theory, because it responds to people's deepest metaphysical concerns. It does so, in part, by continually reinscribing the boundary between the social and the natural, the world created by us and the world we imagine to exist beyond our control. 'Science' and 'politics' can then be treated as separate and distinct forms of activity rather than as strands of a single, tightly woven cultural enterprise through which human beings seek to make sense of their condition. ... Fitting technology into this picture makes for further quandaries, since humanity's material productions affect both what we know and how we behave. S&TS scholars have differed importantly in how they view the role of the material and the inanimate in constituting social order, and the degree of agency that they are prepared to grant to non-humans ...

... [T]here is no univocal position on these matters in current work in the co-productionist idiom. Instead, [writers] show from varied perspectives that the co-productionist idiom can shed light on the constitution of varied social orders, such as international regimes, imperial or comparative politics, science and democracy, and the boundary between public and private property; equally, this approach can illuminate situated interactions between scientific and other forms of life, in settings ranging from laboratory conversations and patients' discourses to the courtroom. Similarly, the co-productionist approach can address the formation of widely varied elements of natural order: for example, climate change, human intelligence, endangered species or sugar cane propagation.

References

Hacking, I. (1999) The Social Construction of What?, *Cambridge, MA, Harvard University Press.*

Woolgar, S. (1988) Knowledge and Reflexivity: New Frontiers in the Sociology of Knowledge, *London, Sage.*

Reading source

Jasanoff, 2004, pp. 19–22

Jasanoff begins by making quite a dense critique of **social constructivism** – the idea that 'social interactions' and 'social practices' alone can explain the circulation and use of specific forms of scientific knowledge and technologies. She does this on two grounds: theoretical and practical.

Theoretically, according to Jasanoff, 'social constructivism' often assumes a causal primacy for the social – in other words the social and social processes are thought to proceed and shape our understanding of the natural world. The problem with this conception is one of 'infinite regression' – if everything is constructed by the social then what precedes the social?

The practical problem identified by Jasanoff is the way that aspects of the social (for example, class, gender or interests) become 'black-boxed'. In S&TS a **black box** is the term used to describe any artefact, process or concept that can be seen as performing its function without any awareness of its internal workings or complexities on the part of the user. We can simply treat it in terms of its inputs and outputs. Many of the technologies we commonly use in our homes can be treated as 'black boxes' – we do not really need to understand the inner complexities of a DVD or video recorder in order to enjoy a film. Jasanoff argues that a social constructivist account may allow us to treat social concepts in this way – as concepts that become so comfortable that we never bother to re-examine their internal workings and complexities. In contrast, a co-productionist account would point to the production of knowledge as being simultaneous to both the material and social orders.

3 Security, the 'risk factor' and epidemiology

Many of the protagonists involved in the contagion and anti-contagion debates of the nineteenth century were forerunners of a particular type of expert that would today be called an epidemiologist: they use a variety of techniques to investigate and trace the environmental origin of outbreaks of infectious diseases so that these can be controlled. In this respect they could be though of as medical ecologists. More generally, epidemiology can be thought of as the scientific study of factors affecting the health and illness of individuals and populations.

While investigative epidemiologists seeking to trace the source of infectious disease outbreaks are still important in public health (particularly in developing countries), a new type of epidemiological expertise appeared in the latter part of the twentieth century. This was partially reflected in major changes in patterns of mortality (rates of death) from the middle of the nineteenth century. Simply put, the rate of deaths caused by acute infectious illnesses declined sharply from about 1850 onwards. In the first decades of the twentieth century, in most western nations, non-infectious chronic illnesses (most notably coronary heart disease and cancers) for the first time overtook acute infections as the leading causes of death. The reasons for the decline of infectious diseases are still the matter of some debate, but it has been suggested that a combination of clean water, sanitary sewage disposal, a suppression of the mosquito, and increasing food safety, through refrigeration and pasteurisation, all played a role.

The investigation of these non-infectious causes of death led to a new type of epidemiology – one that has implications for the security of social worlds that go far beyond the publications of a few obscure medical researchers – the birth of the 'risk factor'. The use of the risk factor in the post-Second World War epidemiology has been characterised by the investigation of things or processes that raise the probability of the individual or population developing a disease or illness. Using this type of approach there is no need to directly explain or even understand the biological cause of any particular disease. The main aim is simple: to find a probabilistic relationship between the disease (for example, coronary heart disease or CHD) and the various factors (diet, environment, habits or genetics) that may play a role in its progression. This is done in order to explain why some people become ill and others do not. Risk factors are derived by using highly complex statistical equations and logistic regression formulae to make sense of data that often contain millions of items of information on thousands of people. The use of complex statistical techniques were needed to explain the often weak relationships between 'risk factors' and diseases.[1] The importance of risk factors is that they are increasingly viewed as diseases in their own right, as direct threats to the security of the individual and populations.

Today if we asked you about the causes of heart disease, you would probably be able to suggest a list of possible factors. You might mention things like fats in people's diet, the stress of particular jobs, smoking, drinking, a lack of exercise, a family history of similar illness, or even the affluence or deprivation of a particular lifestyle. You might also point out that many of these threats to an individual's health could potentially be modified or even prevented. However, as late as the 1950s, CHD was commonly framed in medicine as a chronic, degenerative disease that was beyond prevention – it was merely a specific and often random way in which some (unfortunate) people aged (Aronowitz, 1998). Little was known about the cause of this illness apart from the raw and crude statistics collected by governments and the insurance industry. These limited sources of information were, however, highly disturbing – by 1951 heart disease accounted for around 22 per cent of deaths in the USA, making it the leading cause of mortality (Oppenheimer, 2006). Similar situations existed in many industrialised countries. Based on the anecdotal experiences of doctors and insurance actuaries, a speculative and partial list of possible contributors to CHD began to emerge. These were summed up by Dr Paul Dudley White, founder of the American Heart Association, who in 1957 said:

> We practitioners know from our own experience that basic factors behind CHD are of very great importance. These include the possible influence of race, the sure influence of heredity, of sex and age ... of environmental factors. ... [They] include stress and strain, about which we know relatively little, exercise, which some of us believe

> important, but just how and why we do not know, local customs and personal habits, for example the use of tobacco and alcohol, and proper programs of rest and relaxation, and diet. ... We have talked for years about the relationship of the ways of life to the development of coronary atherosclerosis.
>
> (quoted in Oppenheimer, 2006)

In addition to this highly speculative list of possible causes it was also becoming known in popular discourse that 'heart attacks' were a particular threat to the security of middle-aged males, a group who also happened to be well represented in the legislative bodies that determined research funding. As one medical researcher later reflected:

> In those days, funds were not as short as they are now. Congressmen and Senators were getting heart attacks, and they would say, hey, you know, we got to look into this ... they were actually throwing money at us. Do you need some more money? Could we give you some more money to help?
>
> (Kannel, quoted in Aronowitz, 1998, p. 129)

The belief that CHD was a consequence of multiple causes led to a new kind of study. If a large population who shared a number of characteristics could be studied and followed over a long period of time, the appearance of CHD could be followed and traced – this was the longitudinal community cohort study, a number of which were established in the late 1940s and early 1950s. The most famous of these was that conducted in Framingham, Massachusetts, which involved the enrolment of 5000 residents without CHD for a study that started in early 1950 and continues to the present day. The study was a collaboration between the Massachusetts Department of Health, the US Public Health Service, and Harvard University's Department of Preventive Medicine.

To begin with, the goals of the Framingham study were modest and involved only a desire to test the efficacy of new and existing diagnostic tools, to accurately determine the prevalence of CHD, and to identify some of the factors that might predict heart disease. Indeed the more ambitious goals and methods that came to be associated with Framingham, especially the birth of the 'risk factor', were not present at the start of the study but evolved gradually, along with other changes in medical science and lay understandings of disease. Framingham was a good example of the co-production of social and material ordering.

The evolution of these new techniques emerged in part because developments in other areas of science allowed new tests to be carried out and new understandings of the material body. Thus the development of a quick and relatively cheap test for the level of

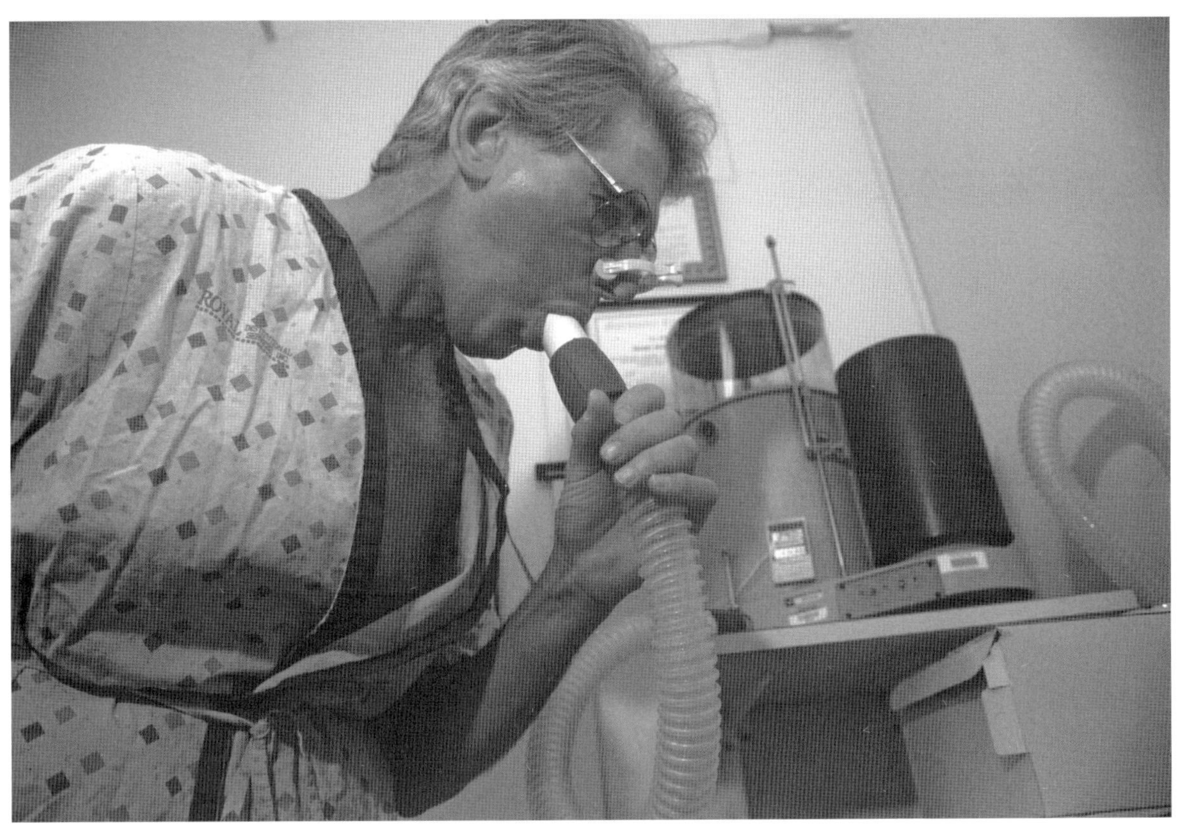

Figure 5.3
Framingham, Massachusetts: Howard Hirsch having a Spiral Breathing Test at the Framingham Heart Study Clinic

cholesterol in blood allowed this factor to be measured regularly in the 5000 Framingham residents. Individual clinical observations made by doctors, such as a reduction in the build-up of fat in the walls of the heart arteries after blood pressure was reduced, could also be fed into the ongoing analysis. Less apparent were developments in the discipline of statistics and mathematical modelling techniques that allowed increasingly complex inferences to be drawn from the data sample. The statisticians working on the Framingham data set were eventually employed directly by the project and were encouraged to invent 'new techniques for analyzing multiple, simultaneous effects and to adapt existing economic methods' (Aronowitz, 1998, p. 128).

Hence the form of research carried out in the Framingham study increasingly used complex mathematical analysis of a very large data set (each resident would have hundreds of pieces of information collected about their medical history, habits, lifestyle and environment). Such analysis would be inconceivable without the use of computers. In the 1950s computers tended to be bulky and prohibitively expensive; computer analysis was carried out by reserving and buying time on someone else's computer. The Framingham study used the computer located in the Department of Biometrics and the National Institute of

Health (NIH) in Bethesda, Maryland. This division in the practicalities of conducting research also led to conflicts over the control of analysis between the NIH and the Framingham investigators.

This also reminds us that this new type of health investigation – the large-scale epidemiological study – required substantial funds and resources to be successful. Two of the key resources for research of this type was the existence of bureaucracies (such as the NIH) that could fund research of this type and other bureaucracies that could marshal particular types of expert into social worlds where the research could be carried out (such as university departments, health departments and public health services).

These different social and material practices were intertwined and co-produced one another, allowing the 'risk factors' to come into being. These new 'risk factors' contributed most to knowledge about the development and trajectory of heart disease in the developed world and, as we shall see, altered the ways in which the health security of individuals and populations came to be viewed. The risk factor both 'embeds' and was 'embedded in social practices, identities, norms, conventions, discourses, instruments and institutions' (Jasanoff, 2004).

Read the following extract by Gerald Oppenheimer.

Reading 5.3 Gerald Oppenheimer, 'Profiling risk: the emergence of coronary heart disease epidemiology in the United States (1947–70)'

The language of risk, specifically, the probability of developing CHD, given the presence and magnitude of certain personal attributes, permeated early Framingham publications. The idea of 'risk', if not the term, was implicit in the study's initial 28 hypotheses developed in 1949, e.g. hypothesis 8, 'degenerative cardiovascular disease appears earlier and progresses more rapidly in persons who habitually use tobacco'. In their 1957 report, Dawber and co-authors [Dawber and Kannel were the two initial investigators on the Framingham study] used the term 'risk' at least 18 times, generally to mean 'probability', as in 'there is an increased risk of [CHD] in persons with elevated cholesterol'. Over the following 2 years, Dawber began systematically referring to clinical and social characteristics possibly associated with the development of CHD – hypercholesterolaemia, hypertension, place of residence – as 'factors'. In a July, 1961 publication, Kannel and Dawber employed 'factors of risk', meaning 'characteristics of increased risk' for a given disease. In the same article, they created a contracted phrase – 'risk factor'. This was done in a rather casual manner. Kannel, the lead author, claims to have soon forgotten that they had coined the term, or at least first applied it to epidemiology, until reminded some years later. In fact, in another article the same month, Dawber used the term 'risk characteristic' to express the same idea.

In 1961, 'risk factor' seemed to capture a moment. It was a phrase that signalled a new approach to disease. It was more felicitous than terms like 'actuarial predictions of risk', a short-hand formula that could be applied aptly to each dimension of CHD epidemiological thought, a term that joined them together. In the absence of a known agent for CHD or the clinical ability to observe the development of underlying disease processes, 'risk factors' represented discrete characteristics linked to the probability of overt heart disease. Within a few years, 'risk factors' were also perceived as tools for inferring, in general, the degree of arterial atherosclerosis in populations and individuals, an external sign of an inner process.

Reading source

Oppenheimer, 2006, p. 725

You can see from this short extract that the 'risk factor' was, to coin a phrase, becoming an 'external sign of an inner process'. What was originally a constructed artefact for studying large populations was becoming a marker of inner threat to individual security and health. It was then a short step for this marker of disease to be actually taken as the disease itself. Thus, today, an individual who both feels and appears healthy can visit their doctor where a check-up, using what are standard and routine tests, reveals some 'risk factor', such as an elevated blood cholesterol level. This individual will then find themselves at the beginning of an asymptomatic illness trajectory that will see them modifying their diet and maybe even beginning to regularly take drugs to lower their cholesterol. They will also no doubt experience both anxiety about their new status as part of a 'risk group' and some disruption to their own sense of personal security. In short the existence and revelation of their own 'risk factor' will have an immediate effect on their social and material identity.

The period since the end of the Second World War has seen the 'risk factor' come to dominate many aspects of social worlds that go beyond the initial focus of the Framingham investigators. Today the 'risk factor' is used to link many different types of chronic illness to a variety of social and material histories, habits, lifestyles and environments.[2] Using the risk factor to make links is done for a variety of purposes; the chances are very high that everyone reading this who has ever applied for a mortgage, a loan, life insurance or a pension scheme will have

Figure 5.4
Framingham, Massachusetts: Evelyn Langley, an 87-year-old original member of the Framingham Heart Study, with her family

answered a variety of questions whose basis are 'risk factors'. This type of knowledge is used to shape the health security of various social worlds:

> Risk factor knowledge today serves many functions besides prognosis. Risk factors serve as the basis for national efforts to prevent ... [disease] through lifestyle change ... Risk factor knowledge also guides government policy toward new drugs and food labelling. Insurance companies use risk factor data to compute the actuarial risk of individuals and populations in order to determine premiums ... [risk factor] predictions are used to formulate health policy and plan new clinical studies ... In sum, risk factors are a central part of modern clinical, public health, and financial strategies for predicting and managing individual variation in disease predisposition and experience.
>
> (Aronowitz, 1998, p. 118)

There is another way of regarding the rise of the risk factor – in terms of a series of mediations. As we have seen in other chapters in this book, mediation can be used in a variety of ways. In S&TS, mediation implies articulation or linking combined with transformation or translation. At its broadest level, this idea describes those processes that allow statements, concerns or material entities to pass from one social world into another, and then 'disciplining or maintaining that translation' in order to stabilise a particular network or association of relationships (Star, 1991, p. 32). But in the movement between social worlds both the entities travelling and the social worlds would be transformed or translated. Thus, to use an earlier example, the introduction of the new microbe mediated the idea of the social because it linked together previously isolated groups via the possibility of contagion – with the advent of the microbe 'the rich' could suddenly become infected by 'the poor' who were their servants. In this way the social space of the city was transformed because 'the rich', 'powerful' and 'privileged' could only be rendered secure by a series of material and social changes, such as the construction of sewers and the introduction of hygiene measures and new public health laws. Within S&TS, these types of mediations are sometimes referred to using the concept of translation.

This concept of translation describes a movement with deformation between social worlds. Thus we could reconsider the story of the risk factor in terms of a series of mediations or translations that allowed statements to pass between social worlds and do so by using a fictitious example. American politicians in Congress and the Senate might begin with:

> We notice that people like us (middle-aged men) often die quite suddenly from heart disease. We would rather this didn't happen anymore.

This becomes translated by epidemiologists into:

> We epidemiologists are the ones who can find out why heart disease is such a killer and, in the process, maybe prevent this in the future.

And this in turn becomes:

> Now grant us our autonomy; support us by giving us time (a long time) and funds (a lot of funds) and then learn from us.

But even this final statement gets further translated into:

> Recruit 5000 people from the same community, follow them for a generation and learn everything about them; keep up on changes in medical diagnostics, clinical experience and statistics; continue to lobby for support from well-endowed state and other bureaucracies; and publish in prestigious medical journals.

What begins as a semi-public concern about the rise of a new way of death and threat to health security in the mid-twentieth century is rapidly translated into the minutiae of conducting new kinds of medical research, together with ensuring support for these activities. Analysis of this type – that follows a series of translations – is often associated with the S&TS approach known as **actor-network theory** (ANT).

4 Actor-network theory

ANT takes as its starting point many of the issues we have already discussed in this chapter. Over the last two decades it has been a major analytical framework in sociology for examining science and technology. It takes the principle of symmetry and radically extends it into an explanatory framework that makes no distinction between the various actors involved in analysis – human or non-human, individuals or organisations, the social or the material, bacteria or scientists. All should be analysed by sociologists in the same terms and using the same principles. For many sociologists this principle of generalised symmetry causes some unease – for example, should we really analyse humans and non-humans in the same terms? ANT considers how the circulation, movement and translation of material objects such as scientific texts, instruments and technologies serve to produce a durable pattern of relations or a network. This network, then, stabilises the identities of different actors (who may be human or non-human).

Descriptions of ANT can be rather abstract and challenging, so let's consider a brief example. Earlier in this chapter we looked at the debates between the contagionists and anti-contagionists that occurred in the period before the modern idea of infection was established. Bruno Latour (Latour, 1983, 1988) uses an ANT framework to provide an analysis of how Louis Pasteur helped established the infectious microbe as a disease-causing entity at the end of the nineteenth century. In his analysis, Latour concentrates on how Pasteur successfully 'invented' anthrax as a disease by making a series of moves or translations (Bucchi, 2002). Pasteur's first move was to problematise anthrax by characterising it as a possible infection rather than something caused by miasmas. However, this translation in itself was not enough to advance his project. Pasteur had to take his laboratory into the field (in this case literally). Here he was able to acquire the local, and largely un-codified, knowledge of the veterinarians and farmers who regularly worked with the animals that contracted anthrax. He translated this local knowledge into his own speculative and emerging understanding of infections as caused by microbes or bacteria. This was then taken back to the laboratory where he reproduced the anthrax disease in animals. Once he had carried out these various translations of knowledges, microbes and laboratory instruments, he was in a position to begin enrolling allies into a 'network' with his own laboratory at the centre. He was then able to reformulate the interests of farmers or veterinarians in a new way:

> If you wish to solve your anthrax problem, you have to pass through my laboratory first. Like all translations there is a real displacement through the various versions. To go straight at anthrax, you should make a detour through Pasteur's lab.
>
> (Latour, 1983, p. 146)

For Pasteur to further stabilise his network and ensure the enrolment of allies, he had to go back to the field and provide a demonstration of the efficacy of his theory by providing a vaccine that prevented sickness. His laboratory, although small, metamorphosed into something more powerful as his vaccine and theory became widely available. Through his various translations and network-building, the identities of various actors (veterinarians, microbes, sick animals, farmers, and so on) have been translated and stabilised in new ways. Indeed it could be argued that 'society, in some of its important aspects, has been transformed through the displacements of a few laboratories' (Latour, 1983, p. 153). This also shows how ANT can question the often assumed status of categories like 'science', 'society', 'nature' or 'the social'. The make-up of these entities, according to an ANT approach, cannot be un-problematically assumed in advance because they mutually co-produce each other. The make-up of these complex categories is always an empirical question best answered by closely following the various actors as they build their networks.

4.1 ANT, asthma and the metered dose inhaler

ANT approaches can be used to examine many of the artefacts and entities that commonly mediate the security of social worlds. We are probably familiar with a wide variety of artefacts that mediate our health security: the vaccinations given to our children or to travellers, the sunscreens we apply to prevent skin damage, toothpastes used to prevent dental caries, and even the seatbelts and child-seats we use to protect ourselves in cars.

People who suffer from particularly severe asthma have to be constantly vigilant about their own security – innocuous everyday objects such as pollen, pet hair or house dust may trigger an asthmatic attack that can leave the sufferer struggling for breath. A severe attack can prove fatal. The advent of the modern metered dose inhaler (MDI) allows asthmatics to self-medicate either to prevent or treat attacks. The MDI is a small device that releases a precisely measured mist of therapeutic drug particles that can be inhaled directly into the lungs.

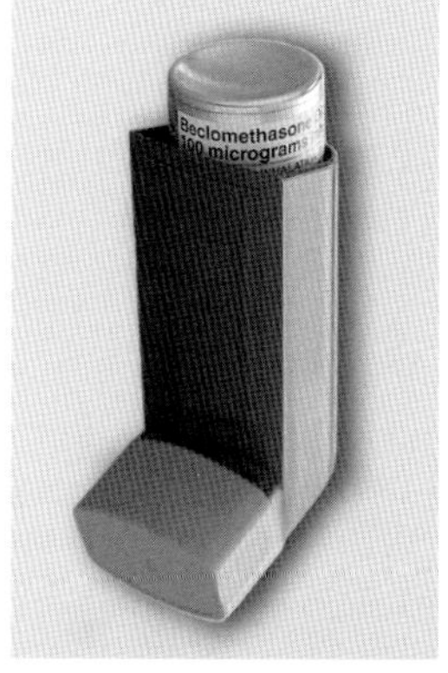

Figure 5.5
A metered dose inhaler

Read the following extract by sociologist Alan Prout, who carried out an ANT analysis of the MDI. Many descriptions of ANT emphasise slightly different aspects of this challenging approach, and so it may be useful to begin by letting Prout explain what he takes as the central problem of ANT.

Reading 5.4 Alan Prout, 'Actor-network theory'

ANT can be characterised as a form of relational materialism. It is concerned with the materials from which social life is produced and the processes by which these are brought into relationship with each other. Because it wishes to avoid *a priori* assumptions about what these materials and means are, ANT is sceptical about many commonly employed forms of sociological explanation, especially those which mobilise ready-made abstractions, for example 'power' and 'organisation' (Law, 1992, p. 380). From an actor-network viewpoint these are not explanations but phenomena themselves in need of explanation. ...

... ANT rejects the assumption that society is constructed through human action and meaning alone. In contrast, 'society' is seen as produced in and through patterned networks of heterogeneous materials; it is made up through a wide variety of shifting associations (and dissociations) between human and non-human entities. Indeed, so ubiquitous are associations between humans and the rest of the material world that all entities are to be seen as hybrids – what Latour (1993) has termed 'quasi-objects' and 'quasi-subjects' – where the boundary between the human and the non-human is shifting, negotiated and empirical. Social life cannot, therefore, be reduced either to the 'purely' human or to the 'purely' technological (or animal, vegetable, mineral, abstract ...). Neither the human nor the technological determines the overall patterning or ordering that results from their combination. Sociological approaches which try to make one or the other do all the explanatory work result in reductionism.

... [The S&TS] literature examined particular devices or techniques and the social processes of laboratories, design departments and similar milieux within which these devices are produced. As this literature developed it became clear that no hard and fast distinction between 'social relations' and 'technology' could be made. Laboratories and design departments, for example, are already hybrid phenomena within which the 'technological' and the 'social' relations are mutually constitutive and inextricable. They are, so to speak, 'embedded' in each other, each constituting and shaping the other (Bijker and Law, 1991). From this insight a more rigorously monistic strand of thought, ANT, has developed. This proposes an expanded form of semiotics in which both human and non-human entities participate. The aim of this is to explore the processes by and through which human and non-human entities involved in social life relate to each other.

Actor-network writers have evolved, *inter alia,* three key concepts with which to examine these relations: these can be labelled 'punctualisation'; 'delegation' and 'translation'. The first of these, punctualisation, holds that in any specification an entity (such as a device or a person) entails the substitution of a network by a point (Law, 1992, p. 385). In the flow of everyday life we tend to treat other entities as if they were a single unified block or point. But behind and beyond each such point there lies a complex network which orders people and things – and without which social life would not be possible. Normally these networks are effaced ('punctualised') in order that the flow of life can continue but on some occasions the networks do become visible. Often this happens when a device fails. For example, normally I treat the computer on which I am writing this paper as a single block. When, however, it recently broke down and I had to call on the supplier's guarantee, part of the network (made up of people, things and their organisation) that stands invisibly behind the machine were revealed. Similarly, when as social scientists we want to know how a device came into being and what goes into its existence, the unpicking (at least partially) of the punctualisations which efface the networks behind it becomes a key task.

In fact ANT sees social life as ordered but shifting and complex sets of associations and dissociations between all kinds of entities that are simultaneously points and networks. However, despite being able (partially) to unpick networks, it has to be recognised that social life would be impossible unless 'network packages' were to be treated as single entities that have (relatively speaking) stability and durability. A device, therefore, can be seen as packaging a network and extending it through time and space; it can 'delegate' a network, standing in for it, repeating it and performing its work in times and places remote from its origination (Latour, 1991, p. 261).

These device packages involve what actor-network writers refer to as 'translations'. This term is used to refer to the processes by which entities mutually enrol each other into a combination of some type, claiming to speak for each other, interpreting, configuring and reconfiguring each other. An essential part of the approach is to stress mutuality in the constitutive relationships between machines and people.

References

Bijker, W.E. and Law, J. (eds) (1991) Shaping Technology/Building Society: Studies in Sociological Change, *Cambridge, MA, MIT Press.*

Law, J. (1992) 'Notes on the theory of the actor-network: ordering strategy and heterogeneity', Systems Practice, vol. 5, no. 4, pp. 379–93.

Latour, B. (1991) 'Where are the missing masses? Sociology of a few mundane artefacts' in Bijker, W.E. and Law, J. (eds) Shaping Technology/Building Society: Studies in Sociological Change, *Cambridge, MA, MIT Press.*

Latour, B. (1993) We Have Never Been Modern, *Hemel Hempstead, Harvester Wheatsheaf.*

Reading source

Prout, 1996, pp. 200–02

Notice how Prout identifies three key concepts within ANT: 'punctualisation', 'delegation' and 'translation'. Punctualisation refers to the way in which often complex networks are assumed to be single points – they become, to use a term we explored earlier, 'black-boxed'. The second term used by Prout is delegation. This refers to the way in which artefacts can come to stand in for the work of humans in times and places that may be distant from their originators. A good example of this would be a device such as a door closer used to close fire doors, keep warm air in buildings or prevent children from wandering into dangerous areas. Responsibility for closing doors is 'delegated' to the device and if this did not happen a human would have to take on the obligation of closing these doors. We have already considered translation, but Prout draws attention to the way in which this concept allows entities to enrol each other and then how this allows them to speak on behalf of others. Thus epidemiologists, following their research, could claim to speak on behalf of diseased hearts, or after the emergence of germ theory, Pasteur could claim to speak on behalf of microbes.

Another term that you may have noticed is 'hybrid'. The idea of the hybrid is often used in S&TS to denote times and places where the boundaries between material objects, the social and humans become blurred. For example, someone suffering from a severe form of asthma may be unable to survive or exist for long periods without their inhaler. Under such circumstances might it be possible to think of a human–inhaler hybrid? The point that Prout (following Latour) makes is that these hybrids are ubiquitous and that their boundaries constantly shift.

Read the following extract, which continues from Reading 5.4. Let's see how Prout applies an ANT analysis to the case of the metered dose inhaler (MDI).

Reading 5.5 Alan Prout, 'The socio-technical embedding of the metered dose inhaler'

ANT suggests that by looking at the MDI – a complex, hybrid network which associates a variety of material and human elements – its simultaneously technical and social character becomes clear. The MDI ... associates a large number of different entities, some human (patients, biomedical clinicians, technicians and scientists ...) and others technical or material (aerosol gases, the Bernoulli principle, metering valves, lungs ...). In this section I will show that the ordering of these heterogeneous elements into a specific device is not determined in a simple way but in a complex interaction which from the start is inextricably both social and technical. At the centre of this process is the attempt to make a connection between various domains of biomedical work and the everyday lives of asthma patients, a connection which entails them becoming inhaler users.

The biomedical construction of the problem of treating asthma was one caught in a contradiction: on the one hand it was thought necessary to ensure that therapeutic substances could be administered at the most appropriate time (i.e. before an asthma attack begins or at the point when it is beginning); at the same time it was necessary to control access to such substances, regarded as potentially dangerous and to be taken under medical supervision. As it was later put by a specialist in inhalation therapy:

> ... the pressurized metered dose inhaler (MDI) was a major innovation ... For the first time the potential existed for patients to target precise quantities of medication directly to the lungs using a small, portable and unobtrusive delivery system. Inhalation facilitates rapid onset of drug action, and because less drug needs to be administered to achieve a therapeutic effect, side-effects are substantially reduced.
>
> (Baum, 1989, p. 20)

The MDI can, therefore, be seen in the first instance as a means of delegating (Latour, 1991) biomedical work. In particular it could be thought of as 'standing in' for biomedical control of the therapeutic substance by encoding the ability to meter a dose. This, however, entails a trade-off between, on the one hand, patient access and, on the other, medical control of therapeutic substances. The MDI is an attempt to balance these considerations: substances were made available in a form which gave a certain amount of autonomy to the patients but at the same time were contained in such a way that they were to be released in biomedically pre-determined quantities. The work of controlling the dose available was given to the device but the device was placed in the hands of the user. Control over the drug contained in the MDI was given up but in a way that attempted to limit user autonomy by the metering abilities of the MDI which in turn encoded biomedical judgements, concerns and purposes.

Although the language of 'metering' tends to obscure the point, such encoding of biomedical control over the amount of a therapeutic substance to be taken is not novel. Arguably it is one of the most basic tasks of any therapeutic substance delivery technology. The pill, for example, does exactly the same sort of delegated work. At the time the MDI was invented, asthmatics often carried bottles of tiny ephedrine hydrochloride tablets which they were enjoined to take at the onset of an asthmatic attack. The amount of ephedrine in each tablet can also be seen as an attempt at control over the dose taken, though arguably one less powerful than the MDI and without the advantages of topical application.

Neither, as I pointed out above, are inhaler devices per se new. Drug inhalation can be accomplished by turning the substance into smoke, powder or 'medical dusts' (as they were known) or mist (such as that produced by the handbulb nebulizer). Each of these could also encode (more or less successful) attempts to limit autonomous access to the drug by packaging it in a specified dose. In this sense the MDI was an attempted new solution to an old biomedical problem. Seen [from] a biomedical point of view, its immediately obvious advantages over previous solutions were that it appeared to control dosages of therapeutic substances to higher degree [of] accuracy, remained available for repeated use without any extensive preparation on the part of the user and yet remained topical in application.

Efficacy was, of course, also important and early clinical accounts stress the relief from symptoms reported by patients. But efficacy was not exhausted by the success or failure of the inhaler to bring such relief to its users. The MDI was praised not only because it benefited patients for whom previous therapeutic modes had been ineffective but also because in so doing it enhanced the power of biomedical practice. As Freedman noted:

> The results (of the trial) are especially impressive when one considers that many of the patients had become extremely critical of all medical treatment ...
>
> (1956, p. 668)

The MDI, then, can be seen as a device for treating both asthma and criticism of biomedicine. Critical patients could be re-enrolled (and new ones enrolled) into a relationship with biomedicine because the relief they were interested in became available through clinicians. At one point in the network biomedical practitioners were the obligatory passage point through which [sufferers] had to pass in order to gain access to the MDI; and at others the MDI was a combination of human and technological materials ordered, enrolled and spoken for ('translated') into biomedical purposes.

Reference

Baum, E.A. (1989) 'Design, development and testing of a new breath test actuated inhaler' in Inspiration: Development in Inhalation Therapy, *Oxford, The Medicine Publishing Foundation, Symposium Series 26.*

Freedman, T. (1956) 'Medihaler therapy for bronchial asthma: a new type of aerosol therapy', Postgraduate Medicine, *vol. 20, pp. 667–73.*

Latour, B. (1991) 'Where are the missing masses? Sociology of a few mundane artefacts', in Bjiker, W.E. and Law, J. (eds) Shaping Technology/Building Society: Studies in Sociotechnical Change, Cambridge, MA, MIT Press.

Reading source

Prout, 1996, pp. 206–07

Prout concludes by making the interesting observation that the MDI not only treated the individual asthmatic but also criticism of medicine itself. Before the invention of the MDI, people suffering from asthma were highly critical of their health prospects and the lack of medical support for their life-threatening situation. With the introduction of the MDI these critical patients could be enrolled into a relationship with biomedicine with clinical practitioners becoming an obligatory passage point through which the asthma sufferer must now pass (just as farmers wishing to ensure the health of their animals had to 'pass' through Pasteur's laboratory). Thus the MDI not only safeguards the security of particular patients but also the security of medicine itself.

5 Conclusion

This chapter began by using the example of cholera arriving in Britain in the first part of the nineteenth century to show that the often acrimonious debates over health security were intertwined with arguments about the economy and free trade; about how theories on the nature and causation of disease were linked to debates about how an economy should be organised. However, we also used this case study to make a point about how such controversies or debates in science should be studied by sociologists (or any social scientists); when we study the reasons why scientific knowledge comes to be accepted as 'correct', we must use the same methods and principles of inquiry that we use when considering those knowledges that eventually come to be seen as 'erroneous'. This approach is known as the principle of symmetry.

This brought us on to a related issue from Science and Technology Studies – the concept of co-production. This argues that we should be equally wary of either socially or materially determinist accounts of social worlds. In explaining the making of social worlds we should always pay attention to the ways in which the material and the social are intertwined – social action is in part shaped by the material while the material is itself changed and modified by the social environment. To illustrate this we examined the emergence of the 'risk factor' in the study of a particular threat to health security in the twentieth century. Here we saw how the study of coronary heart disease by epidemiologists led to new techniques of investigation and these in turn had far-reaching effects on issues such as social policy and insurance actuaries.

Finally we looked at one usage of the concept of mediation as a form of translation to introduce the S&TS approach known as actor-network theory. Using asthma as a case study of danger to personal security, we introduced some of the key concepts of ANT (punctualisation, delegation, translation and hybrid) to show how material artefacts like the metered dose inhaler not only ensure the security of the individual patient but also the security of biomedicine itself.

End-notes

1 However, the discovery of the most famous 'risk factor', that between smoking and lung cancer, was such a strong relationship that no complex statistical techniques were needed to uncover the link between factor and disease (Doll and Hill, 1950).

2 Epidemiology has often become the site of disputes over the status and meaning of health knowledge. For example, it has frequently become embroiled in differences of opinion between interest groups, community physicians, politicians and civil servants in order to establish their 'claim-making' activities around contemporary issues such as inequalities in health (Bartley, 1992).

References

Ackerknecht, E.H. (1948) 'Anticontagionism between 1821 and 1867', *Bulletin of Historical Medicine*, vol. 22, pp. 562–93.

Annan, K. (2002) 'Problems without passports', *Foreign Policy*, September/October, pp. 30–1.

Aronowitz, R. (1998) *Making Sense of Illness: Science, Society and Disease*, Cambridge, Cambridge University Press.

Bartley, M. (1992) *Authorities and Partisans: Debate on Unemployment and Health*, Edinburgh, Edinburgh University Press.

Bloor, D. (1976) *Knowledge and Social Imagery*, London, Routledge & Kegan Paul.

Bucchi, M. (2002) *Science in Society: An Introduction to Social Studies of Science*, London, Routledge.

Budd, W. (1856) 'On intestinal fever: its mode of propagation', *The Lancet*, pp. 694–5.

Cooter, R. (1982) 'Anticontagionism and history's medical record' in Wright, P. and Treacher, A. (eds) *The Problem of Medical Knowledge*, Edinburgh, Edinburgh University Press.

Crosby, A.W. (1972) *The Columbian Exchange: Biological and Cultural Consequences of 1492*, Westport, CT, Greenwood.

Doll, R. and Hill, B. (1950) 'Smoking and carcinoma of the lung: preliminary report', *British Medical Journal*, vol. 2, pp. 739–48.

Jasanoff, S. (ed.) (2004) *States of Knowledge: The Co-production of Science and Social Order*, Abingdon, Routledge.

Lancet, The (1831) 'History of the rise, progress, ravages etc. of the blue cholera of India', *The Lancet*, pp. 241–84.

Latour, B. (1983) 'Give me a laboratory and I will raise the world' in Knorr-Cetina, K. and Mulkay, M. (eds) *Science Observed*, Beverly Hills, CA, Sage.

Latour, B. (1987) *Science in Action: How to Follow Scientists and Engineers Through Society*, Buckingham, Open University Press.

Latour, B. (1988) *The Pasteurization of France*, Cambridge, MA/London, Harvard University Press.

Mann, J. (1995) *The Coming Plague: Newly Emerging Infections in a World Out of Balance*, London, Virago.

Morris, R. (1976 [1832]) *The Social Response to an Epidemic*, London, Croom Helm.

Oppenheimer, G. (2006) 'Profiling risk: the emergence of coronary heart disease epidemiology in the United States (1947–70)', *International Journal of Epidemiology*, vol. 35, no. 3, pp. 720–30.

Pelling, M. (1978) *Cholera, Fever and English Medicine, 1825–1865*, Oxford, Oxford University Press.

Pemble, J. (1987) *The Mediterranean Passion: Victorians and Edwardians in the South*, Oxford, Clarendon Press.

Prout, A. (1996) 'Actor-network theory, technology and medical sociology: an illustrative analysis of the metered dose inhaler', *Sociology & Illness*, vol. 18, no. 2, pp. 198–219.

Rosenberg, C. (1962) *The Cholera Years: The United States in 1832, 1849 and 1866*, Chicago, IL, University of Chicago Press.

Star, S. (1991) 'Power, technology and the phenomenology of conventions: on being allergic to onions' in Law, J. (ed.) *A Sociology of Monsters: Essays on Power, Technology and Domination*, London, Routledge.

Strauss, A.L. (1978) 'A social world perspective', *Studies in Symbolic Interaction*, vol. 1, pp. 119–28.

Tomes, N. (2001) 'Merchants of health: medicine and consumer culture in the United States, 1900–1940', *The Journal of American History*, vol. 88, pp. 519–48.

United Nations (2001) 'Global crisis – global action: declaration of commitment on HIV/AIDS', A/RES/S–26/2, New York, NY, United Nations.

Afterword

Simon Carter, Tim Jordan and Sophie Watson

Contents

1	Introduction	180
2	The story so far	180
3	Security in making social worlds	184
References		187

1 Introduction

Our lives are embedded in the social worlds we move through and security is a part of these worlds. We hope that after reading the contributions to this book you will agree that social worlds, and the forms of security in them, are not solely defined by formal institutions or geography but may also be primarily constituted through shared commitments or practices. Case studies have helped us to explore social worlds and security, alongside three sociological concerns: mediation, matter and the individual. We have argued that these sociological concerns are useful tools or framing devices for understanding the ways in which security helps to constitute contemporary social worlds. This book has argued that even though the complexity of security means that it may sometimes appear to be a nebulous concept, we can understand it more clearly by examining how it is made socially, culturally and materially.

This afterword will remind you of some of the specific arguments described by the authors in previous chapters. This will both review and reinforce our claims about security. We will do this by looking at examples of the three sociological concerns that have informed so much of our discussion. The afterword is not a comprehensive overview of the whole book, rather it offers some of the many ways of linking different chapters using the sociological concerns. We will conclude by focusing directly on the overall argument of the book that security is complex; it changes constantly in the creation of our social worlds. This will also allow us to make a final ethical point about analysing security sociologically.

2 The story so far

Thinking about security is never simple, as demonstrated by the wide range of contexts in which security has been analysed in preceding chapters. Security has been explored at a range of 'social sizes' from the individual psyche (as we saw in Chapter 1) to the geopolitical (as we saw in Chapter 2). Given our argument that security is constructed from social, cultural and material practices, this book has attempted to investigate what kinds of practices are involved in the forms of security that make up the social, and how particular social interactions generate these practices. To retain a view of this complexity we have followed security as it has wound its way through various social worlds and been implicated in the exploration of matter, in the translations of mediation and in the definitions of individuals. Looking back, what have we discovered about security in relation to these three sociological concerns?

The ideas of mediation are deployed in different ways in different contexts. For example, mediation can be interpreted as the media – as television programmes, newspaper articles, radio reports, films, computer games and more. Mediation also refers to the ways in which information – ideas, knowledge, viewpoints, events, and so on – are represented through various cultural artefacts such as the press and the television. In this context sociologists are concerned with understanding the ways in which the media construct particular versions and interpretations of social worlds. Of importance here is what lies behind different representations in such things as news reports, films and books. Whose interests do they serve? What is being highlighted or obscured? What versions of truth are thereby produced? Readers who are well versed in media studies will be familiar with this understanding of mediation. A slightly different use of mediation refers to translations of entities into each other (including both human and non-human entities). This notion of translation is based on the view that all experience is mediated. This means we need to explore what kinds of mediations are made in our social worlds and a repeatedly useful way of doing this is to follow the translations that are made as one entity turns into another.

Chapter 4 included a number of illustrations of mediation. It pointed to the ways in which individuals and groups who differ from a dominant culture in particular social worlds can be represented as dangerous and threatening. This then produces new forms of segregation in the city and new strategies for maximising the personal safety and security of a few groups. In these processes, Watson noted a role for the media. For example, advertising for sports utility vehicles (SUVs) promotes them as safe and secure havens, thereby exploiting the fears and anxieties held by some contemporary city dwellers. In a different example, Watson explored opposition to the use of CCTV cameras by the Surveillance Camera Players, who use theatrical plays (another form of media) to highlight the lack of privacy that CCTV cameras create in many social worlds. In Chapter 2 we similarly saw how the idea of national security was translated by politicians to legitimise political actions and interventions to protect a particular political regime or a territorial space, such as in the case of the asylum seekers and refugees in Australia. Prime Minister John Howard used television time to translate immigrants from people who many would claim were vulnerable 'victims' into callous 'others'. We saw how the definition of these categories of people as threatening and dangerous was carried by the media and was used to construct particular notions of security, which in turn had serious implications for the lives of refugees who found themselves on a sinking ship.

The use of mediation as translation is often informed by science and technology studies (S&TS) and actor-network theory (ANT), as discussed in Chapter 5. It focuses attention on the role of agencies that function to 'translate' narratives, understandings, knowledges, artefacts or practices from one social world to another. This framework for studying science and technology makes no distinction between the various actors involved in an analysis whether they are human or non-human, social or material. Within ANT, the concept of mediation as translation describes those statements, concerns and/or images that pass from one social world to another, and also the ways in which that translation is stabilised by a particular network or association of relationships. Another way of looking at this concept is to consider the means by which one entity (human or non-human) gives a role to other entities (human or non-human). Of course, the media is also a key form in which translations occur.

In Chapter 5 we saw how various ideas about the spread of disease mediated between different conceptions of reality and tactics for fighting the spread of cholera. Contagionist and anti-contagionist views radically distinguished how illness and public health were secured. Chapter 1's similar analysis of soil poisoning described how scientific tests create alignments and connections between all kinds of social actors, from microbes to local government officials. These connections produced translations that constituted differing social worlds in which allotment-grown food was 'safe' or 'dangerous' to eat. Security and insecurity were produced by two different laboratory tests that translated from the matter of dirt into figures that health authorities interpreted as indicating danger.

From this latter example we can see that mediation in the sense of translation can be connected to the question of matter, another of the sociological concerns used in this book. Chapter 1 told a story of the transformation of matter, the soil, from something secure – even life-giving and 'good' – to something that was re-inscribed as dangerous, life-threatening and 'bad' via a series of tests undertaken by a range of social actors. Through this example we were introduced to Michel Callon and Bruno Latour's ANT notion of the sociologist as someone who studies associations and disassociations, not just those between humans but also between humans and material and technical objects.

The ANT approach is addressed at greater length in Chapter 5. We saw how the contagionist view emphasised a material entity that passed between humans carrying cholera; this view was opposed by the anti-contagionists whose ideas on the spread of the disease were characterised as the 'miasma theories' in which poisonous vapours were the culprit. In turn, these debates reflected contemporary views about the appropriate form of political, economic and social ordering of contemporary worlds. Contagionist views implied social policies that curtailed the movement of people and things, which ran counter to the prevailing economic discourses of free trade. As such, these theories were an anathema to the rising industrial bourgeoisie. This discussion led to another useful concept within the ANT approach, that of co-production. This is the idea that the ways in which we know the world are inseparable from how we live within it. The development of germ theory, for example, depended on a complex mixture of social and material practices, where the social was itself mediated and transformed by the idea of the newly discovered microbes and the implications they had for security and health.

The significance of material practices in sociology is not restricted to ANT approaches, as is illustrated across a number of the chapters in this book that do not draw on ANT. For example, Chapter 4 explored the materiality of bodies and ways in which these contribute to stereotypes of the 'other' or stranger. The fear that bodies bring contamination has shaped the ways in which cities have been built and planned since their inception. Jews were confined to the Venetian Ghetto since they were assumed to carry disease, and in Victorian London working-class slum dwellings were characterised as sites of illness and squalor. This gave rise to interventionist models of urban planning that sought to rid the city of the 'threat', as the middle and upper classes saw it, of social unrest on the one hand and ill health on the other. Throughout Watson's account, the city as a built material form – as bricks and mortar, as roads and houses – emphasised that this kind of matter is thoroughly implicated in the shaping of social worlds. Gated communities, for example, are seen as a solution to the growing ethnic and racial diversity in global cities, where those that are represented as threatening can be excluded. Here the sociological concerns of matter and mediation are mutually implicated in the making of contemporary social worlds. Similarly the deployment of surveillance cameras in the street as a solution to a perceived increase in crime, violence and vandalism represents a material and technical response to problems that are socially produced.

Chapter 3 similarly drew attention to the centrality of matter to sociological inquiry. It focused on the role of information and communication technologies in domestic space that mediate the public and private spheres. While critical of the duality implied by these terms deployed separately, and of their implied homogenous view of the household, Elizabeth B. Silva emphasised the ways in which objects such as computers are essential for everyday routines and the functioning of domestic life. This functioning is a key component in the construction of senses of security, as explored through the concept of ontological security.

Matter and mediation are also implicit in the nature of individuality in social worlds. Chapter 1 explored how the Harry Potter brand participates in the inner emotions of children. As children pass through certain key developmental stages, particularly independence from family and developing relations with peers, their identity is at risk. This risk can be mediated through a range of material practices, which in the case study flows from reading Potter books, watching Potter films, playing Potter games, purchasing Potter merchandise, and so on. The mediation that these material artefacts allow is to symbolically explore the psychic, developmental tensions that a child might face. For example, by following the adventures of orphaned Harry, a child can symbolically inhabit the possibility of a life without parents. Through such explorations each child develops their individuality, using the fantasy of novels and films to create their identity. This individuality or identity can be more or less secure, depending on how the child negotiates these phases of development and how the resources of a fantasy literature like the Potter series play a role in these phases.

We saw other ways in which individuality was explored and how this connected the construction of an individual to the social practices that create and maintain individuality. The accounts of everyday routines in Chapter 3, as retold by the two families interviewed by Silva, demonstrated how each individual – in this case, in their individuality in being a mother or a father – is bound by other individuals and the resulting social relations. In each family, the time spent with children or at work is crucial to the sense that each mother and father has of their role in their familial social world. This time is itself dependent on arrangements with spouse, workplace and school times. Not only is the nature of individuality something that shifts both throughout our lives and across the different social worlds we inhabit, but the individual is also bound into a relationship with the social.

Here we have presented examples of the three sociological concerns, drawn from the five chapters of this book. This does not in anyway exhaust the possibilities for finding other such connections. Rather it illustrates that security in social worlds is complex and how matter, mediation and the individual are useful ways of understanding that complexity.

3 Security in making social worlds

The core object of this book has been the role of security in the making of social worlds. In placing security at the centre of our analysis, we are of course not claiming that security is the only way to organise contemporary debates about the nature of society. There are many other ways of analysing society, for example in ideas about attachment

(**Redman, 2008**) or conduct (**McFall et al., 2008**). Rather than suggesting that security is *the* keystone concept for sociology, we wish to argue that sociology is one of the key ways of understanding and analysing security.

In the contemporary world security has emerged as a prevalent concern for many people, as reports of the potential risks arising from global warming, terrorist attacks, war and pandemics such as bird flu proliferate. Security is important not only for its seemingly ever-increasing role in a globalised world, but also for the way that it can be used to legitimise and de-legitimise social and political claims. Chapter 2 most clearly helps us to see this ethical point. Starting with the macro or global level, Matt McDonald unpacks the centrality of the concept of security to world politics and shows how a particular conception of security dominates international politics on the one hand, and the work of security intellectuals on the other. Central to his argument is the point that particular articulations of security can create particular types of relationships between individuals and wider political communities, thus mediating individual and national responses to specific events. As such, understandings of security, as other chapters also show, have significant effects that are by no means neutral. Rather, the meaning of security gets to the heart of questions of 'belonging, values and the boundaries of ethical responsibility in global politics', as was clear in the cases of asylum seekers and global climate change. Similarly, in Chapter 1 we saw how security allows us to explore food health and how brands seek to exploit emotional development. In Chapter 3 we found concerns about the nature of ontological security in a world of family change. In Chapter 4 we found the very roads and walls of the city creating definitions of who is a threat and needs to be excluded. And in Chapter 5 we found the nature of health being secured or threatened by a range of social and material forces. How security is defined in any one context, and the means through which particular ideas about security are enabled and legitimated, is clearly important in deciding the nature of our social worlds.

Security shifts meaning across different social worlds and it is this complexity that a sociological approach allows us to see. This is important not only because security seems to grow ever-more pivotal in the early twenty-first century, but also because security is often used to close down discussion and debate and to enforce a particular and specific type of social world.

Fear of others who are different, particularly ethnically or racially, in an increasingly globalised world represents another way in which a social world's sense of security may become threatened. Under these circumstances a sense of security can be articulated to pronounce some ethnicities as being inherently safe and others as dangerous. Many forms of 'otherness' can be produced in similar ways. In Chapter 4 we saw how fears in the city mobilised new strategies of behaviour and urban policies in search of an imagined greater security; where dangerous others could be excluded or kept at bay. Chapter 5 drew attention to the long association between health, illness and security where individual threats of illness have underpinned the making of local and global social worlds. Allowing concepts of security to remain unanalysed is one way of allowing them to unreflexively determine the nature of our social worlds without due discussion of the social, cultural, political and material practices they comprise. The sociological analysis pursued in this book accordingly refuses to close the discussion of the nature of security.

We have considered that security is complex and multifaceted, and that consideration of security issues raises ethical questions. These issues touch all aspects of our lives because they are connected to the social worlds we make. Here we meet again the overarching argument of this book, that security is part of the making of social worlds. These worlds should not be understood as ones made out of formal memberships, out of geographies, localities, bloodties or political allegiances. Rather they are forged from shared practices and commitments. In Chapter 1 the allotment holders share practices like digging in the soil and making compost heaps. Chapter 2's asylum seekers share desperate practices of travel and immigration. In Chapter 3 families share routines built around school and work hours. Chapter 4's SUV drivers share a questionable sense of safety based on the materiality of large cars. In Chapter 5 epidemiologists use increasingly complex statistical techniques and measurements of physical characteristics to understand coronary heart disease.

Throughout all these practices and all these social relations, various social worlds are built within which conceptions of security play crucial roles. By refusing to 'black-box' security as something that requires compliance, we have been able to employ sociological analysis and better understand the complexity and importance of security in our social worlds.

You might now consider the following questions. How secure are you? How secure do you feel? In which places and performing what practices do you feel safe, at risk, in danger or at peace? What do you mean by security in these different times and places? If you walk down the street and you see two police officers walking towards you, do you relax or feel tense? When you read about a bomb going off in a metropolitan area, do you feel more or less inclined to visit city streets? Do arguments about organic food make you want to improve what you eat or do they make you feel a little guilty?

This book has shown that such questions could be multiplied indefinitely. It has also shown that this is because the analysis of security demonstrates its complexity. Security exists at the level of the nation-state and at the level of the unconscious and at all points in between and beyond. The definition of security shifts across all these contexts, invoking varied collections of elements such as risk, danger, peace, safety, and so on. The aim of this book is to show that the answer to someone who asks 'how secure are you?' means opening up the worlds in which we live and seeking out what it is that makes us secure and insecure in our social worlds.

References

McFall, L., du Gay, P. and Carter, S. (eds) (2008) *Conduct: Sociology and Social Worlds*, Manchester, Manchester University Press/Milton Keynes, The Open University (Book 3 in this series).

Redman, P. (ed.) (2008) *Attachment: Sociology and Social Worlds*, Manchester, Manchester University Press/Milton Keynes, The Open University (Book 2 in this series).

Acknowledgements

Grateful acknowledgement is made to the following sources:

Text

Reading 1.1: from 'Unscrewing the big Leviathan: how actors macro-structure reality and how sociologists help them to do so', Callon, M. and Knorr-Cetina, K. in *Advances in Social Theory and Methodology: Toward an Integration of Micro- and Macro-sociologies*, Knorr-Cetina, K. and Cicourel, A.V. (eds). Copyright © 1981 Routledge & Kegan Paul. Reproduced by permission of Taylor & Francis Books UK; *Reading 1.2:* Rustin, M. and Rustin, M. (2001) *Narratives of Love and Loss: Studies in Modern Children's Fiction*, H. Karnac. Copyright © Margaret Rustin and Michael Rustin; *Reading 1.3:* Reproduced by permission of Sage Publications, London, Los Angeles, New Delhi and Singapore, from Barnes, B., *Understanding Agency: Social Theory and Responsible Action*, Copyright © Barry Barnes 2000; *Reading 2.1:* Waever, O. (1995) 'Securitization and desecuritization' from Lipschutz, R. (ed.) *On Security*. Copyright © 1995 Columbia University Press. Reprinted with permission of the publisher; *Reading 2.2:* Booth, K. (1991) 'Security and emancipation', *Review of International Studies*, Vol. 17, No. 4. Copyright © British International Studies Association, reproduced with permission; *Reading 3.2:* From 'Information and communication technologies and the moral economy of the household', Silverstone, R., Hirsch, E. and Morley, D., in *Consuming Technologies: Media and Information in Domestic Spaces*, Silverstone, R. and Hirsch, E. (eds). Copyright © 1992 Routledge. Reproduced by permission of Taylor & Francis Books UK; *Reading 4.1:* Bauman, Z. (2003) *Liquid Love: On the Frailty of Human Bonds*, Polity Press; *Reading 4.3: Discipline and Punish: The Birth of Prison* by Michel Foucault, translated by Alan Sheridan (first published as *Surveiller et Punir*: *Naissance de la Prison* by Editions Gallimard 1975, Allen Lane 1975) Copyright © Alan Sheridan, 1977, Penguin, London. *Discipline and Punish* by Michel Foucault. English Translation copyright © 1977 by Alan Sheridan (New York: Pantheon). Originally published in French as *Surveiller et Punir*. Copyright © 1975 by Editions Gallimard. Reprinted by permission of Georges Borchardt, Inc., for Editions Gallimard

Readings 5.4 and 5.5: Prout, A. (1996) 'Actor-network theory, technology and medical sociology: an illustrative analysis of the metered dose inhaler', *Sociology of Health & Illness*, Vol. 18, No. 2. Blackwell Publishing Ltd.

Figures

Figure 1: Copyright © Justin Guariglia/Corbis; *Figure 1.1:* Copyright © The Garden Picture Library/Alamy; *Figure 1.2:* adapted from

Environmental Science and Technology, Vol. 30, No. 2, 1996, American Chemical Society; *Figure 1.3 (top left)*: Copyright © Ferruccio/Alamy; *Figure 1.3 (top right):* Copyright © Bjorn Holland/Alamy; *Figure 1.3 (bottom):* Copyright © A.T. Willett/Alamy; *Figure 1.4:* Copyright © Peter Brooker/Rex Features; *Figure 2.1:* Copyright © Reuters/Corbis; *Figure 2.2:* Copyright © Jason Reed/Reuters; *Figure 2.3:* Copyright © Pal Hermansen/Stone+/Getty Images; *Figure 2.4:* Copyright © Mario Tama/ Getty Images; *Figure 3.1:* Copyright © Michael Boys/Corbis; *Figure 3.2:* Copyright © Huntley Hedworth/Getty Images; *Figure 3.3:* Copyright © Greg Watts/Rex Features; *Figure 3.4:* The Ronald Grant Archive; *Figure 4.1:* Copyright © Renaud Le Goix; *Figure 4.2:* Copyright © Scott van Dyke/Beateworks/Corbis; *Figure 4.3:* Copyright © Gregory Bull/AP/PA Photos; *Figure 4.4:* Copyright © Tribune Media Services, Inc. All Rights Reserved. Reprinted with permission; *Figure 4.5:* Copyright © Howie Twiner; *Figure 4.6:* Copyright © Martin Bond/Photofusion Picture Library/Alamy; *Figure 4.7:* Surveillance Camera Players; *Figures 5.1 and 5.2:* Wellcome Library, London; *Figures 5.3 and 5.4:* Copyright © Mark Peterson/Corbis; *Figure 5.5:* Copyright © Gustoimages/Science Photo Library.

Every effort has been made to locate all copyright-owners, but if any have been overlooked the publishers will make the necessary arrangements at the first opportunity.

Index

Note: Emboldened words in the index and main text indicate key words in the interactive glossary which is available for students on the DD308 *Making Social Worlds* course.

accountability, and agency 43
Ackerknecht, Erwin, 'Anticontagionism between 1821 and 1867' 150–5, 156–7
actor-network theory (ANT) 24, 168–75, 176, 181–3
  asthma and the metered dose inhaler 169–75
Afghanistan, refugees from 52, 61
agency, individuals and the social world 39–40, 42–4
airport security 10–14
air travel, and the complexity of security 3
allotment security 14, 18–27, 28, 44
  black boxes and social actors 24–6
  and the individual 39, 40, 41
  matter and 19–27
  and mediation 28
animal testing 22
ANT *see* actor-network theory (ANT)
anthrax 168–9
architecture of enclosure 126
arms race, emancipation and security 69, 71–2
Aronowitz, R. 162, 166
art, social world of 5
association 4, 20, 25–6, 89, 17, 167, 170–2, 182
  one-dimensional (Gesellschaft) 113
  and soil safety in allotments 20–1
asthma, and the metered dose inhaler 169–75
asylum seekers/refugees 14, 49, 51–63, 68
  and the Australian government 51, 54–6
  destinations of 52
  and global security 53–4, 76
  and mediation 181
  and refugee status 51–2
Australian government, 'securitisation' of asylum 51, 54–6, 61–2, 181
Ayres, Chris 130

Bailey, Joe 94
Baptiste, Hilson 119–20
Barnes, Barry 38, 40–1
  Understanding Agency 42–4
Bauman, Zygmunt 128, 129
  'Togetherness dismantled' 117–19, 121
Bentham, Jeremy, *Panopticon* 134, 135, 136
bioaccessibility 21
  Environment Agency report on 23
biomedicine, and metered dose inhalers 173–5
black box 24, 172, 186
  and social constructivism 160
  and social actors 24–6
Blade Runner 120
Blandy, Sarah 125
Bloor, Davis 155, 156
Blunkett, David 129
Booth, Ken 49, 65, 67, 73, 74, 75, 76
  'Security and emancipation' 68–72
Boulding, K. 69
Bow Quarter, East London 127–9
brands, Harry Potter and psycho-social security 32–6, 184
Bull, H. 70
Bush, George W. 65–7, 73

Callon, M.
  and Latour, Bruno 20, 21, 27, 182
    'Unscrewing the big Leviathan' 24–6
Campbell, D. 50
cars, sports utility vehicles (SUVs) 130–2, 181, 186
Castells, M. 116
CCTV **surveillance** 124, 133–41, 181
  and gated communities 125, 127
  in north London 136–9
  and the panoptic effect 133–6
Chambers family, home-life routines 85–9, 92–3, 101
Chambers, Iain, *Migrancy, Culture and Identity* 123–4
Chicago School of Sociology, and the concept of social worlds 4

children's fiction, Harry Potter and psycho-social security 14, 27–38

China, and the Kyoto Protocol 66

Chirac, Jacques 117, 118, 119

choices, and home-life routines 84, 93

cholera 146, 175
  contagionist and anticontagonist debate 147–60, 168, 182–3
  epidemics 148, 149
  and modern germ theory 153–5, 156–7
  modern understanding of 147–8
  and quarantines 150–1, 153
  symmetry and co-production in the study of 155–60

city and security 15, 112–41, 186
  contrasting rural and urban life 112
  and materiality 140–1, 183
  and mediation 181
  origins of city planning 113
  race and ethnicity 113–14, 117, 120
  social consequences of nineteenth-century urbanisation 112–13
  see also fear in the city

civil rights, and CCTV surveillance 139

climate change 2, 14, 62–75, 77
  and ethical responsibility 63, 66, 67, 74
  scale and effects of 63–5
  the United States and the Kyoto Protocol 65–7

Clinton, President Bill and Kyoto Protocol 66

cold war, and global security 48–9, 58, 69, 70, 71–2

colonial planning, and segregation 113–14

community 113
  as selling-point 125
  Gemeinschaft 113
  Hogwarts school 37
  of similarity 129, 136
  political 51, 53, 57, 67,72,75
  threat to 124
  world 68, 72
  see also gated communities

computers
  computer analysis of the Framingham study 163–4
  and the moral economy of the household 100
  and security 2, 3–4

Condition of the Working Class in England, The (Engels) 112

Cooper, Clare 94

Cooter, Roger 155

Copenhagen School, and securitization 51, 54, 62

co-production, in Science and Technology studies 156–60, 169, 176, 183

coronary heart disease (CHD), risk factors for 9, 15, 161–8, 176

Country and the City, The (Raymond Williams) 112

crime, fear of 117–19, 128
  and CCTV surveillance 133, 138–9
  and gated communities 128, 129–30

Davis, Mike 120

delegation, and actor-network theory 171, 172, 173–4

Dickens, Charles, description of cities 112

difference
  and stereotypes 122–4
  urban divisions and fear in the city 119–21

disease prevention 3, 53, 146

distanciation, and stereotypes 122

domestic violence, and ontological security 95–6

Downer, Alexander 55

Duras, Marguerite, *The Sea Wall* 114

Eastern Europe, Sonnenfeldt doctrine for 70

emancipation, security as 67–72, 76–7

emergency services, and airport security 12

emotional development in children, and psycho-social security 28–38

employment, and home-life routines 84, 85–93

energy security 2

Engels, Friedrich, *The Condition of the Working Class in England* 112

Environment Agency, report on bioaccessibility 23

environmental protection rules, and soil testing 19–20

environmental security 2, 3
  and climate change 63–75

epidemiology, and the 'risk factor' 160–8, 176, 186
Erikson, Erik 94
ethnicity *see* race and ethnicity
European Union, and asylum seekers 62
expert systems, and ontological security in the home 102, 107

family routines 84
fear in the city 15, 115–39
  and CCTV surveillance 124, 125, 127, 133–41, 181
  and gated communities 124–30
  making of 115–16
  psycho-social accounts of 121–4
  and sports utility vehicles (SUVs) 130–2, 181, 186
  and urban divisions 119–21
food safety, and allotment soil 18–19
Foucault, Michel 132
  'Panopticism' 133–6
Fox News Channel, and the Iraq War 7
France
  and fear in the city
    CCTV surveillance in Lyon 139
    French presidential election (2002) 117–19
free will, and the individual 39, 40
Freudian theory, and fear in the city 122
Freud, Sigmund 37
fuel consumption, and sports utility vehicles (SUVs) 130–2
Furedi, Frank 121

gated communities 124–30
  Bow Quarter, East London 127–9
  as communities of similarity 129
  Mexico City 126–7
  and mixophobia 128, 129
  public attitudes to 127
  in the USA 124–5, 126
gender, and home-life routines 84
Giddens, Anthony 83, 84, 92, 93, 95, 99, 102, 106
Gilman, Sander 123
global capitalism, and fear in the city 116
globalisation
  and fear in the city 119–20, 140
  and health security 146
global security 14, 48–77, 185–6
  and asylum seekers 49, 51–63
  changing definitions of 49
  and climate change 2, 14, 63–75, 77
  and the cold war 48–9, 58, 69, 70, 71–2
  and emancipation 67–72, 76–7
  and international politics 75–7, 185–6
  performative definitions of 49–50
  and speech acts 57, 58–61
good-enough environments, and healthy individuals 96–8, 106
Graham, Stephen 132
Greenham Common women 71–2
Gregory, Derek 116

Harry Potter and the Prisoner of Azkaban 30–2, 37
Harry Potter and psycho-social security 14, 27–38, 44
  and the individual 39, 40, 41, 184
  and mediation 27–8, 38, 184
  and Potter as a brand 32–6
health, illness and security 15, 146–76, 186
  and actor-network theory (ANT) 168–75, 176, 181–3
  and cholera 146, 147–60, 175, 182–3
  and disease prevention 3, 53, 146
  epidemiology and the 'risk factor' 160–8, 176, 186
  and infectious diseases 146, 160
  and the Venetian Ghetto of the Renaissance 114
  and Victorian urban policy intervention 113
Hirsch, Eric *see* Silverstone, Roger, Hirsch, Eric and Morley, David
Hobbes, Thomas 58, 68, 72
Home is Where We Start From (D.W. Winnicott) 95
homelessness, and security in the city 120
home life and security 6, 14–15, 82–107
  and changes in household composition 82
  home-life routines 83–93, 101
  in the individual and the social 94–8, 105–6, 184
  and materiality 98–101, 107, 183
  see also ontological security
household composition, changes in 82

House of Lords Science and Technology Committee 2
housework, and ontological security 96
housing, in gated communities 124–30
Howard, John 55, 56, 62, 181
human rights, and asylum seekers 62
Hurricane Katrina 66, 73–4, 77
Huysman, Jef 62
hybrids, in actor-network theory 172

identity, documentation and security management 7–8
imaginary 15, 27, 106, 112, 114, 121, 140, 141
India, and the Kyoto Protocol 66
individual, the 6, 9–10, 39–44, 180
  and agency 38–9
  Harry Potter and psycho-social security 39, 40, 41, 184
  home life and security 82, 84, 94–8, 105–6, 184
  identity and airport security 12–13
  and panopticism 134–5
infant experiences, and ontological security 95, 97, 98
information and communication technologies, and the moral economy of the household 99–101, 106–7
Intergovernmental Panel on Climate Change (IPCC) 63
internet security 2
Iran, refugees in 52
Iraq war 2, 7, 73, 132

Jackson, Paul 132, 139
Jasanoff, Sheila 146–7, 156
  'Ordering knowledge, ordering society' 157–60
Jewish Ghetto, in Renaissance Venice 114, 183
Jospin, Lionel 117, 118, 119

Kant, Immanuel 70, 72
King, Anthony 113–14
King, Sir David 64
Klein, Melanie 122
Koch, Robert and germ theory of disease 153
Kristeva, Julia 121–2
Kuwait, Iraqi invasion of 69
Kyoto Protocol, and the United States 65–7, 74

Laing, R.D. 94
Lancet, The, article on cholera 149
language differences, and mediation 7
Latour, Bruno 20, 21
  and actor-network theory 168–9, 170
  see also Callon, Michel, and Latour, Bruno
LBH (London Borough of Hackney), and soil testing of allotments 18–19, 19–21, 23, 24, 27, 39
Lebranchu, Marylise 118–19
liberty, and home-life routines 84
London
  Bow Quarter, East London 127–9
  CCTV in north London 136–9
  Hackney allotments 18–19, 19–21, 23, 24, 27, 39
  slums in Victorian London 112
Los Angeles, as a militarised city 120
Luttwak, Edward 68
Lyon, CCTV surveillance in 139

McCarthyism and the Cold War 58
McFall, Liz 184
materiality
  and security in the city 140–1, 183–4
  and security in the home 98–101, 107, 183
material objects, in airports 12–13
material practices 8
matter 6, 8–9, 180
  and allotment security 19–27
  and the individual 41
maturation, and the healthy individual 96–7
MDIs (metered dose inhalers) 169–75
media, mediation as 7, 8, 28, 181
mediation 6, 7–8, 181–2
  and the airport 11, 13
  and allotment security 28
  Harry Potter and psycho-social security 27–8, 38, 184

and the individual 41
as media 7, 8, 28, 181
and risk factor knowledge 166–7
and social worlds 131
as translation 7–8, 181–2
and matter 182–4
metered dose inhalers *see* MDIs
'The metropolis and mental life' (Georg Simmel) 113
Mexico City, gated housing in 126–7
miasma theories, and cholera 149, 151
Migrancy, Culture and Identity (Chambers) 123–4
migration, and contemporary urban fear 116–17
mixophobia, and gated communities 128, 129
modernity, and urban policy intervention 113
Morley, David *see* Silverstone, Roger, Hirsch, Eric and Morley, David
Mumford, Lewis 128

national security 44, 49, 60, 71, 77, 181
nation-states
and airports 12, 13
and global security 49, 53
newspapers, on the importance of security 2
New York Surveillance Camera Players 139–40
Nike as a brand 32–3, 34

object relations theory 122
ontological security 15, 94, 101, 106–7
and fear in the city 121–4
in the home 102–5, 183, 185
in the individual and the social 94–8
and information and communication technologies 99, 100
Oppenheimer, Gerald 162
'Profiling risk: the emergence of coronary heart disease epidemiology in the United States' 164–7
others
contaminating 113
fear of 116–19, 126, 128–9, 140, 181, 183, 186
foreigners 121–4, 181
urban 120–21

Pakistan, refugees in 52
panoptic effect, and CCTV surveillance 133–6
parenting, and home-life routines 84, 86–93
Parkes, Henry 55
passports
and airport security 12–13
and the individual 9–10
and material practices 8
and mediation 7–8
passwords, and computer security 2, 4
Pasteur, Louis 153, 168–9, 172
PBET (physiologically based extraction tests) 21–4, 27, 39, 41
performative definitions, of global security 49–50
personal security 44
plate tectonics, asymmetrical explanation of 156
police, and gated communities 129–30
power
and home-life routines 84, 101
and panopticism 134, 135
and resistance 132
principle of symmetry 175
probability and causes of disease 161
prostitution, and security in the city 113, 120
Prout, Alan, 'Actor-network theory, technology and medical sociology: an illustrated analysis of the metered dose inhaler' 170–5
psycho-social
and fear in the city 121–4
and Harry Potter 14, 27–38, 39, 40, 41, 44, 184
punctualisation, and actor-network theory 171, 172, 176

quarantines, and cholera 150–1, 153

race and ethnicity
and difference 123–4
and security in the city 113–14, 117, 120, 136, 138
rational choice theory 40
rationality, and the individual 39, 40, 41, 42
Redman, Peter 103, 122, 184
refugees *see* asylum seekers/refugees

Reith, Peter 55, 62
Renaissance Venice, Jewish Ghetto in 114, 183
resistance, and power 132
Rice, Anita 127–8, 129
risk factors, and epidemiology 160–8, 176, 186
routines, in home life 83–93
Rowling, J.K., Harry Potter books 27–38, 39, 40, 41, 44
Ruddock, Phillip 55
Russia, and European energy security 2
Rustin, Margaret and Michael 27, 28, 29
  'The inner world of Harry Potter' 36–8
Rwanda, genocide in 75

Saddam Hussein 56, 69, 71, 73
Sandercock, Leonie 114
science and technology
  and home life 83–4
  and matter 8–9
  and PBET (physiologically based extraction tests) 21–4
Science and Technology Studies (S&TS) 15, 146–7
  and actor-network theory 168–75
  mediation in 166–7, 181–2
  symmetry and co-production in 155–60, 175–6
Sea Wall, The (Duras) 114
securitisation 51
  and asylum seekers 51–63, 181
security
  and the airport 10–14
  complexity of 2–4, 180
  importance of 2
  in making social worlds 184–7
  and social worlds 6
  see also ontological security
segregation, and colonial planning 113–14
self, the 83
Sennett, Richard 114, 129
September 11 terrorist attacks 4, 119
  and asylum seekers 51–6
  and fear in the city 115, 116, 119
  and global security 14, 75–6
Short, John Rennie 117
Sibley, David, 'Images of difference' 122–4
Silverstone, Roger, Hirsch, Eric and Morley, David, 'Information and communication technologies and the moral economy of the household' 99–101
Simmel, Georg, 'The metropolis and mental life' 113
Slipper, Peter 56
slums, and security in the city 112, 113, 119–20
'smart houses' 101
Smith, Neil 120
social actors
  and black boxes 24–6
  see also actor-network theory (ANT)
social class, and anti-contagonist views of cholera 155
social constructivism, and co-productionism 157–8, 159–60
social contract, and security 67–8
social worlds vii–viii, 180–6
  and agency 42–4
  and individual 39, 44, 82, 106–7
  as a 'framing device' 5–6
  concept of 4–6, 26, 147
  material and social 176
  mediating 131, 170
  of the airport 11–12
  routine 94, 96
  security in making 24, 113, 129, 184–7
  translation 167
society, and the individual 9
soil poisoning 9, 14, 18–27, 182
  and PBET (physiologically based extraction tests) 21–4, 27, 39, 41
South Africa, CCTV surveillance in Johannesburg 133
speech acts
  and global security 57, 58–61
  and securitisation 51
sports utility vehicles (SUVs) 130–2, 181, 186
Starbucks as a brand 32–3
states
  security and climate change 65–7
  security and emancipation 68–72, 76–7
stereotypes, and psycho-social thinking 122–4
Strauss, Anselm L. 147
surveillance *see* CCTV surveillance

SUVs (sports utility vehicles) 130–2, 181, 186
symbolic interactionism 4
symmetry, in Science and Technology studies 155–60, 168, 175

Tampa, asylum seekers and Australian security 54–6, 61
telephones, and the moral economy of the household 100
terrorist attacks
  and airport security 12
  compared with the effects of climate change 64–5
  and the complexity of security 4
  and fear in the city 115, 116
  and the importance of security 2
  and travel security 3
  war on terrorism 50, 61
  see also September 11 terrorist attacks
Thatcher, Margaret 71–2
translation
  and actor-network theory 171, 172, 174–5
  mediation as 7–8, 181–2
    and matter 182–4
  in S&TS 167
travel security
  airports 10–14
  complexity of 2–3
Truman Show, The (film) 102–5, 106

unconscious motives, in security assessment 27
unemployment, and urban divisions 120–1
United Nations
  defining refugees/ asylum seekers 51–2
  and global security 49
  and health concerns 146
  State of the World's Cities report 119
  UNHCR 51–2
United States of America
  and climate change policies 65–7, 74
  Dead Cities in 120
  Framingham study of coronary heart disease 162–4, 165, 166
  gated communities in 124–5, 126
  and Hurricane Katrina 66, 73–4
  and international politics 75–6
  McCarthyism and the cold war 58
  New York Surveillance Camera Players 139–40
  and sports utility vehicles (SUVs) 130–2
  and travel security 2

Vaillant, Daniel 118–19
Venice, Jewish Ghetto in Renaissance Venice 114, 183
violence, security and climate change 65
Virilio, Paul 126
virtual identities, airport passengers 12–13

Waever, Ole 51, 76
  'Securitization and desecuritization' 56–61
Watson, Sophie 115, 137, 138, 181, 183
wealth, inequality in the distribution of 119–20
Wekerle, Gerda 132, 139
Wells family, and home-life routines 89–93, 101
Wells, Karen 137, 138
White, Dr Paul Dudley 161–2
Williams, Raymond, *The Country and the City* 112
Winnicott, D.W. 95, 102, 106
  'The concept of a healthy individual' 96–8

young people, and urban divisions 121

Zunes, Stephen 73